Steroids and Doping in Sports

Recent Titles in the
CONTEMPORARY WORLD ISSUES
Series

Books in the **Contemporary World Issues** series address vital issues in today's society such as genetic engineering, pollution, and biodiversity. Written by professional writers, scholars, and nonacademic experts, these books are authoritative, clearly written, up-to-date, and objective. They provide a good starting point for research by high school and college students, scholars, and general readers as well as by legislators, businesspeople, activists, and others.

Each book, carefully organized and easy to use, contains an overview of the subject, a detailed chronology, biographical sketches, facts and data and/or documents and other primary source material, a directory of organizations and agencies, annotated lists of print and nonprint resources, and an index.

Readers of books in the **Contemporary World Issues** series will find the information they need in order to have a better understanding of the social, political, environmental, and economic issues facing the world today.

CONTEMPORARY WORLD ISSUES

Society

Steroids and Doping in Sports

A REFERENCE HANDBOOK

David E. Newton

ABC-CLIO

Santa Barbara, California • Denver, Colorado • Oxford, England

Copyright 2014 by ABC-CLIO, LLC

All rights reserved. No part of this publication may be reproduced, stored in a retrieval system, or transmitted, in any form or by any means, electronic, mechanical, photocopying, recording, or otherwise, except for the inclusion of brief quotations in a review, without prior permission in writing from the publisher.

Library of Congress Cataloging-in-Publication Data

Newton, David E.
   Steroids and doping in sports : a reference handbook / David E. Newton.
        pages cm. — (Contemporary world issues)
   Includes bibliographical references and index.
   ISBN 978-1-61069-313-4 (hardcopy : alk. paper) —
ISBN 978-1-61069-314-1 (ebook)   1. Doping in sports—Handbooks, manuals, etc.   2. Anabolic steroids—Health aspects—Handbooks, manuals, etc.   3. Steroid drugs—Handbooks, manuals, etc.   I. Title.
   RC1230.N48 2014
   617.1'027—dc23

                                2013006849

ISBN: 978-1-61069-313-4
EISBN: 978-1-61069-314-1

18   17   16   15   14   3   4   5

This book is also available on the World Wide Web as an eBook. Visit www.abc-clio.com for details.

ABC-CLIO, LLC
130 Cremona Drive, P.O. Box 1911
Santa Barbara, California 93116–1911

This book is printed on acid-free paper ∞

Manufactured in the United States of America

FIGURES

Swifter, Higher, Stronger. That motto was first suggested for the Olympic Games by their modern founder, Pierre de Coubertin. It was officially introduced to the event in the games of 1924, held in Paris. The motto might also be appropriate for the concept of athletic competition in general. Whether one competes in swimming, the javelin throw, pole vaulting, speed skating, downhill slalom, mixed doubles tennis, or any of dozens of other sports, the goal is always the same: run or swim faster; jump higher; or lift heavier weights than anyone else in the competition.

Sports historians believe that humans have engaged in athletic contests as far back as civilization exists. And it seems likely that athletes have always searched for ways in which to extend their natural talents, to run a bit faster, jump a bit higher, or lift a bit more weight than their bodies seem naturally capable of doing. For example, 2,000-year-old records show that Greek athletes consumed the testicles of bulls prior to an athletic competition in the belief that so doing would transfer some of the best attributes of that animal to their own physical skills.

At times, efforts to improve one's own performance have gone to the extreme, reaching ludicrous levels. In the marathon event at the 1904 St. Louis Olympics, for example, American runner Fred Lorz was awarded the gold medal for the astonishing time of 3 hours 13 minutes. He held that honor only for a brief time, however, as he was discovered to have completed

11 miles of the 26.2-mile race in a friend's car. Olympic officials banned Lorz for life for this "practical joke," as he called it, although they later changed their mind and relented on this penalty.

And cheating in sports is hardly limited to human events. Animals used in sporting events, such as greyhounds and race-horses, may also be "doped" by their trainers to improve their performances. In 2012, for example, *The New York Times* ran a series of articles detailing the use of anabolic steroids and other performance-enhancing drugs among quarter horses, a practice that had resulted in the death of more than 3,000 horses between 2009 and 2011.

Throughout history, most sports authorities have argued that the use of performance-enhancing substances, such as anabolic steroids, and practices, such as "blood doping," are unfair and contaminate the fundamental purity of athletic competition among men and women. They have created a host of regulations that prohibit such substances and practices, almost always accompanied by a variety of tests by which such banned substances and procedures can be detected. The discovery of an athlete who has cheated in competition or in preparation for competition usually results in that individual's being banned from competition for some period of time and being stripped of any honors earned as a result of the illegal practice.

While entirely admirable, these efforts often fail in their basic objective of reducing or eliminating the use of performance-enhancing substances and practices in sports. The reason for this deficiency is that competitors and their allies in the battle—sports promoters, trainers, and research chemists, for example—almost always try to stay one step ahead of the regulatory agencies. No sooner than substance A is banned by an antidoping agency than is a new substance, B, discovered and put into use by athletes. When regulatory agencies find out about substance B, they place it on the prohibited list also, unaware that substance C (and D and E and so on) has just been made available in the black market of performance-enhancing drugs.

This issue has become even more complicated in recent decades as an increasing number of athletes, trainers, coaches, academics, sports ethicists, and other experts interested in the topic have begun to question whether currently banned substances really need to be legally prohibited. These individuals put forward a number of arguments for their position. They say that the adverse physical effects of drug use are grossly overstated. They point out that athletes have used performance-enhancing substances and practices since the beginning of time. They argue that such substances and practices do not actually increase a person's skills; they only help the person reach his or her natural limits in sport, and so on. In the second decade of the 21st century, then, a policy that would seem to have been settled long ago—the banning of performance-enhancing substances and practices—is once more up for debate.

The purpose of *Steroids and Doping in Sports* is to provide the reader with the information and resources about performance-enhancing drugs and practices, especially the class of compounds known as anabolic steroids, which allow one to continue research on this topic. In addition to the introductory chapters on the history and background of anabolic steroids, their use in athletic events, and rules and regulations that have been developed against them, the book includes chapters on the chronology of anabolic steroids in athletics, important individuals and organizations interested in this topic, print and electronic resources available on the use of anabolic steroids in sports, and a glossary of important terms. One chapter of the book, Chapter 3, also presents the viewpoints of a number of individuals with specific interests and viewpoints on the topic of anabolic steroids in athletics.

Steroids and Doping in Sports

Taylor seemed abnormally upset. His parents could not understand how their normally happy, optimistic 16-year-old athlete-son could have become so depressed. And his health had taken a turn for the worst. He complained of aches and pains much of the time, although he otherwise seemed in the best of health. Perhaps it was just the pressure of trying to become the high school baseball team's number one pitcher. When the symptoms did not pass, they convinced Taylor to see a psychiatrist. There he confessed the probable source of his unhappiness and distress: steroids. Believing that he probably had to become physically stronger, Taylor had started injecting himself with anabolic steroids (AS). Now there seemed to be only one way out: he had to give up on the drugs.

Taylor's parents were hopeful that the problem had been solved. Then, about six weeks later, they discovered how wrong they were. When Taylor failed to come down from his bedroom one morning, his parents found that he had hung himself. The probable cause of Taylor's suicide: a deep depression caused by his withdrawal from steroid use. (The true story of Taylor Hooton's death is chronicled at a number of sites. See, for example, Willey 2012.)

Welsh cyclist Arthur Linton, pictured ca. 1894, who died shortly after winning the 1896 Bordeaux to Paris road race. Coached by Choppy Warburton, whose famous "little black bottle" for his athletes may have contained strychnine or other substances thought to improve performance, Linton's death is considered to be the first sports fatality caused by the use of performance-enhancing drugs. (Hulton Archive/Getty Images)

When Taylor Hooton died in Plano, Texas, in 2003, concerns about the use of AS for the enhancement of athletic performance were just reaching their peak. During the decade, a number of the world's greatest athletes would see their fame diminished or destroyed by evidence or suspicion that their accomplishments were the result not solely of their own natural skill and dedicated training programs, but also the consequence of synthetic chemicals that artificially increased their muscle mass, strength, endurance, speed, and other physical attributes. Where, how, and when did this movement to enhance physical performance with synthetic chemicals begin? How did it develop? Where does it stand today? And what does it foretell for the future of amateur and professional sports, as well as for the physical and psychological well-being of those who choose to use AS? These are some of the questions posed—and, to some extent—answered in this book.

The History of Performance-enhancing Drugs

It is probably impossible to say precisely when competitive sports first appeared among humans. Some observers have argued that competition is an innate human characteristic, so it should hardly be surprising that competitive athletic events were common as far back as the earliest stages of human civilization (Skills for Life 2012). Certainly, there is abundant archaeological evidence for the existence of competitive sports dating to at least the second millennium BCE (Carroll 1988). Another ancient sport is hurling, sometimes called the oldest (and fastest) of all European sports. Broadly similar to the North American sport of lacrosse, hurling dates to at least 1400 BCE in Ireland (A Brief History of Hurling 2012).

Dating to at least the same period in Mesoamerica was a group of games played with balls and, sometimes, sticks in large open or enclosed arenas that sometimes resulted in the deaths of members of the losing teams. One well-documented discovery traced a still extant ball field to about 1400 BCE near

Chiapas, Mexico (Hill, Blake, and Clark 1998). A primitive form of football was also played in ancient China in the pre-Christian era. The game, called cuju, was first mentioned in a first century BCE document, the *Shi Ji* (Historical Record) as being a very popular sport played by both men and women (a bit unusual in and of itself in a predominantly male-oriented era) (Speak 1999, 32–33; The Culture of Cuju 2012).

One might like to believe that there was once a time in human history when competition was pure and simple, when races were won by the swiftest of competitors and wrestling awards went to the strongest of participants. But that view seems somewhat unlikely. A number of observers have commented on the fact that men and women who engage in competition do so because they want to win; they want to be the best among their peers. As one historian of the use of performance-enhancing substances in sports has written:

When humans compete against one another, either in war, in business, or in sport, the competitors, by definition, seek to achieve an advantage over their opponent. Frequently they use drugs and other substances to gain the upper hand. In sport such conduct . . . has existed for as long as sport has been organised. (Yesalis and Bahrke 2002, 42)

Still, reliable reports of the specific ways in which athletes can cheat to win a competition are essentially nonexistent until the first millennium BCE in Greece. During that period, historians began to record a number of strategies by which competitors unfairly took advantage of their opponents, most commonly perhaps by simply bribing an opponent to run more slowly, fall down during a boxing match, or intentionally drive a chariot less quickly than possible (Case Analysis: Instances of Cheating in the Olympic Movement 2012). It was also at about this time that what is apparently the first specific reference to the use of performance-enhancing substances was mentioned.

A prescription widely attributed to perhaps the most famous of all classical physicians, Galen, called for preparation of a mixture consisting of "the rear hooves of an Abyssinian ass, ground up, boiled in oil, and flavored with rose hips and rose petals." This preparation, Galen said, was likely to improve an athlete's performance in any sport. (This prescription is cited in many sources. See, for example, Buti and Fridman 2001, citing the International Olympic Committee multimedia presentation "Olympic Gold: A 100 Year History of the Summer Olympic Games.")

Many classical athletes also adopted a vaguely homeopathic (or, more properly, an organotherapeutic) approach to substance use. In preparation for a competition, they were likely to adopt a diet that included specific items that were related to strength, endurance, speed, and other desirable physical traits in other animals. The assumption was that the consumption of an animal's testicles, as an example, would confer upon a person the manly qualities that they gave to a bull, ram, stallion, or other male animal. Similarly, a person might consume animal brains to improve one's own intelligence or animal hearts to improve one's courage.

Athletes relied on performance-enhancing substances other than animal organs. Charmis, the winner of the stade race in the Olympic Games of 668 BCE, for example, existed almost entirely on a diet of figs in preparation for the competition. Another champion, Dromeus of Stymphalos attributed his success in winning seven Olympic races to a diet consisting almost entirely of meat (a very unusual diet for the times). Other athletes relied on cheese, wheat meal, brandy and wine mixtures, sesame seeds, or hallucinogenic mushrooms for the special boost they needed in a competition (Yesalis and Bahrke 2002, 44–45).

These practices were by no means limited to the ancient Greek civilization. As early as about 1400 BCE, for example, the Indian physician Sushruta recommended the consumption of testicular tissue as a means of curing impotence and improving one's masculinity. Athletes from a number of cultures also relied on plant materials to produce enhanced physical characteristics. The legendary Berserkers from ancient Norse tradition are known to have consumed the drug bufotenin obtained from the *Amanita muscaria* mushroom to increase their fighting strength "12-fold." Under the influence of the drug, they became such fierce warriors that their behavior is preserved in the modern word "berserk." Similar use of plant-based drugs to improve an individual's physical skills has been traced to early cultures throughout Europe, Africa, and Mesoamerica (Bøje 1939; Prokop 1970; Yesalis and Bahrke 2002, 44–45).

Doping in the Modern Era

The rise of Christianity in Europe during the late Roman Empire, according to some observers, had the consequence of eliminating or reducing sports competitions, largely because they were viewed as pagan events that distracted a person's attention from more important religious activities. Among the events most commonly cited by such observers was the banning of the Olympic Game by Emperor Theodosius in 393 CE, apparently for just that reason (Gertz 2012).

It was not, therefore, until the 18th century that sports competitions again became widely popular and, perhaps as an inevitable consequence, the use of performance-enhancing substances once more became common. An event that is sometimes cited as the first documented case of doping in the modern era occurred in 1865 when some contestants in a swimming competition at an Amsterdam (Netherlands) canal were suspected of having taken an "unknown" substance (now thought to have been caffeine) to improve their performances (Prokop 1970). (Other writers tell a somewhat different story, claiming that the 1865 doping event actually involved swimmers at a race in the British Channel; see Müller 2010, 3.)

Over the next seven decades, there were isolated reports of drug use in athletic competitions, sometimes with terrible consequences. In 1886, for example, the first death attributed to the use of performance-enhancing drugs was recorded when a European cyclist (reported to have been either Dutch or French) died after using a combination of heroin and cocaine, a mixture known as a "speedball" (Lee 2012; von Deutsch, Abukhalaf, and Socci 2012, 493). One of the most notorious individuals involved with doping at the time was the English cyclist and trainer, Choppy Warburton. Warburton was a highly success-ful runner who won more than 500 races in his career. When he retired from track and field, he began a second career as a cycling coach. He achieved notable success in that field also, at least partly because of the infamous "little black bottle" that he shared with his athletes. Although the bottle supposedly con-tained magical powers, no one knows what the bottle actu-ally contained. But judging from its effects on the cyclists who used it, the contents may have been something more dangerous even than black magic, perhaps cocaine, heroin, trimethyl, or strychnine, all common performance enhancers of the time. In any case, at least three cyclists are thought to have died after having taken a draft of the "little black bottle," and Warburton is now widely thought to have been the first coach or trainer to have systematically supplied performance-enhancing drugs to his charges (Moore and Ritchie 2011; Rosen 2008, 5–7).

The first known case of doping in the Olympics Games occurred in the 1904 St. Louis event. During the marathon, American runner Thomas Hicks appeared to be so tired that his assistants gave him a dose of strychnine in brandy to "perk him up." When that treatment didn't have much effect, they gave him a second dose of the same mixture. Hicks quickly regained his stride and won the gold medal. (Hicks actually finished sec-ond to Fred Lorz, who was disqualified for having ridden in a car for more than half of the race distance.) Hicks collapsed after crossing the finish line as a result of the doping experience. Medical experts later pointed out that one more dose of strych-nine would almost certainly have killed him (Cronin 2012).

One of the sports in which performance-enhancing drugs took root early and widely was cycling. The demands of long distance races, such as the Tour de France, place enormous stress on a person's physical body, and it is easy to see how competitors would constantly search for any means by which they can survive and win such contests. One of the most famous doping cases of the first quarter of the 20th century occurred in connection with the 1924 Tour de France. Three French brothers who participated in the race, Henri, Francis, and Charles Pélissier, gave a somewhat unusual interview to journalist Albert Londres, a reporter for the newspaper *Le Petit Parisien*. The Pélissier brothers told Londres that the only way they could keep going was with drugs, and they showed their "stash," consisting of aspirin, chloroform, strychnine, cocaine, "horse ointment," and other drugs. Londres published the results of this interview in *Le Petit Parisien* under the headline "Les Forçats de la Route" ("The Convicts of the Road").

The Pélissier brothers later said that they were just kidding around when they spoke with Londres. But other evidence suggests that they were probably describing the situation more accurately than they were willing to admit. By 1930, for example, tour organizer Henri Desgrange found it necessary to make note in the tour rule book that race officials would not supply drugs to contestants and that they would be responsible for those substances themselves (Maso 2005).

In spite of a few dramatic incidents like these, there are relatively few known cases of doping in sports until almost the middle of the 20th century, especially in comparison with the number of such cases that have been uncovered since that time. One observer of the topic has suggested that reports of the disastrous consequences of using drugs may have scared off many competitors from using such substances. On the contrary, he suggests, such reports may simply have made athletes far more secretive about their activities, resulting in many fewer reports of drug use than was actually the case (Lee 2012, 9).

In any case, the story of drug use by athletes after the 1930s underwent a dramatic change from anything that occurred prior to that time. The turning point in that history was the discovery and synthesis of testosterone and its analogs. (Drug analogs are chemical compounds that are structurally similar to some parent compound, such as testosterone, but that have relatively modest molecular modifications that change their properties slightly or substantially from those of the parent compound.) Prior to the discovery of testosterone, the purpose of taking a performance-enhancing drug was to activate or inactivate body systems that contribute to success in sporting events. For example, strychnine has the tendency to stimulate the nervous and muscular system, increasing the efficiency with which the body functions. It seemed a reasonable decision, then, to give athletes very small doses of the substances to increase their participation. Indeed, some sports authorities at the time thought that athletes probably could not compete successfully in some endurance sports, like the marathon, *without* using a drug like strychnine (de Mondenard 2000).

Other drugs were used to reduce the pain and discomfort associated with athletic events, just as modern-day professional athletes may (usually illegally) receive an injection of a narcotic analgesic, such as heroin, morphine, or oxycodone, that will allow them to return to competition with a sore arm, a twisted ankle, or a broken bone. Testosterone and its chemical cousins have a totally different effect: they actually initiate the production of new cells and tissue in the body, resulting in an increase in body muscle mass. This change, in turn, increases a person's strength, speed, endurance, and other physical traits. Testosterone and related compounds not only help a person become better at what he or she does with his or her body, but fundamentally alters that body to raise the bar as to what one's maximum achievement can be.

The Road to Testosterone

The Early Years

The first inklings that animals may possess some sort of material responsible for primary and secondary sexual characteristics dates to at least the fourth millennium BCE. At some point in time, farmers discovered that castration of a male animal alters (often dramatically) many of that animal's behaviors, such as aggressiveness, interest in sexual mating, vocalization, and display. The first scientific study designed to study this phenomenon was conducted in 1767 by the famous English physician and surgeon John Hunter. Hunter removed the testes from two male chickens and transferred the tissue to the abdominal cavity of two other roosters, who were otherwise not altered. Hunter found that the roosters who received the testicular tissue experienced no behavioral changes, while the two roosters from whom the tissue was taken lost many of their natural male characteristics. In a word, they "grew fat and lazy" (A Brief Description of Testosterone 2012). Hunter was actually not very interested in the demasculinization effects produced in the experiment, as he was primarily interested in learning more about the process of tissue transplantation (Freeman, Bloom, and McGuire 2000, 371).

Hunter's experiment was repeated and refined some eight decades later by the German physiologist Arnold Berthold. In 1849, Berthold castrated six young chickens. From four of the chickens he removed both testes; from the other two, he removed only one of each pair of testes. He noted that castration had observable effects on all six birds, reducing their aggressiveness toward other birds and their sexual interest in females. Their combs and wattles (both sexual organs in chickens) both continued to grow, although at a much slower rate than normal and with virtually no color.

Berthold next transplanted the testes removed from the young chickens into the abdominal cavities of two of the castrated birds, a procedure similar to that of Hunter. He found that this procedure caused a reappearance of male sexual characteristics in the birds that had received the transplantations. When these birds were sacrificed, he found that new connections had developed between the transplanted testes and the animal's circulatory system. He concluded from this research that the testes provided some substance that circulated in the bloodstream and evoked male sexual characteristics in an animal (Berthold 1944).

Perhaps the first experiment of this type performed on humans was reported in 1889 by the French neurologist and physiologist Charles E. Brown-Séquard. In a letter to the British scientific journal *The Lancet*, Brown-Séquard told how he had injected himself (he was 72 at the time) with extracts taken from the testes of dogs and guinea pigs. He reported that

> a radical change took place in me. . . . I had regained at least all the strength I possessed a good many years ago. . . . My limbs, tested with a dynamometer, for a week before my trial and during the month following the first injection, showed a decided gain of strength. . . . With regard to the facility of intellectual labour, which had diminished within the last few years, a return to my previous ordinary condition became quite manifest. (quoted in Cussons et al. 2002, 678)

Brown-Séquard said that he had achieved similar results with three additional subjects, aged 54, 56, and 68 years, although he found no such results in two elderly men injected with pure water as a placebo.

Brown-Séquard has long been the subject of some debate, with many authorities questioning whether the results he reported were the result of the injections or were, in fact, themselves placebo effects. In 2002, a group of Australian researchers reported on a study that suggests that the amount of testosterone injected by Brown-Séquard was far less than needed to produce the effects of which he wrote (Cussons et al. 2002, 679).

Whether Brown-Séquard's reports represented true phenomena or were merely artifacts based on the placebo effect, they soon had a profound effect on medical practice worldwide. Men of all ages saw in his research a way of regaining or enhancing the masculine qualities that were seemingly never great enough for most men. The new field that arose from

Brown-Séquard's research was called *organotherapy*, the improvement of life by using organ extracts. Before long, medical entrepreneurs were offering such extracts taken not only from the sex organs, but from almost every part of the body. These extracts were being recommended for the cure of an almost endless list of diseases, including epilepsy, tuberculosis, diabetes, paralysis, gangrene, anemia, arteriosclerosis, influenza, Addison's disease, hysteria, and migraine (Hoberman and Yesalis 1995, 78). Within a year of Brown-Séquard's *Lancet* article, more than 12,000 medical practitioners were producing and selling some version of his rejuvenating fluid, soon given the name Elixir of Life (Tattersall 2009, 730).

Reports about experiments with the Elixir of Life soon began to pour in from around the world. Some observers reported remarkable changes in men who received injections from dogs, rats, guinea pigs, lambs, and other animals. Others saw no improvement in subjects' conditions. But, in a not-unexpected reaction, men around the world concerned about the (natural) loss of their masculine powers, thronged to medical practitioners who promised to solve this problem for them with a simple injection or two (or three or more) (Lefler 2012; for an interesting contemporary description of the state of affairs, see "Elixir of Life—The Brown Sequard Discovery," 2012; for Brown-Séquard's own account of the discovery and benefits of the elixir, see Full Text of the "Elixir of Life").

Demand of the Elixir of Life was so great that a new problem arose: a deficiency of testicular tissue needed for making the extracts from which the elixir was made. In the early 1920s, Viennese physiologist Eugen Steinach suggested a solution for this program. Based on an extended series of experiments on guinea pigs, rats, and other laboratory animals, Steinach argued that vasoligation of the vas deferens (tying off the tubes through which sperm is released) would allow the materials responsible for male sex characteristics to be retained in the body, permitting a rejuvenation of the male body. (The so-called Steinach operation is generally similar to the procedure used in a vasectomy today.) As with the Elixir of Life, Steinach's operation soon became widely popular with such famous figures as Sigmund Freud and William Butler Yeats receiving the treatment (Lock 1983, 1964; Turner 2012).

The Search for Testosterone

Even as practicing physicians were putting to use the empirical discoveries of Brown-Séquard, his predecessors, and his successors, another line of research was directed in a more mechanistic direction, the effort to discover and characterize the specific material responsible for the observable changes caused by "testicular fluids." The key introductory step in that search occurred in 1902 when English physiologists William Maddock Bayliss and Ernest Henry Starling discovered a substance (which they called secretin) that caused the pancreas to secrete water and bicarbonate (as it normally does), even after all nerve connections to the organ had been severed. They concluded that the action of the pancreas was controlled not by messages from the nervous systems, but by some type of material, which they called a "chemical messenger." Some years later, British physiologist William B. Hardy suggested the name *hormone* for these "chemical messengers." It became apparent to medical researchers at that point that both male and female sex organs produced their effect on the human body by releasing one or more hormones into the body. These hormones then travel throughout the body, where they act on other organs that are responsible for primary and secondary sexual characteristics.

Interest in the discovery of sex hormones was of considerable interest to a number of major pharmaceutical companies. The raging success of the Elixir of Life formulas and the Steinach operation made it clear to such companies that, even when treatment effectiveness was somewhat in question, there was great demand for these products and procedures. Thus, companies such as Organon, in the Netherlands; Ciba, in Switzerland; and Schering, in Germany, began to pour money into research on the still mysterious sex-giving hormones. The first breakthrough in this race occurred in 1929 when a team of researchers led by American biochemist Edward Adelbart Doisy isolated the hormone responsible for female sex traits from hundreds of liters of female urine. Doisy called the hormone *theelin*. Only a few months later, an identical discovery was announced by German chemist Adolf Butenandt. Butenandt suggested the name *oestron* (now, estrone) for the hormone, a name that has been retained. For this and later discoveries, Butenandt was awarded a share of the 1939 Nobel Prize in Chemistry.

Butenandt then turned his attention to the comparable male sex hormone, which he first isolated in 1931. He called that hormone *androsterone* (based on the terms *andro-*, for "male," *-ster-*, for the chemical structure of the molecule, and *-one*, the suffix used for ketones, the chemical family to which the compound belongs.) It is now known that androsterone is a metabolite of testosterone with no androgenic or anabolic properties of its own. (A metabolite is a substance formed as the result of the breakdown of some other substance, as when testosterone breaks down in the body to produce androsterone [and other products].) Butenandt's success in isolating androsterone is rather remarkable since it involved the collection of anywhere from 15,000 to 25,000 liters (L) (authorities differ with regard to the exact number) of urine from local policemen (Dotson and Brown 2007, 764).

The final step in this phase of the testosterone story occurred in 1934, when Croatian biochemist Leopold Ružička, starting with readily available relatively simple organic compounds, synthesized androsterone. For the first time, scientists had an essentially complete knowledge of a single sex hormone, androsterone. At the same time, they had extensive evidence to suggest that androsterone was not the hormone responsible for male sexual characteristics.

The discovery of that substance was actually well under way by the time Doisy, Butenandt, and Ružička had completed their studies. As early as 1926, two researchers at the

Leopold Ružička, winner of the 1939 Nobel Prize for chemistry for isolating testosterone, a hormone he later successfully synthesized. (Corbis)

University of Chicago, Fred Koch and Lemeul C. McGee, had begun their own search for the male sex hormone. They were fortunate in the fact that, residing in Chicago, they had access to one of the world's largest supplies of the raw product needed for such studies, the testicles of domestic bulls headed for the slaughter house. They began by purchasing 40 pounds (lb) of bull testicles from the Chicago Stockyards and then developing processes for extracting the hormone found in the testicles. They obtained a minuscule sample of 20 milligrams (mg) of the substance which, when injected into capons (neutered roosters) restored the bird's normal masculine characteristics, such as a pronounced comb and wattles. They then expanded their experiment by starting with an even larger supply of bull testicles—more than 1,000 lb—from which they were able to extract a much larger amount of the male sex hormone. Again, they tested this hormone on experimental animals and, eventually, on a male eunuch (a castrated male). In all cases, they found that the hormone produced the masculinizing effects for which they had been searching. They had clearly demonstrated that some type of male sex hormone exists.

Determination as to the precise nature of that hormone was resolved by another group of researchers at the Organo pharmaceutical firm, in Oss, Netherlands, led by Ernst Laqueur, a founder of the firm. In 1935, the Organo research team announced that they had isolated a new substance with powerful androgenic properties. The term *androgenic* refers to any substance that promotes the development of masculine physical properties, such as the growth of body and facial hair, deepening of the voice, enlargement of the larynx, increase in muscle mass and strength, and broadening of the shoulders in humans. They reported their results in a now classical paper in endocrinology, "Über krystallinisches mannliches Hormon aus Hoden (Testosteron) wirksamer als aus harn oder aus Cholesterin bereitetes Androsteron" ("On crystalline male hormone from testicles (testosterone) effective as from urine or from cholesterol").

The search was almost over. The male sex hormone had been found, its physiological properties had been demonstrated, it had been named, and it had been prepared in crystalline form. All that remained was for someone to synthesize the substance in the laboratory, and testosterone could be said to be completely understood. That final step occurred in 1935 when Butenandt and Ružička independently synthesized testosterone, the former completing his work only a week before the latter. This achievement was at least partially responsible for the joint award of the 1939 Nobel Prize in Chemistry to these two researchers.

What Is Testosterone?

Testosterone is an anabolic, androgenic steroid found in mammals, reptiles, amphibians, birds, fish (in a slightly different form), and other vertebrates. The term *anabolic* is derived from the word *anabolism*, which refers to the process by which living cells convert relatively simple chemical compounds, such as sugars and amino acids, to more complex organic compounds, such as carbohydrates and proteins. Its molecular formula is $C_{19}H_{28}O_2$, and its structural formula is shown in Figure 1.1. In this chemical formula, a carbon atom is present (but not shown) at the intersection of any two lines, and one or more hydrogen atoms are attached to each carbon atom, but, again, not usually shown in the chemical formula. Its systematic chemical name is (8R,9S,10R,13S,14S,17S)-17-hydroxy-10,13-dimethyl-1,2,6,7,8,9,11,12,14,15,16,17-dodecahydrocyclopenta[a]phenanthren-3-one, and it is now commercially available under a variety of trade names, including Androderm, Androlin,

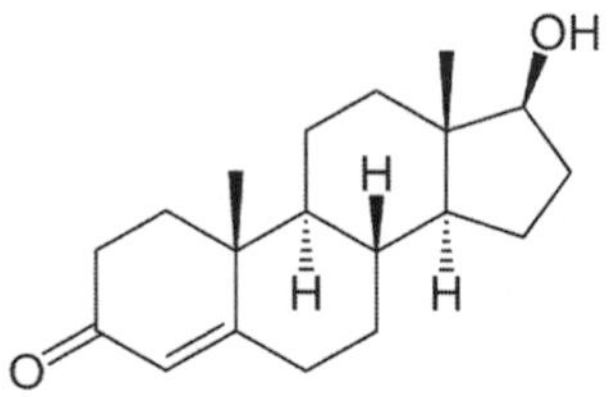

Figure 1.1   Testosterone

Mertestate, Testoderm, Testosteron, Oreton, Synandrol F, trans-Testosterone, and Andronaq.

Testosterone is a member of the steroid family of biochemical compounds. The steroids all share a common core structure consisting of four rings consisting of carbon and hydrogen atoms called the *gonane* nucleus. (Depending on the spatial arrangement of the four rings, the structure may also be called the *sterane* nucleus.) Figure 1.2 shows the chemical formula of the gonane nucleus. Again, for the sake of simplicity, carbon and hydrogen (usually) atoms are not shown in the formula, but are present as described for the testosterone formula above.

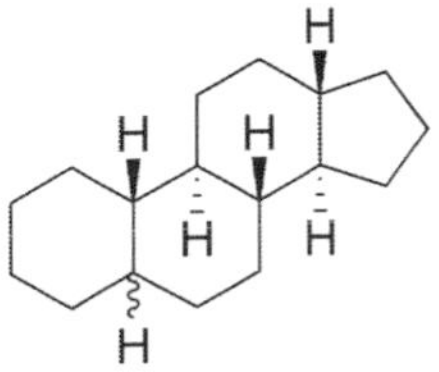

Figure 1.2   Gonane

Various steroids differ from each other on the basis of atoms and groups of atoms that have been substituted for one or more hydrogen atoms in the gonane system. Compare, for example, the formulas for testosterone (Figure 1.1) and cholesterol (Figure 1.3), both of which contain the gonane nucleus and are, therefore, steroids. Testosterone has a hydroxyl (-OH) group attached at one end of the gonane nucleus and a double-bonded oxygen at the other end. Cholesterol also has a hydroxyl group at one end of the gonane nucleus, but a long string of seven carbon atoms at the other end of the gonane nucleus.

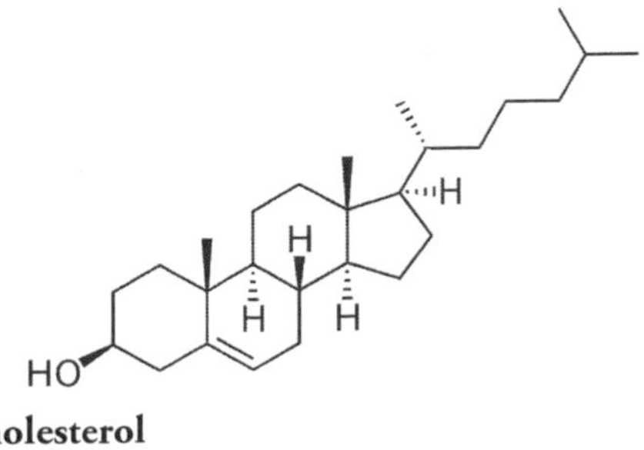

Figure 1.3   Cholesterol

Don't worry. There's no quiz on this information. But it will help you understand the next topic, the analogs of testosterone, which *can be* of both interest and concern.

Derivatives of Testosterone

The testosterone molecule has two points of chemical activity. One is the hydroxyl group at one end of the molecule, attached to the number 17 carbon atom in the molecule (don't worry about the numbering system in this explanation). The other is the carbonyl (C=O) group in position number 3 in the molecule. Both of these positions can react with other substances to form a number compound, a derivative of testosterone. For example, almost any acid will react with the number 17 hydroxyl group to produce a product known as a *testosterone ester*. In chemistry, an *ester* is simply a compound formed when an alcohol (a compound with a hydroxyl group) reacts with an acid. If testosterone is treated with acetic acid, for example, the product is the ester called testosterone acetate. The most widely prescribed testosterone derivative is testosterone enanthate, an oil-based injectable drug that is very effective at building muscle tissue and is legally used to treat hypogonadism and other disorders of androgen deficiency. (Hypogonadism is a condition in which a person's sex glands produce a deficient quantity of sex hormones. It is often treated with pure testosterone or a testosterone derivative.)

Another common class of testosterone derivatives consists of the alkyl testosterones. The term *alkyl* refers to a hydrocarbon radical, such as the methyl ($-CH_3$), ethyl ($-C_2H_5$), or propyl ($-C_3H_7$) group. Adding a methyl group of testosterone at the number 17 hydroxyl group, for example, produces methyltestosterone, a compound that is used with individuals who do not have adequate levels of testosterone in their blood. It is marketed under the trade names Android, Testred, and Virilon.

Two other close relatives of testosterone are also used to make testosterone derivatives: dihydrotestosterone (DHT) and nortestosterone. DHT has two more hydrogens than does testosterone, and nortestosterone has one carbon atom less than testosterone. So the three compounds are all quite similar structurally. Both DHT and nortestosterone can undergo alkylation and esterification as can testosterone itself.

So what's the point of making testosterone derivatives, such as a testosterone ester? The point is that these derivatives have slightly different physical, chemical, physiological, and pharmacological properties from pure testosterone itself. They may

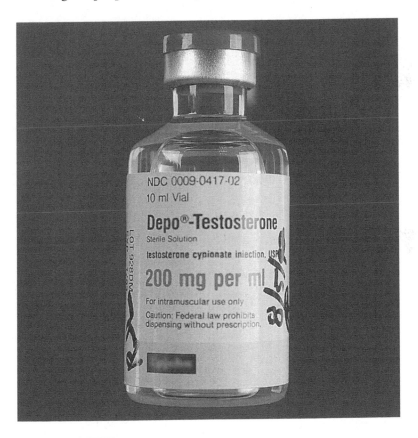

The anabolic steroid DEPO-testosterone. In an effort to curb the use and abuse of anabolic steroids, particularly in sports, the Anabolic Steroid Control Act of 2004 established a comprehensive list of steroids as controlled substances, making their possession and use a federal crime. (U.S. Drug Enforcement Agency)

have stronger or weaker anabolic or androgenic properties; they may have more severe, less severe, or just different side effects; they may be absorbed by the body more or less easily; they may be more or less soluble in water; they may cause more or less irritation at the injection site; they may be more or less easily detectable in standard doping tests; or they may differ from pure testosterone in some other way.

Some of the most commonly used of the hundreds of testosterone derivatives currently available are the following:

- Testosterone cypionate has the longest side chain (the cypionate group) of any testosterone ester. For that reason, it takes the body a long time to complete metabolizing the compound (about two weeks), allowing it to produce its effects on the body over a long period of time.

- Testosterone heptylate is currently produced by only one pharmaceutical firm in France, under the trade name Theramex. Although effective as an anabolic product, it also has the disadvantage of producing somewhat excessive androgenic effects.

- Testosterone undecanoate was developed by Organon in the 1980s. Compared to other testosterone derivatives, it has relatively mild anabolic and androgenic effects and can, therefore, be expensive to use in order to achieve significant muscle-mass-building effects.

- Fluoxymesterone is sold by the Upjohn pharmaceutical company under the trade name Halotestin. It differs from testosterone at three positions in the gonane nucleus with a fluorine atom (hence its name) at the number 9 carbon atom. It has strong strength and endurance properties, but is not very effective at building muscle tissue. The presence of the fluorine atom also makes it toxic to the liver, so it can be used in only small quantities at a time.

- Oxandrolone was first developed by Searle Laboratories, but it now produced by Savient Pharmaceuticals and sold under the trade name of Oxandrin. It is prescribed for weight gain for patients who have lost weight as the result of surgery, injury, or disease. Its androgenic and anabolic effects are both relatively mild, but it tends to be effective at reducing fat content in the body.

- Trenbolone enthanate is on almost everyone's list of "best of" and "worst of" AS. Trenbolone itself is a testosterone derivative in which there are small changes in the gonane nucleus itself, but no changes in the hydroxyl and carbonyl groups. It is usually sold in the form of the ester, trenbolone enthanate. It is "the best" because it has powerful anabolic effects, producing up to five times the muscle-building capacity of testosterone itself. But it is also "the worst" because of its serious side effects, such as damage to the liver and heart.

- Stanozolol, also known as Winstrol, is a derivative of DHT. It is quite unusual structurally in that it contains a fifth ring attached to the gonane nucleus. This configuration makes it more stable in the body, capable of remaining longer in the bloodstream. It also cannot be attacked by aromatase, and so cannot be converted into a female sex hormone, eliminating the possibility of gynecomastia.

- Oxymetholone is another derivative of DHT. It is currently regarded as the most powerful of all AS with the most pronounced androgenic effects. It is the only anabolic androgenic steroid (AAS) to have been classified as a possible carcinogen (cancer-causing agent). It is sold commercially as Anadrol-50.

- Trenbolone is a derivative of nortestosterone with a strong tendency to promote nitrogen retention in muscle tissue, a key to the development of new muscle tissue. It is also thought to act as an anticatabolic substance that blocks the action of glucocorticoids, such as cortisol (see the following page). Finally, it is thought to promote the action of the growth-promoting substance, insulin growth factor 1 (IGF-1).

- Deca-durabolin is the decanoic ester of nortestosterone. It is widely known simply as "Deca." It has been used successful to treat wasting in patients with HIV/AIDS infection and is very popular with weight lifters and bodybuilders as a reliable substance for weight gain.

In conclusion, researchers have synthesized hundreds of derivatives of testosterone, DHT, and nortestosterone over the past century. In general, the most important objective of this research has been to find testosterone derivatives that have greater anabolic effects and reduced androgenic effects. To a considerable extent, that search has been successful, and the medical profession now has an arsenal of products that can be used for a wide variety of medical disorders, ranging from muscle-wasting disorders, damaged myocardium in heart disorders, and growth retardation to bone marrow failure disorders, end-stage renal disease, and deficient plasma protein production. (For an excellent review of the history of testosterone derivative development and current applications, see Shahidi 2001.)

How Testosterone Works in the Human Body

The human body grows and develops as the result of a complex network of chemical reactions made possible by a number of specialized substances known as *enzymes*. The processes by which testosterone is produced in the body and by which it exerts its effects on the body are an example of that pattern of events. Testosterone is produced in males almost exclusively in Leydig cells (also called *interstitial cells*) of the testes and in the ovaries, in females. Very small amounts (usually less than 5 percent) of the testosterone in the male body come from other sources, such as the breakdown of other androgens. The term *androgen* refers to any hormone that stimulates the production of primary or secondary male sexual characteristics.

The amount of testosterone produced by the male body is many times greater than that produced in the female body, an average of 300–1,000 nanograms per deciliter (ng/dL), or

3–7 milligrams per day (mg/d) in the average male. In females, the rate of testosterone production is about 25–90 ng/dL, or 0.1–0.4 mg/d (Kicman 2010, 28–29; Virtual Muscle 2012). Testosterone production is very much a function of age, with an early peak occurring in the first six months of life, followed by a decline and a second peak at the onset of puberty. As males age, their level of testosterone production declines continuously. Testosterone production is also a diurnal function, meaning that the amount of testosterone produced varies cyclically throughout a 24-hour (hr) period (Winters 2012).

Testosterone is synthesized in Leydig cells through a series of chemical reactions that begin with another familiar steroid, cholesterol. One of two pathways is possible, the most common of which involves eight steps, each made possible (is "catalyzed") by a specific enzyme:

cholesterol → pregnenolone → 17-hydroxypregnenolone → dehydroepiandrosterone (DHEA) → androstenediol → progesterone → 17-hydroxyprogesterone → androstenedione → testosterone.

Each step involves a small discrete change in a molecule, adding or removing a single hydrogen atom, for example. Overall, the series of reactions illustrates the way in which the body makes important biochemical changes one step at a time.

The second pathway by which testosterone is formed parallels the one shown above. It consists of the following steps:

cholesterol → progesterone → 17-hydroxyprogesterone → androstenedione → testosterone.

Notice that a number of substances are involved in the synthesis of testosterone. These substances are known as *precursors*, compounds that "go before" the final product itself, or, if the final product is a hormone, they are called *prohormones*. Prohormones that lead to the formation of testosterone generally have weak or no androgenic or anabolic effects themselves. They may still be desirable as performance-enhancing drugs, however, because they increase the amount of testosterone that forms in the body.

The amount of testosterone produced by the body is ultimately a function of the number of Leydig cells available in the testes. That number, in turn, is determined by the action of two hormones, luteinizing hormone (LH) and follicle-stimulating hormone (FSH), produced by the hypothalamus and pituitary glands. Genetic disorders, diseases, or injuries that affect the production of these hormones, then, can result in a reduction in the number of Leydig cells produced and, hence, the rate of testosterone production. In such cases, and the disorder known as hypogonadism is one, testosterone can be supplied externally (exogenously) to compensate for the loss of natural (endogenous) testosterone.

A very great majority of the testosterone produced in the testes is converted to a bound form with albumin and globulin proteins. This reaction is a simple one, $T + A \rightarrow TA$ and $T + G \rightarrow TG$, in which testosterone essentially becomes biologically inactive. These reactions appear to serve a number of important functions in the body, such as protecting testosterone from degradation by enzymes produced in the liver or increasing the solubility of testosterone, improving the ease with which it is transported in the bloodstream. Something less than 5 percent of all the testosterone synthesized each day, then, exists in a "free" form in the blood, so-called *serum testosterone*. When a test is performed to determine the amount of testosterone in a person's blood, it is generally a test for serum testosterone.

Testosterone produces its physiological effects when it is delivered to individual cells. Testosterone molecules pass through the membrane of a cell and enter the cytoplasm. Then, in some cases, the testosterone is converted by the enzyme 5-alpha-reductase to a closely related androgen, DHT, which is many times more potent as an androgenic substance than is testosterone itself. In cells that lack 5-alpha-reductase, testosterone remains in its original form. Next, either testosterone or DHT attaches itself to a protein molecule that contains a special "recognition site" called an *androgen receptor*. The binding of the testosterone or DHT to the receptor site of the molecule initiates a cascade of reactions in which genes in DNA in the nucleus of the cell are activated to begin producing amino acids which, in turn, are used to synthesize new protein in the cell. (For an excellent technical review of this subject, see Kishner 2012.)

The precise proteins produced depend on the specific cells involved. In the skin, scalp, and prostate, for example, it is the action of DHT on DNA that is thought to be responsible for the production of both primary and secondary male sexual characteristics. In muscle cells, protein synthesis results in the formation of new actin and myosin molecules, the substrates from which muscle tissue is formed. It is precisely this series of reactions that bodybuilders, weight lifters, and other athletes are hoping for when they take AS to improve their performance.

One of the practical issues with which athletes have to deal is that, in a normal, healthy male, a very large fraction of androgen receptor sites are already engaged by endogenous testosterone or other AS. In such a case, the addition of exogenous AS may have little or no effect, since there are few or no binding sites remaining on androgen receptors. Anabolic effects of the exogenous steroids occur, then, only because of other biochemical changes, such as reducing catabolic changes that may be taking place within cells (Calfee and Fadale 2006).

Another chemical reaction involving testosterone of considerable interest and importance occurs in cells that contain the enzyme aromatase. Aromatase is an enzyme that converts androgens (male sex hormones) to estrogens (female sex hormones). Specifically, it converts testosterone to estradiol and androstenedione to estrone. If you compare the structural formula of estradiol (Figure 1.4) with that of testosterone, you will see three major differences, one of which is the one of the gonane rings (the one farthest to the left) has double bonds (=) lacking in the testosterone molecule. A ring with three double bonds is called an *aromatic* compound, which is how aromatase gets its name.

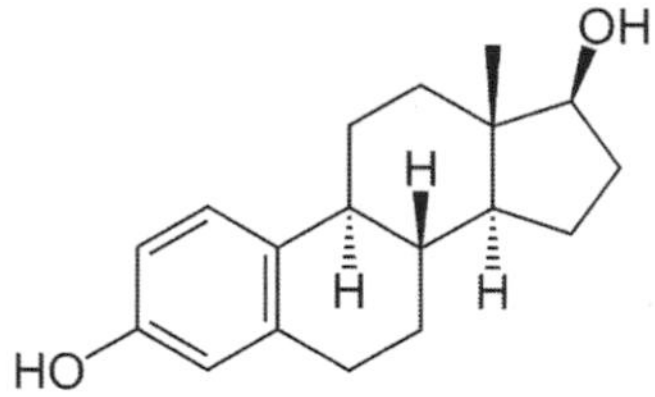

Figure 1.4   Estradiol

This action of aromatase poses a problem for athletes who choose to use AAS in their training programs. With an increase in the amount of testosterone in the bloodstream, the likelihood of aromatization occurring significantly increases. As that process becomes more common, more and more female sex hormones are produced within the body, and a person's body begins to take on more feminine characteristics, such as a reduction in body hair, increase in voice pitch, narrower shoulders and broader hips, and increase in breast size. The last of these changes is probably of greatest concern to athletes who use steroid supplements, because it clearly distracts from the characteristically masculine body that most men strive for. The condition is given the name of *gynecomastia*, from the two Greek words for "breast" and "woman."

One of the most common complaints among athletes who use steroid supplements is that they do not achieve the results promised by the product. There are a number of reasons for this situation, but one is that many of those who complain about the problem do not realize that improvement on body muscle mass, strength, endurance, and other properties is a process that actually has two components. One, around which this discussion has centered so far, is anabolism, the processes by which the body converts simple chemical compounds into more complex compounds needed to build new tissue. The second component is catabolism, the normal bodily function by which bodily tissue and the complex compounds of which it is made are degraded to simple compounds, which are then eliminated from the body. Catabolism, then, is the process by which body tissues "wear out" and break down. Taking supplements to increase anabolic reactions in the body are of little or no value if catabolic reactions result in a loss of comparable or more body tissue.

For this reason, experts in sports medicine sometimes recommend the addition of anticatabolic supplements to a person's diet to reduce the amount of muscle tissue lost by catabolism. Sometimes, these supplements are chemicals that actually block or disrupt the function of enzymes that cause catabolism. Perhaps the best example of the action of AS as anticatabolites is in their action on cortisol. Cortisol is a hormone that belongs to the class of compounds known as the corticosteroids, steroids that are produced in the adrenal gland of vertebrates. They are, more specifically, members of the family of glucocorticoids, corticosteroids that contain a sugar-like component. Cortisol has a number of important functions in the body, one of which is the catabolism of proteins in tissue to release amino acids, which are then available for anabolic reactions that result in the formation of new protein and new tissue. AS can interfere with the action of cortisol because it can displace cortisol from its position on cortisol receptors, preventing it from producing its catabolic functions.

AS have a number of other effects on the body in which they increase the concentration of substances that contribute to the growth of body tissue. For example, they may increase the amount of the enzyme creatine phosphokinase (CPK), that increases the rate of muscle tissue growth, and IGF-1, which also regulates the growth of cells (Kishner 2012). Given the fact that, as noted above, androgen receptor sites are often full, or nearly full, in a healthy adult male, these anticatabolic and metabolic functions may actually be more important in increasing body muscle mass than are the anabolic reactions discussed earlier in this chapter. In fact, one expert in the area has suggested changing the name of AS to *anticatabolic steroids* because their effects are more of the latter type than of the former kind (Miller 2012).

Effects of Anabolic Steroids on the Human Body

Perhaps the most fundamental question one might ask about AS is "How effective are these substances in accomplishing the purposes for which people take them?" That is, do they increase muscle mass, strength, endurance, speed, balance, and other physical traits for which they are supposedly designed? Do athletes who use AS actually perform better in their sports than those who do not use drugs?

Over the past half century, hundreds of studies have been conducted in an attempt to answer these questions. At first, those studies focused on performance. What evidence was there that people who use AS are most successful in athletic competitions than are those who do not? Over time, the focus of research shifted to asking questions as to how the use of AS affects a person's body composition. Do these drugs increase a person's muscle tissue, nervous response, metabolic rate, or other physiological characteristics? Over the last two decades or so, the research emphasis has shifted once again, this time to the potential adverse effects associated with prolonged use of AS.

In addition to the many individual research studies that have been conducted, other researchers have attempted to review large groups of such studies and glean general conclusions from them. A handful of those reviews, published since the 1980s, provide a summary of the information that researchers have obtained about the way in which AS affect the human body (and the bodies of other animals) and performance in physical exercises and athletic events.

One of the interesting conclusions to be drawn from all these studies and reviews with regard to the efficacy of AS on body composition and performance is: It's hard to say. Every review of research on AS emphasizes the ongoing problems associated with such research. Here are some of the problems with research design and execution that are commonly mentioned in reviews:

- Subjects of many research studies are not typical of the type of individuals who use AS for performance enhancement on an everyday basis. A college professor might select, for example, a group of men and women who work out at a local gym and who also take AS to improve their athletic skills. These individuals are unlikely to have the same characteristics as the Mark McGwires, Barry Bonds, and Arnold Schwarzeneggers who might consider the use of AS to improve performances that are already among the highest in the world.

• Much of the research on AS effects, in fact, is not even conducted with humans but, instead, with experimental animals, such as laboratory rats, mice, guinea pigs, and frogs. The reason for this kind of research is obvious. The researcher can sacrifice an animal at the end of an experiment and actually examine anatomical changes that have taken place in the animal's brain or other organs. But it is generally not clear how or to what extent the discoveries made in this kind of research apply to comparable changes in the human body that has been exposed to AS.

• Research that *is* conducted with professional athletes must somehow take into consideration the fact that such athletes are already participating in intense training programs that include the most effective training schedules and nutritional programs known to sports science. Separating gains from such programs from the use of AS is sometimes difficult.

• Most research is hampered by the fact that researchers cannot or do not use the level of AS that athletes themselves use. It is not unusual for controlled experiments on AS use to provide their subjects with less than 10 percent the dose used by practicing weight lifters, bodybuilders, or other professional athletes. Indeed, one observer has suggested that "[a]thletes attempting to bulk up reportedly consume doses 100 to 1,000 times those prescribed for medical purposes [which is typically less than 5 milligrams]" (Sender 2012). Doses that exceed levels that occur naturally in the body are known as *supraphysiological* or *suprapharmacological* doses. One of the main reasons that researchers cannot and do not use supraphysiological doses in their experiments is that the practice would almost certain violate university and other rules that guide the design of experiments with humans.

- Some observers have even suggested that the very idea that one is taking an AS causes changes in a person's mental state, producing a "psychosomatic" condition that contributes to bodily change that might include gains in muscle mass. This effect is also described as a *placebo* effect, in which real changes in a person's body or behavior may come about because of her or his beliefs about the process that is occurring, rather than anything that AS themselves have done (Fahey 2012).

- Another common problem with AS research is selection criteria. Researchers pretty much have to use people who volunteer to take part in their studies, people who perhaps are highly motivated to improve their body image or performance or individuals who may be strongly opposed to the concept of using performance-enhancing drugs. Researchers may not know very much about their subjects' motivations for participating in a study, although that factor might have an important effect on the study outcome. (For an excellent review of problems with research design and execution for AS research, see Hartgens and Kuipers 2004, 517–518.)

So, are there *any* conclusions that can be drawn from the available research on AS, changes in the body, and athletic performance? As noted above, one theme that runs through most, if not all, review articles is the uncertainty of much of the results from such studies. A 1988 review, for example, noted that "although a large number of studies of the effects of AS on athletic performance have been completed, there are very few that have been well controlled and randomized" (Rogol 1988, 7). A later review of the research reached a similar conclusion. "The majority of 'evidence' concerning the efficacy of AS as performance enhancing agents," it said, "is anecdotal. In the main, experimental investigations have been poorly designed scientifically, clinically and statistically" (Mottram and George 2000, 55). A still later report came to the conclusion that "[a]t this time, scientific support for the ergogenic or anabolic use of steroid precursors does not exist" (Powers 2002, 305). A 2006 article about the use of AS also reaches a somewhat similar conclusion in which the author says that, while AS have found a number of useful applications in treating medical conditions, "their efficacy still needs to be demonstrated in terms of improved physical function and quality of life" (Kicman 2008, 502).

(It should be noted that questions about the efficacy of AS among scientific and medical professionals has not prevented enthusiasts for these drugs from publishing their own lists of the "most effective" AS, and the categories in which they are especially effective. See, for example, Steroid Effectiveness Chart 2012 for one of the more thoughtful of such efforts.)

Given these research results, how do scientists explain what appear to be the fairly massive changes in women and men who "bulk up" after use of AS? Some authorities suggest, as noted above, that a well-designed training and nutrition program can be credited with significant improvement in muscle mass, strength, endurance, speed, and other physical properties. A number of researchers have come to the conclusion, however, that there is now growing evidence that the use of AS does, indeed, contribute significantly to the growth of new muscle tissue and can be a real factor in the "bulking up" that occurs among individuals who use AS.

One of the best expressions of this position can be found in a paper by Cynthia M. Kuhn, at the Duke University Medical Center. In a 2002 review of research on AS, Kuhn begins by acknowledging long-standing concerns about the research design and execution of research on AS. She also notes that "[t]he anabolic effects of restoring normal physiologic levels of testosterone in hypogonadal men are uncontested" (Kuhn 2002). Hypogonadal men are men who have much lower than normal levels of testosterone in their bodies, so the additional exogenous testosterone (or other AS) would be expected to have observable and measurable effects on physical properties attributable to the action of testosterone (such as muscle mass). The same statement can be made for women in general who, of course, have a much lower level of testosterone in their blood than do men. Studies are relatively clear that supraphysiological doses of AS can significantly increase a woman's muscle mass and athletic performance.

Kuhn then goes on, however, to challenge the traditional view among scientists that AS are really not very effective in improving muscle mass and athletic performance among men who are eugonadal, that is, who have normal levels of testosterone in their bodies. She cites a number of studies that appear to show that the use of supraphysiological doses of AS can have measurable and observable effects on body structure and athletic performance in eugonadal men. She concludes her review with the observation that

> Studies in AAS [anabolic androgenic steroid]-using human subjects as well as experimental model systems have refuted the decades-old assertion that suprapharmacologic dose regimens of AAS are not anabolic in normal men or are only anabolic due to the impact of their CNS effects on motivation to train. The physiopathology of suprapharmacologic doses of AAS is clearly demonstrated and predicted by the beneficial effects on the same systems when AAS are used in hypogonadal men. (Kuhn 2002, 432)

Kuhn then concludes her review with the observation that perhaps the most interesting point about this whole debate is that there has been so little research on the anatomical, biochemical, pharmacological, and physiological changes produced by AS on the human brain. (An excellent source of the most recent research news about AS is Anabolic Steroid News 2012.)

It should be noted that the individuals who are probably most interested in getting accurate, up-to-date information about the efficacy of AS are men and women who have committed substantial amounts of time to weight lifting, bodybuilding, and related sports. The Internet is now flooded with websites advertising such products for sale and, not so incidentally, often providing surprisingly accurate and useful information about steroids. These websites are often very helpful for men and women trying to decide which AS to purchase and use, in what amounts the product should be taken, by what means it should be taken, whether it should be taken alone or with other steroids and, if so, in what pattern, and so on. In many cases, the advice available at these sites is accurate and reliable, although the efficacy of the advice provided is always, and inherently somewhat, limited. (See, for example, websites such as anabolicsteroids-hormoneknowledge-bigmuscles-drugs.com/testosterone_esters.html, Anabolex.com, EliteFitness.com, isteroids.com, Steroid.com, and SteroidAbuse.com. For a particularly good example of this phenomenon, see Shugarman 2012.)

Therapeutic Uses of Anabolic Steroids

The goal of using AS for increasing body mass, strength, and other physical attributes is important, of course, in fields other than sports and athletics. For nearly a century, researchers have been looking for ways in which such substances can be used to treat and cure a wide variety of physical disorders. The medical applications of AS can be classified into one of three general categories: treatment of hypogonadism in males, treatment of other disease conditions in eugonadal males, and treatment of nonhypogonadal elderly males. The first of these applications is generally known as androgen replacement therapy (ART) because it is used with individuals whose serum testosterone levels are significantly less than those found in a normal male. A number of conditions are responsible for hypogonadism, including the genetic disorder known as Klinefelter's syndrome, castration, diseases of the testes (such as testicular cancer), medical treatments that affect testicular function (such as chemotherapy or radiation therapy), and the action of certain drugs such as cytotoxins and spironolactone. Hypogonadism may also be caused by a number of other medical conditions, such as tumors of or surgery to the pituitary or hypothalamus gland, morbid obesity, the use of illicit drugs or AS, and certain genetic disorders. ART has been used with hypogonadal males since the 1950s with generally good success. According to one source, treated individuals can expect to gain about 1.7 kg (3.7 lb) of body mass, often with a corresponding increase in strength and decrease in body fat mass (9151: Medical and Illicit Use of Anabolic Steroids).

A decrease in serum testosterone also tends to occur in association with certain diseases and injuries, such as HIV infection, chronic obstructive pulmonary disease (COPD), burns, renal failure, cancer, liver failure, and postoperative recovery. Treatment of such conditions with testosterone and its derivatives is called pharmacological androgen therapy (PAT) and, like ART, has been quite successful for well over a century in raising serum testosterone level of individuals with these conditions. Weight gain, increased bone mass and bone density, improved strength, and other advances are commonly associated with the use of PAT. One recent study has noted, however, that the use of AS in PAT has become somewhat less popular not because of its poor track record, but that it is so inexpensive that drug companies prefer to offer more expensive (and, thus, more profitable) options for achieving the same results (Handelsman 2006, 436).

The third application of testosterone therapy is used with aging males who have normal serum testosterone levels for individuals of their age, but who may be candidates for the treatment for a variety of physical and mental reasons. For example, males who are recovering from surgery may benefit from increased muscle mass and body strength provided by AS treatments. At this point, the use of AS for such purposes is somewhat controversial. It is also, according to one view, hampered by an inadequate level of research which, in turn results from the unfavorable view of illegal AS use by bodybuilders, weight lifters, and other athletes (9151: Medical and Illicit Use of Anabolic Steroids).

Risks Associated with the Use of Anabolic Steroids

As noted above, the emphasis of research on AS in the recent past has shifted to a considerable extent to the question of adverse effects of steroid use on the human body. The implicit argument behind at least some of that research seems to be that, whether or not AS have positive effects on the human body, such as increasing muscle mass and strength, it also is responsible for a number of negative physiological and psychological effects. This recent line of research has produced a number of findings that seem to suggest that the deleterious effects of AS use are great enough to be of concern to anyone who chooses to use those substances and to the parents of young people who might consider their use.

One of the strongest official statements along this line is one provided by the New York State Department of Health. On its website, "Anabolic Steroids and Sports: Winning at Any Cost," the department lists more than three dozen adverse effects associated with the use of AS, ranging from increased blood pressure, impaired liver function, and liver tumors to male pattern baldness, striae (stretch marks), and HIV infection to mood swings, aggression, and depression. ("Anabolic Steroids and Sports: Winning at Any Cost" 2012. Other websites and publications with similar themes include DrugFacts: Steroids [Anabolic-Androgenic]; Anabolic Steroids: A Dangerous and Illegal Way to Seek Athletic Dominance and Better Appearance; Dangers of Anabolic Steroids 2012; and Are Steroids Worth the Risk?)

Although documents such as those found on the Internet may sometimes seem overly melodramatic or unduly cautionary, there is probably little doubt that misuse of AS can have a host of deleterious physical effects on users, including cardiovascular, reproductive, nervous, hormonal, hepatic, and orthopedic complications. Perhaps even more troublesome are a number of psychological and psychiatric problems that include aggression, violence, depression, and suicide (9151: Medical and Illicit Use of Anabolic Steroids). Among the best known of these may be so-called 'roid rage (from "android rage"), a condition of unusual violence and aggression associated with the use of supraphysiological amounts of AS. Some authorities suspect that the murder-suicide of professional wrestler Chris Benoit's family in 2007 was the result of Benoit's having gone on a 'roid rage, killed his wife and son, and then committed suicide (Hitti 2012). Depictions of 'roid rage events are available on the Internet (see, for example, http://www.youtube.com/watch?v=gfJTXDppVNA), although they are sometimes age restricted because of their violent nature. Other observers suggest that 'roid rage and other psychological effects of AS are either exaggerated or completely incorrect, and that the use of AS is essentially never associated with psychopathic or sociopathic behavior. David Handelsman, at the University of Sydney Concord Clinical School of Medicine, for example, has called the theory of 'roid rage "street folklore" that serves "mostly as an excuse for bad behavior" (Handelsman 2001; see also Johnson 2012). Those who doubt that 'roid rage really exists argue instead that the phenomenon occurs not because of AS, but because people who were combative and aggressive before they started using supplements simply have a new outlet for their antisocial feelings. As one observer has said, "I would imagine that someone who is kind of a jerk to begin with, he's going to be a bigger jerk when he's 20 or 40 pounds heavier" (Roid Rage a Myth? 2012, at 1:25 minutes).

More generally, some researchers have suggested that the risks posed by use of AS by athletes may have been exaggerated in the past. In one of the best available presentations of this viewpoint, Jay R. Hoffman and Nicholas A. Ratamess at The College of New Jersey have identified a number of factors that may have resulted in a disconnect between medical research-ers studying the effects of AS on the human body and actual practices of amateur and professional athletes. One factor that Hoffman and Ratamess identify is differences in dosage and patterns of usage between athletes and medical researchers. As noted above, athletes typically use much larger doses of AS than researchers do or can use in their own research. Athletes also use steroids in a variety of distinctive way, such as in various forms of cycling, pyramiding, and stacking. Also, researchers tend to study steroid effects on relatively short-term bases, while ath-letes are more likely to use such drugs for extended periods of time. Time factors may also account for the fact that researchers limit their observations to periods of use only and do not fol-low up on long-term effects of steroid use. As a result, Hoffman and Ratamess say, researchers miss the fact that most of the side effects that are reported are transit and that long-term studies would probably show many fewer and less severe consequences of steroid use (Hoffman and Ratamess 2006, 189).

Overall, Hoffman and Ratamess suggest, actual users of AS are probably well ahead of most medical researchers in their knowledge of the products available and the effects of those products on the human body. As a result, athletes are often using performance-enhancing drugs for which researchers have no data and, indeed, about which they may not even know.

Finally, existing research often does not distinguish between correlations and cause-and-effect. For example, assume that the data show that coronary problems are more common among athletes who use AS than those who do not. That finding ex-presses a correlation between two variables, coronary problems and steroid abuse. But those data do not necessarily show a cause-and-effect relationship. It is entirely possible that the athletes involved in this study had coronary problems *before* they began using steroids, and steroid use is unrelated to such problems.

This disconnect between medical research and actual prac-tice among athletes is not an entirely benign phenomenon.

One consequence of the disconnect, according to Hoffman and Ratamess, is that steroid-using athletes tend to ignore the advice of medical professionals, relying instead on gym trainers, training partners, other athletes in the field, and other nonprofessional sources (perhaps another reason for the glut of blogs about steroids on the Internet). This problem is unfortunate, Hoffman and Ratamess say, because athletes who use AS on a regular basis can benefit from monitoring by medical professionals, which neither they nor the professionals themselves are inclined to provide.

Some support exists for the concerns raised by Hoffman and Ratamess. A 2004 study by researchers from the Harvard Medical School and the Duke University Medical Center asked 80 weight lifters how they assessed the expertise of their own physicians both in the field of medicine in general, and with regard to AS in particular. A majority of respondents rated their physicians' overall knowledge of medicine highly, but trusted their knowledge about AS no more highly than they did that of their trainer, friends, sources of drugs, or Internet sites. Four out of ten respondents trusted their drug supplier at least as much, and usually more, than they did any physician they had ever seen. Indeed, more than half of all respondents (56 percent) had never informed their own physician of their use of steroids. Researchers concluded from these results that such attitudes "compromise physicians' ability to educate or treat Anabolic steroids users," and that physicians can be of greater help to their possible Anabolic steroids-using patients "by learning more about these substances" (Pope et al. 2004, 1193).

Appearance and Performance-enhancing Drug (APED) Use

The discussion of AS use thus far has focused almost entirely on therapeutic applications and the use of AS to improve athletic performance. Yet there is another, relatively new and rapidly growing use for AS: in the improvement of a person's overall physical appearance. For a variety of reasons, many children and adolescents today are dissatisfied with their own bodily appearance and would like to be more physically attractive. While gaining strength, endurance, speed, and other athletic attributes may be part of this effort, they are secondary to the goal of simply matching more closely the cultural norm as to what the "good-looking" boy or girl, man or woman, is "supposed" to look like. The use of AS to "burn fat," add muscle, and improve strength and stamina is central in such an effort.

Research directed at a better understanding of the causes, features, and treatment of APED is still quite limited. The evidence produced so far suggests that three factors are associated with the condition. First, those who are concerned about APED tend to be individuals who are significantly more dissatisfied with their bodily appearance than are most children and adolescents. Given that many or most adolescents are somewhat unhappy with the way they look to others, APED is an issue primarily with those who have unusually strong feelings in this regard. Second, those who fall into this category are likely to rely heavily not only on AS, but also on a number of other substances which they believe will help alter their physical appearance, substances such as insulin and insulin-like products, human growth hormone, xanthines (caffeine-like substances), sympathomimetics (such as ephedrine and ephedra), and thyroid hormones. Finally, those with concerns about their physical appearance generally commit themselves to a relatively intense program of physical exercise and nutritional diet to go along with the use of AS (Hildebrandt and Langenbucher 2012; Hildebrandt et al. 2011a). As of late 2012, the medical and psychiatric communities are just beginning to recognize the seriousness of the APED syndrome and starting to develop diagnostic tools and programs for treatment of the condition (Hildebrandt et al. 2011b).

One of the most interesting pieces of data about APED may be its prevalence. From the fact that so little is known about it and so little research has been conducted on the topic, one might assume that APED is only a modest contributing factor to the general problem of AS abuse. One review of the literature published in 2010 suggests that such is almost certainly not the case. In that review, P. A. Hammer, of Wilamette University, in Oregon, found that APED is actually a more common cause of steroid use among high school students in the United States and other parts of the world than is athletic motivation. He summarizes the results of his research by noting that recent research indicates that "the risk of AAS use is lower for those involved in organized sport than for the general adolescent population and that AAS use is more like part of a broader syndrome of problem behaviours than a response to situation-specific goals such as success in sport" (Hammer 2010, 31).

Prevalence of Anabolic Steroid Use

Beginning in the 1950s, a number of studies were conducted to determine the prevalence and, sometimes, incidence of AS use in the United States and other parts of the world. (The term *prevalence* refers to the number of individuals involved in an activity at the present time and *incidence* means the number of individuals who took part in that activity for the first time within some period of time, usually the last year.) The vast majority of these studies have focused on children and young adults. There are at least two reasons for that fact. One is that it is often easier to collect data from youngsters than it is from adults. Most children attend school, so questionnaires and interviews are relatively easy to distribute, collect, and analyze. Also, adults tend to be concerned about steroid use (and other illegal and undesirable behavior) among children and adolescents, so they may want to know how widespread the problem is.

Almost certainly the most important single source of information available about AS use among youngsters can be found in the article by P. A. Hammer mentioned above. In that article, Hammer relied on two important surveys by Charles E. Yesalis and Michael S. Bahrke and by Patrick Laure for pre-2000 data. Those surveys covered more than two dozen discrete research studies of teenagers in the United States and ten more in other countries of the world, including Australia, Canada, South Africa, Sweden, and the United Kingdom. As one might expect because of differing research design, the number of AS users in these surveys varied considerably, with the one general finding that steroid user was almost without exception higher among males than among females. The prevalence rate in the approximately three dozen individual surveys ranged from a low of about 1.5 percent to a high of about 4.5 percent for males. Based on these percentages, other researchers have estimated that anywhere from 500,000 to 700,000 high school students were using AS in the United States during the 1990s. (These data are presented in Hammer 2010, 26, as compiled from Yesalis and Bahrke 2000 and Laure 2000. The prevalence estimate comes from Foley and Schydlower 1993.)

Hammer also reviewed 19 additional studies between 2000 and 2008 conducted in the United States, Brazil, France, Germany, Norway, Poland, Sweden, and other European countries. The U.S. surveys were conducted nationally, regionally, and within individual states. These 19 surveys reported on AS use by grade level, gender, and from populations overall. They found prevalence rates very much within the range reported by other studies. For males, those rates ranged from a low of 0.5 percent (Germany) to a high of 14.3 percent (Poland), with an average within the 3–5 percent range. For females, they ranged from a low of 0.1 percent (Oregon and Washington) to a high of 11.1 (Poland), with an average within the 1–2 percent range. The broadest surveys, those conducted annually by the Monitoring the Future survey program at the University of Michigan, consistently show a prevalence rate of about 1.5 percent for eighth graders, 1.8 percent for 10th graders, and 2.2 percent for 12th graders (Hammer 2010, Table 1, 28; for results of the Monitoring the Future survey for U.S. data, see Johnston et al. 2012). Hammer concludes his review with an estimate of a lifetime prevalence of AAS use for adolescent males of 4–6 percent and for females of 1.5–3 percent, "indicating a problem involving millions of athletes and a potential epidemic of AAS-related pathologies" (Hammer 2010, 26).

Prevalence surveys among adults are much less common, and they tend to provide somewhat less useful information. Most commonly, these surveys have focused on specific nations, such as those conducted for Nigeria, Poland, South Africa, Sweden, and the United Kingdom, for specific groups, such as athletes training for the Olympic Games. The results of these surveys vary widely depending on a number of factors, including the nationality of the population, the sport for which individuals are training, their professional versus amateur status, and the mode by which data were collected. Prevalence rates for these studies range from a low of about 1 percent for both men and women in Nigeria training for the Olympic Games to more than 50 percent for active weight lifters training for national or international competitions. As an example, a survey conducted in 1997 of 21 gymnasia in England, Scotland, and Wales found an average rate of AS use of 9.1 percent among men and 2.3 percent among women. That rate ranged wildly, however, from site to site, with a low of zero percent at three gymnasia and a maximum of 46 percent of all respondents at another location (Korkia and Stimson 1997; an excellent and comprehensive review of studies on the prevalence of AS use by men, women, elite athletes, and adolescents and children is available from Lenehan 2003, 12–20).

One of the most recent studies on the prevalence of AAS users in the United States confirmed the evolving view that concerns for physical attractiveness are a greater motivating force for the use of steroids than is athletic competitiveness. In a survey of 1,955 male adult nonmedical AS users culled from the Internet, researchers found that the typical AAS user was a "Caucasian, highly-educated, gainfully employed professional approximately 30 years of age, who was earning an above-average income, was not active in organized sports, and whose use was motivated by increases in skeletal muscle mass, strength, and physical attractiveness." Such a finding, the researchers noted, suggests a reconsideration of conventional views about the motivations that drive individuals to use AS.

Finally, a 2011 study raised a new issue about the use of AS for purposes of physical enhancement. In this study, researchers asked a group of physicians how they feel about prescribing steroids to individuals who want the products primarily or exclusively for the purposes of improving their physical appearance. Physicians who participated in the study provided a range of views, extending from the belief that individuals should have the right to use such products if they feel they need them to questions about providing some individuals an advantage with pills that might not be available to other individuals (Hotze et al. 2011).

This study illustrates some of the many social, ethical, legal, and other issues that exist in connection with the use of AS by athletes and nonathletes. Should such drugs be readily available to anyone who wants them? What kinds of regulations, if any, should be imposed on their athletic use; on their nonathletic use? Are special policies and practices needed for adolescents and children who want to use AS for performance enhancement or improvement of physical appearance? Should standards be different for those who want to use the drugs solely for athletic purposes or solely for the purpose of appearance enhancement? These are some of the issues to be considered in Chapter 2 of this book.

References

"9151: Medical and Illicit Use of Anabolic Steroids." http://www.netce.com/coursecontent.php?courseid=684. Accessed on June 11, 2012.

"Anabolic Steroids: A Dangerous and Illegal Way to Seek Athletic Dominance and Better Appearance." Drug Enforcement Administration. http://www.deadiversion.

usdoj.gov/pubs/brochures/steroids/public/public.pdf. Accessed on June 11, 2012.

"Anabolic Steroids and Sports: Winning at Any Cost." New York State Department of Health. http://www.health. ny.gov/publications/1210/. Accessed on June 11, 2012.

"Anabolic Steroids News." http://www.medindia.net/ healthnews/anabolic-steroids-news.asp?language=. Accessed on June 11, 2012.

"Are Steroids Worth the Risk?" TeensHealth. http:// kidshealth.org/teen/drug_alcohol/drugs/steroids. html#a_Dangers_of_Steroids. Accessed on June 11, 2012.

Berthold, Arnold Adolph. 1944. (Translated by D. P. Quiring) "The Transplantation of Testes." *Bulletin of the History of Medicine.* 16: 399–401. http://labs.bio.unc.edu/Goldstein/ Berthold1849.pdf.

"A Brief Description of Testosterone." American Vein and Aesthetic Institute. http://www.medrehab.com/Description_ Testosterone.php. Accessed on June 7, 2012.

"A Brief History of Hurling." Celtia. http://www.ancientsites. com/aw/Post/633637. Accessed on June 4, 2012.

Bøje, Ove. 1939. "Doping: A Study of the Means Employed to Raise the Level of Performance in Sport." *Bulletin of the Health Organization of the League of Nations.* 8: 439–469.

Buti, Antonio, and Saul Fridman. 2001. *Drugs, Sport and the Law.* Mudgeeraba, QLD: Scribblers.

Calfee, Ryan, and Paul Fadale. 2006. "Popular Ergogenic Drugs and Supplements in Young Athletes." *Pediatrics.* 117(3): e577–e589.

Carroll, Scott T. 1988. "Wrestling in Ancient Nubia." *Journal of Sport History.* 15(2): 121–137.

"Case Analysis: Instances of Cheating in the Olympic Movement." http://doc.rero.ch/lm.php?url= 1000,40,38,20090929153921-KN/HSU_Leo_-_5_-_

Appendix_1–_Case_study_of_cheating.pdf. Accessed on June 5, 2012.

Cronin, Brian. "Sports Legend Revealed: A Marathon Runner Nearly Died Because of Drugs He Took to Help Him Win." *Los Angeles Times*. Available online at http://latimesblogs.latimes.com/sports_blog/2010/08/sports-legend-revealed-a-marathon-runner-nearly-died-because-of-drugs-he-took-to-help-him-win.html. Accessed on June 5, 2012.

"The Culture of Cuju." *Cultural China*. http://features.cultural-china.com/cuju/index02.html. Accessed on June 4, 2012.

Cussons, Andrea J., et al. 2002. "Brown-Séquard Revisited: A Lesson from History on the Placebo Effect of Androgen Treatment." *Medical Journal of Australia*. 177(11): 678–679.

"Dangers of Anabolic Steroids." *Taylor Hooton Foundation*. http://taylorhooton.org/dangers-of-anabolic-steroids/. Accessed on June 11, 2012.

von Deutsch, Daniel A., Imad K. Abukhalaf, and Robin R. Socci. 2012. "Anabolic Doping Agents." In Mozayani, Ashraf, and Lionel P. Raymon, eds. *Handbook of Drug Interactions*. 2nd ed. Totowa, NJ: Humana Press.

Dotson, Jennifer L., and Robert T. Brown. 2007. "The History of the Development of Anabolic-androgenic Steroids." *Pediatric Clinics of North America*. 54(4): 761–769.

"DrugFacts: Steroids (Anabolic-androgenic)." National Institute of Drug Abuse. http://www.drugabuse.gov/publications/drugfacts/steroids-anabolic-androgenic. Accessed on June 11, 2012.

"Elixir of Life—A Brief History of Testosterone." http://paperspast.natlib.govt.nz/cgi-bin/paperspast?a=d&d=TAN18890925.2.17&l=mi&e=———10—1———0-all. Accessed on June 7, 2012.

Fahey, Thomas D. "Anabolic-androgenic Steroids: Mechanism of Action and Effects on Performance." *Encyclopedia of Sports Medicine and Science.* Available online at http://www. sportsci.org/encyc/anabster/anabster.html. Accessed on June 11, 2012.

Foley, John D., and Manuel Schydlower. 1993. "Anabolic Steroid and Ergogenic Drug Use by Adolescents." *Adolescent Medicine.* 4(2): 341–352.

Freeman, Erica R., David A. Bloom, and Edward J. McGuire. 2001. "A Brief History of Testosterone." *The Journal of Urology.* 165(2): 371–373.

Full Text of the " 'Elixir of Life.' Dr. Brown-Séquard's Own Account of His Famous Alleged Remedy for Debility and Old Age, Dr. Variot's Experiments . . . to Which Is Prefixed a Sketch of Dr. Brown-Séquard's Life, with Portrait." Internet Archive. http://www.archive.org/stream/ elixiroflifedrbr00dunbuoft/elixiroflifedrbr00dunbuoft_ djvu.txt. Accessed on June 7, 2012.

Gertz, Stephen. "Revisiting the Pagan Olympic Games." *Christian History.* http://www.christianitytoday.com/ch/ news/2004/aug19.html. Accessed on June 5, 2012.

Hammer, P. A. 2010. "Anabolic-androgenic Steroid Use among Young Male and Female Athletes: Is the Game to Blame?" *British Journal of Sports Medicine.* 44:26–31.

Handelsman, David. 2001. "Book Review: Adonis Complex: The Secret Crisis of Body Obsession." *New England Journal of Medicine.* 344: 146–147.

Handelsman, David J. 2006. "Testosterone: Use, Misuse and Abuse." *Medical Journal of Australia.* 185(8): 436–439.

Hartgens, Fred, and Harm Kuipers. 2004. "Effects of Androgenic-anabolic Steroids in Athletes." *Sports Medicine.* 34(8): 513–554. Available online at http://www.afboard. com/library/Effects%20of%20Androgenic-Anabolic%20 Steroids%20in%20Athletes.pdf. Accessed on June 11, 2012.

Hildebrandt, Tom, and James W. Langenbucher. "Appearance and Performance Enhancing Drug Use Schedule." http://www.mssm.edu/static_files/MSSM/Files/Research/Programs/Appearance%20and%20Performance%20Enhancing%20Drug%20Program/APEDUS_Hildebrandt.pdf. Accessed on June 12, 2012.

Hildebrandt, Tom, et al. 2011a. "The Diagnostic Dilemma of Pathological Appearance and Performance Enhancing Drug Use." *Drug and Alcohol Dependance.* 114(1): 1–11.

Hildebrandt, Tom, et al. 2011b. "Development and Validation of the Appearance and Performance Enhancing Drug Use Schedule." *Addictive Behaviors.* 36(10): 949–958.

Hill, Warren D., Michael Blake, and John E. Clark. 1998. "Ball Court Design Dates Back 3,400 Years." *Nature.* 392(6679): 878–879.

Hitti, Miranda. "Chris Benoit: Was Roid Rage to Blame?" WebMD. http://www.webmd.com/mental-health/features/roid-rage-14-questions-and-answers. Accessed on June 11, 2012.

Hoberman, John M., and Charles E. Yesalis. 1995. "The History of Synthetic Testosterone." *Scientific American.* 272(2): 76–81.

Hoffman, Jay R., and Nicholas A. Ratamess. 2006. "Medical Issues Associated with Anabolic Steroid Use: Are They Exaggerated?" *Journal of Sports Science and Medicine.* 5: 182–193.

Hotze, Steven F., et al. 2011. "Doctor, Would You Prescribe a Pill to Help Me . . . ?" A National Survey of Physicians on Using Medicine for Human Enhancement." *American Journal of Bioethics.* 11(1): 3–13.

"How the Different Testosterone Esters Affect Your Blood Level of Testosterone and the Potency of its Effects." anabolicsteroids-hormoneknowledge-bigmuscles-drugs.com/testosterone_esters.html.

http://www.anabolicsteroids-hormoneknowledge-bigmuscles-drugs.com/testosterone_esters.html. Accessed on June 8, 2012.

Johnson, Paul. "Roid Rage: Real or Myth?" http://www.bodybuildingweb.net/blog/roid-rage-real-myth/. Accessed on June 11, 2012.

Johnston, Lloyd D., et al. *Monitoring the Future: National Survey Results on Drug Use, 1975–2011*. Ann Arbor, MI: Institute for Social Research, June 2012. Available online at http://www.monitoringthefuture.org/pubs/monographs/mtf-vol1_2011.pdf. Accessed on June 12, 2012.

Kicman, Andrew T. 2010. "Biochemical and Physiological Aspects of Endogenous Androgens." In Detlef Thieme and Peter Hemmersbach, eds. *Doping in Sports*. Heidelberg; New York: Springer, 25–64.

Kicman, Andrew T. 2008. "Pharmacology of Anabolic Steroids." *British Journal of Pharmacology*. 154(3): 502–521.

Kishner, Stephen. "Anabolic Steroid Use and Abuse." *Medscape Reference*. http://emedicine.medscape.com/article/128655-overview. Accessed on June 9, 2012.

Korkia, Pirkko, and Gerry Vivian Stimson. 1997. "Indications of Prevalence, Practice, and Effects of Anabolic Steroid Use in Great Britain." *International Journal of Sport Medicine*. 18(7): 557–562.

Kuhn, Cynthia M. 2002. "Anabolic Steroids." *Recent Progress in Hormone Research*. 56: 411–434. Available online at http://rphr.endojournals.org/cgi/content/full/57/1/411#SEC4. Accessed on June 11, 2012.

Laure, Patrick. 2000. "Le Dopage: Données Épidémiologiques." *La Presse Médicale*. 29(24): 1365–1371 (in French).

Lee, Yu-Hsuan. "Performance Enhancing Drugs: History, Medical Effects & Policy." http://leda.law.harvard.edu/leda/data/780/LeeY06.pdf. Accessed on June 1, 2012.

Lefler, Leah. "The Elixir of Life: A Brief History of Testosterone." http://leahlefler.hubpages.com/hub/The-Elixir-of-Life-A-Brief-History-of-Testosterone. Accessed on June 7, 2012.

Lenehan, Pat. *Anabolic Steroids and Other Performance-enhancing Drugs.* London; New York: Taylor & Francis, 2003.

Lock, Stephen. "O That I Were Young Again": Yeats and the Steinach Operation." *British Medical Journal.* 287(6409): 1964–1968.

Maso, Benjo. *The Sweat of the Gods: Myths and Legends of Bicycle Racing.* Norwich, England: Mousehold Press, 2005.

Miller, G. Klaud. "Use and Abuse of Anabolic Steroids." http://www.jockdoc.ws/subs/anabolicsteroids.htm. Accessed on June 10, 2012.

de Mondenard, Jean-Pierre. 2000. "History and Evolution of Doping." *Annals of Analytical Toxicology.* 12(1): 5–18.

Moore, Gerry, and Andrew Ritchie. 2011. *The Little Black Bottle: Choppy Warburton, His Mysterious Potion, and the Deaths of His Bicycle Racers.* San Francisco: Cycle Publishing.

Mottram, David R., and Alan J. George. 2000. "Anabolic Steroids." *Clinical Endocrinology and Metabolism.* 14(1): 55–69.

Müller, Rudhard Klaus. 2010. "History of Doping and Doping Control." In Detlef Thieme and Peter Hemmersbach, eds. *Doping in Sports.* Heidelberg; New York: Springer.

Pope, Harrison G., et al. 2004. "Anabolic Steroid Users' Attitudes Towards Physicians." *Addiction.* 99(9): 1189–1194.

Powers, Michael E. 2002. "The Safety and Efficacy of Anabolic Steroid Precursors: What Is the Scientific Evidence?" *Journal of Athletic Training.* 37(3): 300–305.

Prokop, Luxembourg. 1970. "The Struggle Against Doping and Its History." *The Journal of Sports Medicine and Physical Fitness*. 10(1): 45–48.

Rogol, Alan D. 1988. "Anabolic Steroid Hormones for Athletes: Efficacy or Fantasy? *Growth, Genetics, and Hormones*. 4(4): 2–3+.

"Roid Rage a Myth?" http://americaspastimetainted. wordpress.com/steroids-101/roid-rage-a-myth/. Accessed on June 11, 2012.

Rosen, Daniel M. 2008. *Dope: A History of Performance Enhancement in Sports from the Nineteenth Century to Today*. Westport, CT: Praeger.

Sender, Aaron J. "Anabolic Steroids for Non-therapeutic Use." http://www.nyu.edu/classes/jaeger/anabolic_steroids.htm. Accessed on June 11, 2012.

Shahidi, Nasrollah T. 2001. "A Review of the Chemistry, Biological Action, and Clinical Applications of Anabolic-androgenic Steroids." *Clinical Therapeutics*. 23(9): 1355–1390.

Shugarman, Alan E. "Muscle Building Supplement Guide." http://www.nutritionexpress.com/article+index/authors/ alan+e+shugarman+ms+rd/showarticle.aspx?articleid=793. Accessed on June 11, 2012.

"Skills for Life." Andre Burger Cricket. http://www. andreburgercricket.com/psychology.ews. Accessed on June 4, 2012.

Speak, Mike. 1999. "Recreation and Sport in Ancient China: Primitive Society to AD 960." In James Riordan and Robin Jones, eds. *Sport and Physical Education in China*. London; New York: International Society for Competitive Physical Education and Sport, 20–44.

"Steroid Effectiveness Chart." isteroids. http://www.isteroids. com/steroids/Steroid%20Effectiveness%20Chart.html. Accessed on June 10, 2012.

Tattersall, R. B. 2009. "Charles-Edouard Brown-Séquard: Double-hyphenated Neurologist and Forgotten Father of Endocrinology." *Diabetic Medicine*. 11(8): 728–731.

"Taylor's Story." Taylor Hooton Foundation. http:// taylorhooton.org/taylors-story/. Accessed on June 4, 2012.

"Testosterone Ester Report." http://www.timinvermont.com/ fitness/ester.htm. Accessed on June 8, 2012.

Turner, Christopher. "Vasectomania, and Other Cures for Sloth." http://www.cabinetmagazine.org/issues/29/turner. php. Accessed on June 7, 2012.

Virtual Muscle. "All about Testosterone." Body Building.com. http://www.bodybuilding.com/fun/vm12.htm. Accessed on June 9, 2012.

Willey, Jessica. "Man Crusades to Save Kids from Steroids." http://abclocal.go.com/ktrk/story?section=news/ local&id=5903834. Accessed on June 4, 2012.

Winters, Stephen J. "Laboratory Assessment of Testicular Function." Endotext. http://www.endotext.org/male/ male4/male4.html. Accessed on June 9, 2012.

Yesalis, Charles E. and Michael S. Bahrke. 2000. "Doping among Adolescent Athletes." *Baillieres Best Practice and Research. Clinical Endocrinology and Metabolism*. 14(1): 25–35.

Yesalis, Charles E., and Michael S. Bahrke. 2002. "History of Doping in Sports." In Michael S. Bahrke and Charles Yesalis, eds. *Performance-enhancing Substances in Sport and Exercise*. Champaign, IL: Human Kinetics, 42–76.

2 Problems, Controversies, and Solutions

On January 30, 1933, German President Paul von Hindenburg appointed Adolf Hitler Chancellor of the German government. That act confirmed the ascension of the National Socialist German Workers' Party, better known as the Nazi Party, to power. For the next 12 years, the Nazis used virtually every tool available to them to control the everyday lives of the German people, as well as those of the nations they conquered.

In 1934, Croatian biochemist Leopold Ružička partially synthesized androsterone from cholesterol. A year later, researchers at the Dutch pharmaceutical firm of Organon, under the direction of German-born chemist Ernst Laqueur, announced the discovery of a crystalline substance which they called testosterone. Only a few months after the Organon discovery, two separate research teams led by German chemist Adolf Butenandt and Ružička announced the first synthesis of testosterone from cholesterol. Within two years of their coming to power in Germany, the Nazi Party had a powerful new chemical weapon available to them: natural and synthetic sex hormones with the ability to make individuals stronger and more virile with greater power, endurance, and aggressive tendencies.

Olympic champion shot-putter Heidi Krieger of East Germany competes during the Women's Shot-Put event at the 1987 World Indoor Athletics Championships, held in the Hoosier Dome in Indianapolis in early March 1987. Krieger, one of many athletes to participate in the covert but systemic East German doping program, later undertook a sex change operation due to the masculinization caused by years of steroid abuse at the insistence of coaches. (Tony Duffy/Getty Images)

Anabolic Steroids in Nazi Germany

To what extent did the Nazis use these chemical discoveries in shaping their own citizens? To many observers, the answer to that question seems obvious. The Nazis were unscrupulous in their efforts to develop a citizenry of which the nation could be proud and of which the rest of the world would be terrified. The Nazi propaganda machine developed and promoted a vision of Germans as a race of Aryan purity, which was superior in every way to all other nationalities, races, and ethnic groups. It was this belief, of course, that eventually led to the ethnic cleansing in which Jews, gypsies, homosexuals, people of color, and other non-Aryan groups were systematically destroyed in the "Grand Experiment" that led to the Holocaust.

A number of historians have argued that the Nazis made use of sex hormones in this campaign, providing drugs to members of the military with the objective of making German soldiers stronger, more aggressive, more violent, and better suited to prevail in combat. In his 1982 book, *Anabolic Steroids and the Athlete*, for example, William N. Taylor argues that several anecdotal records suggest that testosterone and its analogs were given to Nazi Gestapo and Nazi soldiers to "make them more muscular, sexually aggressive and mean fighters in battle" (Taylor 1982, 181). A similar position was expressed in a more recent book on the use of anabolic steroids (AS) in East Germany by American psychologist and former gymnast Steven Ungerleider, *Faust's Gold: Inside the East German Doping Machine*. He writes that

> During World War II, Hitler issued vast quantities of steroids to the SS and Wehrmacht so that his troops could better resist combat fatigue and be more ruthless in following any order. (Ungerleider 2001, 45; see also Cowart 1987)

These and other historians also argue that Nazi researchers tested the effects of AS on residents in concentration camps. In his 1991 book, *Macho Medicine*, Taylor noted that

In the records of World War II are numerous accounts of hormonal manipulation and experimentation with human prisoners by Nazi scientists. (Taylor 1991, 8)

Such views have also now entered into some of the exchanges that occur on the Internet about the history of AS (see, for example, de Borbon 2012; "The Elixir of Life" 2012).

In fact, there appears to be little or no concrete evidence that the Nazis carried out experiments with AS either on their own military personnel or on individuals held in concentration camps. It appears that the conclusions drawn by Taylor, Ungerleider, and others have been based on rumors, anecdotal evidence, hearsay, and other questionable sources. Daniel M. Rosen, author of an excellent book on the history of doping in sports, has concluded that

Despite the pressure on German athletes, and a medical literature full of the information about the effects of other drugs on human performance, no mention of testosterone or its effects has been found in the German medical literature of the times. (Rosen 2008, 13)

Two of the most eminent historians of drug use in sport, Charles E. Yesalis and Michael S. Bahrke, have confirmed this view. They have observed that the Nazis' puritanical outlook on drugs (and virtually all other kinds of moral sins, at least in principle), in general, probably would have militated against the kinds of steroid use described by earlier historians. They also note that such assertions of their use in the military and among captive peoples "has yet to be documented, in spite of efforts in this regard" (Yesalis and Bahrke 2002, 48). Another well-regarded historian of sport and drugs, John M. Hoberman, observed that

It seems improbable that the enormous achievements of German science over the past two centuries did not culminate in scientific experiments aimed at producing the

super-race of which the Nazis boasted, including
superhuman athletes. Our eagerness to believe that the
Nazis did carry out such a project suggests that the world
outside Germany has projected its own experimental
impulses onto this ultimate gangster regime.... (Hoberman
1992, 213)

A third observer, Rob Beamish, observes that stories of Nazi
use of AS simply have no scientific basis and are, purely and
simply, a myth. The only really important point of that myth,
he says, is that "such opinion leaders as physicians, scientific
researchers, policymakers, and journalists have believed the
myth was true" and shaped their later interpretation of steroid
use by athletes from the Soviet block in the 1950s and beyond
(Beamish 2011, 40; Beamish and Ritchie 2005).

Whatever the military applications of AS used or not used by
the Nazis, there is considerably less doubt about German use
of these products in attempting to improve the performance of
German athletes in a number of sports. Again, no conclusive
evidence exists to support the conjecture, but many historians
of sports believe that German athletes during the 1930s were
provided access to the new drugs being produced in, among
other sites, Germany. Again, the argument tends to be that the
philosophy of supremacy of the Aryan race that dominated
Nazi thinking would likely have encouraged coaches, trainers,
managers, and athletes to take advantage of any means they
had to achieve the maximum athletic potential possible. And,
perhaps more to the point, the use of performance-enhancing
drugs was not yet illegal. (In fact, the number of steroid drugs
available for use by athletes was still quite limited, since the
vast majority of anabolic androgenic steroids [AAS] had not
yet been invented.)

The one bit of data to which many sports historians refer
when discussing this issue is the number of medals won by the
United States and Germany in the 1932 and 1936 Olympic
Games. In 1932, there were no steroidal substances available

for use with athletes. In that year, the United States won a total of 110 medals at the Olympic Games held in Los Angeles, 44 gold, 36 silver, and 30 bronze. Germany placed fourth among competing nations, with 5 gold, 12 silver, and 7 bronze, for a total of 24 medals. By comparison, Germany won the greatest number of medals in the 1936 Games held in Berlin, with a total of 101 medals, 38 gold, 31 silver, and 32 bronze. The United States was placed second behind Germany, with a total of 57 medals, 24 gold, 21 silver, and 12 bronze. Some observers suggest that Germany had the "home-field" advantage in 1936, and the United States, in 1932, a factor that could conceivably account for this discrepancy (see, for example, The 1936 Wrestling Team of Germany during Nazi Rule 2012). (No comparisons for Games *following* the 1936 event are possible since the 1940 and 1944 Games were cancelled and Germany did not compete in the 1948 Games in London.) But other observers say that this dramatic change in medal count may well have been a result of the use of now-illegal drugs by German athletes in preparation for the Olympic Games.

Doping in Athletic Competition, 1950–1970

The debate over the use of testosterone and other performance-enhancing drugs in athletics aside, the fact remains that some such phenomenon now seems to have been inevitable at some point in time. Research on testosterone and its derivatives was moving along in at least three major pharmaceutical firms in Europe: Ciba, in Switzerland; Schering, in Germany; and Organon, in the Netherlands. It seems inconceivable that news of the apparently wondrous physical effects of these substances on the human body would eventually become known—and probably common knowledge—among athletes before very long.

Perhaps the first instance in which testosterone was used to improve athletic competition in a formal event occurred in 1950, when Dr. Axel Mathiesen, trainer for the Danish rowing team at the European championships held in Milan, was accused of providing his crew with "hormone pills" to improve their performance. When the matter was referred to the International Olympic Committee (IOC) for adjudication, Dr. Mathiesen readily admitted the practice of which he was accused. His defense was that giving his rowers hormone pills (identified by the committee as Androstin) did not provide them with extraordinary skills, but only helped them to achieve the highest level of performance of which they were capable. In any case, the committee decided that it was not yet clear what constituted "doping" in an athletic competition and, therefore, was not competent to make a decision about the 1950 rowing incident (Mullegg and Montadon 2012).

Only two years after the Danish rowing incident, the issue of steroid doping was at the fore of international sports debates again. This time, the occasion was the amazing success of the Soviet Union weight lifting contingent at the 1952 Helsinki Olympic Games. Those Games were the first occasion on which the Soviet Union had participated in the Olympics, and they had made a concerted effort to put their best foot forward in Helsinki. They had begun four years earlier by sending a group of observers to the 1948 London Games with the task of determining, not whether they could compete in the Games at all, but whether they could be clear winners and, if so, in what sports (Riordan 2012).

The London observers concluded that the Soviet Union could compete most successfully in various strength sports, such as weight lifting and wrestling. The evidence suggests that they thought success in these fields could come not only from the natural skills of their athletes, but also from the availability and use of certain supplements—steroids—that could produce the muscle bulk and strength needed to win in these competitions.

They turned out to be correct. In 1952, in the first Olympic Games in which the Soviets ever competed, they won the greatest number of weight lifting medals—seven—of any nation, three gold, three silver, and one bronze. By contrast, the United

States won only six medals overall, and no other nation won more than two medals in the sport. In addition, the Soviets won 9 medals in Greco-Roman and freestyle wrestling and 43 medals in gymnastics. Overall, the Soviet Union won 71 medals at the Helsinki Games, just behind the United States (76 medals) and well ahead of any other nation (Hungary was third with 42 medals).

A number of observers were surprised and puzzled by the Soviets' success. Bob Hoffman, who had been assistant coach of the U.S. weight lifting team at the 1948 and 1952 Games and head coach for the 1956 and 1960 Games expressed the view in Helsinki that "I know they're taking that hormone stuff to increase their strength" (as quoted in Elliott Almond, Julie Cart, and Randy Harvey, "Testing Has Not Stopped Use of Steroids in Athletics; Soviets Led the Way, but West Has Caught Up," *Los Angeles Times*, January 29, 1984 and cited in Hunt 2011, 8). He later told a reporter that he felt certain that Soviet lifters were "taking injections of some kind." "They would come out [for the competition] glassy-eyed, like wild men, and lift like crazy" (Quoted in Fair 1993, 4).

Confirmation of this suspicion came in 1954 during the World Weightlifting Championships being held in Vienna, Austria. One evening, over a friendly glass of beer, a Soviet sport physician told Dr. John Ziegler that Soviet weight lifters had been so successful because they had been receiving injections of pure testosterone. Ziegler, a consultant to the U.S. weight lifting team, was familiar with testosterone. In addition to being an avid fitness proponent, he worked on weekends at the CIBA Pharmaceutical Company near his home in Maryland. The company had been providing Ziegler with samples of testosterone with which to carry out his own research on the compound's anabolic properties. Ziegler had queried the Soviet doctor in Vienna at least partly because he was struck by the unusual appearance and behavior of the Soviet weight lifters, unusual to the point that some of them required catheterization in order to urinate, so much had their bodies changed as a result of testosterone use.

That "friendly glass of beer" may have been one of the most momentous social events in the history of sports. Upon his return home, Ziegler decided to seek out a product that could produce the same results he had seen in Soviet weight lifters, but without the grotesque side effects he also observed as a result of the practice. He was looking, that is, for a substance that had the desirable anabolic (muscle-building) properties of testosterone without the undesirable androgenic (masculinizing) properties of the hormone.

Historians of sport differ somewhat as to Ziegler's involvement in the development of the testosterone derivative for which he was looking. Ziegler's background included both a medical degree and research on hormone structure and function (see his biography, Chapter 4). That background would have allowed him to understand the principles and technology involved in the development of such a product. Ziegler's training and experience, then, would certainly justify the title of "Father of Dianabol," the derivative of testosterone eventually developed by CIBA, that some historians have given to him (Dvorchak 2005; Goldman and Goldman 1980, 5, cited in Fair 1993, 2). But it is somewhat unlikely that he had the time, materials, and other resources needed to develop a new product. In fact, the more likely story is that CIBA researchers were already working on analogs of testosterone in their own laboratories and that one eventually became available that met the requirements set out by Ziegler (Yesalis et al. 1990, 97). That compound was (8S,9S,10S,13S,14S,17S)–17-hydroxy–10, 13,17–trimethyl–7,8,9,11,12,14,15,16–octahydro-6H-cyclopenta[a]phenanthren-3-one, better known (for obvious reasons) as methandrostenolone and sold commercially as Dianabol. Although CIBA researchers originally developed Dianabol as a treatment for burn victims, they also knew of Ziegler's interest in modified forms of testosterone for other applications. So they provided him with samples of their new product.

At the time, Ziegler had the ideal setting in which to test Dianabol. He was a member of the York Barbell Club, in York,

Pennsylvania, where he himself worked out and where he knew a number of leading weight lifters of the time. When some of those weight lifters came to Ziegler for advice about improving their performance, he suggested that they try Dianabol pills. The results of this experiment were mixed. One of the first York members to try the new drug was Bill March, a devoted but run-of-the-mill lifter at the time. Within a short period of time, March's muscle mass and strength began to improve dramatically. After a year of working out and taking Dianabol, March had moved to the forefront of U.S. weight lifters. He gained 20 pounds in 11 months and by March 1963 had set a new world record for standing bench press at 354 pounds. He attributed his success not only to the new muscle he had gained from using Dianabol, but also the sense of euphoria he felt after taking the drug (Dvorchak 2005).

Other weight lifters had less remarkable success. One of these was John Grimek, one of the greatest weight lifters of his time, winner of both the Mr. America and Mr. Universe titles. At Ziegler's suggestion, Grimek also began taking Dianabol to increase his weight and strength. He soon decided that he was getting no results from the product and decided to give them up. As he wrote an interviewer some years later, "after six weeks I gave it up. I got no results" (Fair 1993, 5).

Ziegler's experiment with Dianabol was made even more difficult by the fact that York members were also trying out a new system of training at the time, a system known as functional isometric contraction. A number of athletes and trainers had become convinced that isometrics were the training system of the future, a way of increasing one's muscle mass and strength (the same qualities expected from taking a testosterone derivative). Thus, when athletes found that they were gaining weight and strength while using isometric exercises and taking Dianabol, it was not clear to which practice their success could be laid or, more likely, how much success to each of the two practices. (For an extended discussion of this point, see Fair 1993, passim.) In any case, it appears that Ziegler eventually lost interest in continuing his experiments with Dianabol for the rest of the 1950s. One observer has suggested that he had become too involved in his own medical practice to spend time on Dianabol experiments (Todd 1965, as quoted in Fair 1993, 5).

Regardless of Ziegler's personal involvement, news of the success of steroids in promoting weight and strength gain began to spread throughout the sports community. By the early 1960s, steroid use had become widespread and common in weight lifting, powerlifting, competitive bodybuilding, professional football, a number of track-and-field events, and, according to some reports, even swimming and long-distance running (Yesalis et al. 1990, 98). For example, U.S. hammer thrower and gold medal winner in the event in the 1956 Olympic Games, Harold Connolly, testified before a U.S. Senate subcommittee in 1973 that steroid use had become widespread in track and field by the mid-1960s. "By 1968," he said, "athletes in every event were using anabolic steroids and stimulants. I knew any number of athletes on the 1968 Olympic team who had so much scar tissue and so many puncture holes in their backsides that it was difficult to find a fresh spot to give them a new shot" (Schudel 2012). Dr. Tom Waddell, who finished sixth in the decathlon at the 1968 Summer Olympic Games, confirmed Connally's view. He said that more than a third of the athletes at the Lake Tahoe training site for the 1968 games were taking steroids (Scott 1971, 40).

Professional football was another fertile field for the spread of AS use. Perhaps the most famous instance of steroid use by an entire football team was that of the 1963 San Diego Chargers. The 1962 season had been a disaster for the Chargers, winning only four games in a 14-game schedule. During the winter months following that season, however, head coach Sid Gillman vowed to do whatever was necessary to turn that record around. One of those steps was the introduction of intensive weight training, accompanied by the use of Dianabol pills. As one player later recounted, those pills were provided for players in cereal bowls after every meal during training camp (Quinn 2012). The pills obviously had their intended effect. San Diego won the American Football League (AFL) West Division championship with an 11–3 record, and then went on to demolish the Boston Patriots in the AFL championship game by a score of 51–10. (The 1963 championship was the only professional football championship won by the franchise.)

By the time the 1964 Olympic Games were held in Tokyo, rumors were rife about the possible use of steroids among competitors. Many athletes, coaches, and trainers simply assumed by that point in time that the majority of weight lifters almost certainly used drugs to improve their performance. Athletes in other sports, especially those from the Soviet Bloc, also came under suspicion. For example, the Press sisters, Irina and Tamara, were track-and-field competitors from Ukraine who, during the first half of the 1960s, set 26 world records in their sports, shot put, discus, hurdles, and pentathlon. The bodily appearance of the two sisters was so strongly masculine that most observers assumed that they were (1) taking steroids, (2) hermaphrodites, or (3) actually men. Since no drug testing was available for their sports in the 1964 Games, this question was never answered, and when testing programs were introduced soon after the Tokyo Games, the sisters retired from sports competition (Transgender and Intersex Olympians 2012).

Banning the Use of Anabolic Steroids

Concerns about the use of illegal performance-enhancing substances in athletic competitions goes back almost a hundred years. Even before the discovery of testosterone, a handful of sporting organizations had been discussing the problem of doping in their sports and devising methods for reducing this problem. The first organization to adopt such a ban was the International Amateur Athletic Federation (IAAF), which produced a list of substances that were not permitted to be used in competitions under their sponsorship. In the 1928 version of its Handbook, the IAAF said that

> Doping is the use of any stimulant not normally employed to increase the poser of action in athletic competition above the average. Any person knowingly acting or assisting as explained above shall be excluded from any place where these rules are in force or, if he is a competitor, be suspended for a time or otherwise from further participation in amateur athletics under the jurisdiction of this Federation. (Drugs in Sport 2012)

The IAAF action was, to a large extent, symbolic because tests were not yet available for the detection of the vast majority of potential doping agents. About the only way a person could be convicted of violating the IAAF rule was for her or him to admit to the use of an illegal substance, an unlikely event.

In fact, little or no effective action against the use of illegal performance-enhancing drugs occurred until the mid-1960s, when two organizations, the Union Cycliste Internationale (International Cycling Union; ICU) and the Fédération Internationale de Football Association (Federation of International Football Associations; FIFA) took the lead in establishing antidoping regulations for their sports. The ICU, for example, first included an article on doping in the 1960 edition of its rules book. It then added a similar article to its Technical Guide in 1966. A year later, it published a list of prohibited substances and a list of sanctions against riders who violated the association's antidoping rules (Union Cycliste Internationale 2012; Wagner 2010, 321–322). The FIFA also introduced an antidoping regulation in 1966.

Antidoping regulations were also being considered by the IOC in the 1960s. IOC's concerns over the issue had a long history. It had received confirmation that a German male named Herman Ratjen had competed in the 1936 Games (and placed fourth in the high jump) as a female with the name "Dora"

Dora Ratjen's winning jump at the 1937 German Athletics Championships. In 1936, Ratjen, who was later revealed to be male, had been placed fourth in the women's high jump competition at the 1936 Olympic Games. While it is not known whether Nazi officials knew the real gender of Ratjen (who had maintained a female identity from childhood), the scandal illustrates the "win at all costs" mentality that foreshadowed the rampant doping program launched by East Germany later in the 20th century. (German Federal Archive)

(Hunt 2011, 40). The IOC's problem only became worse in the early 1960s when rumors of drugs capable of changing a person's sex (androgenic steroids) had become available to athletes. In a 1961 issue of the IOC *Bulletin,* one writer warned of

> a particularly revolting form of doping that of women athletes who take male hormones which lead to castration of the functional cycle of women and amount sometimes to an atrophy of the ovaries which may cause a chronic disease in the long run and, not accidentally, also vastly improve their athletic prowess.

The use of such drugs, the writer warned, "may bring success in the immediate present but at what a cost!" (Eyquem 2012, 50).

The one organization that might have been expected to take the lead against performance-enhancing drugs was probably the IOC. The committee not only had control over the most important athletic events in the world, the Summer and Winter Games, but also served as an example to national Olympic committees and both national and international sports associations. Yet, the IOC dithered about the illegal drug problem both in its own events and in those of other associations.

As early as 1960, the IOC had been confronted with the issue of drug use in an Olympics event. On August 26 of that year, Danish cyclist Knud Jensen collapsed and died during a trial run for the Rome Games. Officials eventually determined that his death was the result of having taken a drug called Roniacol, which enhances blood circulation. Earlier attempts by the IOC to simply ignore "rumors" of illegal drug use were not sufficient this time, and President Avery Brundage was forced to consider how the IOC would respond to Jensen's death. Brundage was in something of an awkward position because of the IOC's traditional views about illegal drug use. That position was based on two presumptions, first, that drug use was a relatively minor problem that was probably rare enough simply to ignore. Second, the IOC felt that any drug problem that did exist should probably be dealt with by national organizations, rather than the parent international group. In this regard, Brundage wrote in early 1960 that "[t]he initial responsibility is in the hands of the National Federations of a score or more sports in more than ninety countries . . . [among whom] there may be some who are unscrupulous" (Hunt 2007, 8–9). (By "National Federations," Brundage meant the groups that controlled individuals sports worldwide, such as the IAAFs [track and field], Fédération Internationale de Natation [swimming], International Archery Federation, Fédération Internationale d'Escrime [fencing], and Fédération Internationale de Gymnastique [gymnastics].)

Pressure on the IOC continued to mount, however, and in January 1962, Brundage announced that he would appoint a scientific committee to help the IOC determine exactly what constituted doping. That committee was appointed two months later, with Dr. Arthur Porritt of the Royal College of Surgeons as its chair. The choice of Porritt sent a message about the IOC's attitude about doping, since he had long argued that the IOC had no business becoming involved in medical and scientific issues about doping in sports. His tenure as chair only confirmed that view as he failed to carry out some of the most fundamental responsibilities associated with his position, such as attending meetings at which his committee was supposed to give a report (Hunt 2007, 17–19).

While the IOC doping subcommittee made essentially no progress in its mission of defining the problem for which it had been created to study, pressures continued to mount from other sources. In November 1963, for example, the European Council on Doping and the Biological Preparation of the Athlete Taking Part in Competitive Sports called for the establishment of an international commission that would develop rules dealing with the use of illegal substances in athletic competitions. The obvious organization to take on that task, the IOC, however, continued to deflect any responsibility for such a task and, as a result, the 1964 Summer Games in Tokyo came and went with essentially no progress in the problem of dealing with doping (Todd and Todd 2001, 67).

The period between the 1964 and 1968 Games witnessed an increase of pressure on the IOC and other national and international agencies to resolve the doping problem. The point was fast approaching when decisions had to be made as to what these agencies would do, if anything, about the continuing increase in the popularity of performance-enhancing drugs, perhaps most spectacularly, the AS. One of the first post-1964 Games elements influencing this debate came with a report that unofficial random tests during the 1964 Games had found that a number of participants had received injections of substances designed to improve their performance. With this information in hand, the IOC Executive Board concluded that the IOC "ought to have a rule obliging the athletes to submit to a medical examination," and if the results of those tests show that performance-enhancing drugs have been used, "the athlete or the team should be disqualified" (Hunt 2007, 31).

The Board finally acted on this recommendation at a meeting in Teheran on May 1967. It established a Medical Commission, under the leadership of Prince Alexandre of Mérode of the Belgian royal house. The Board also drew up a list of prohibited substances that included alcohol, cocaine, cannabis, amphetamines, and ephedra but not AS. The fact that the Board already had in hand a report on the dangerous side effects of steroids when they made that decision was, according to a leading historian of doping in sports, "quite damning" (Hunt 2007, 35).

At its first meeting in September 1967, the Medical Commission (which still exists today) laid out its plan for testing at the 1968 Winter Games in Grenoble. Participants would have to promise to submit to medical examinations, agree to random drug testing, and arrange for suitable conditions under which to supply urine or blood samples—an agenda much the same as the IOC had proposed in the past. At the same time, the debate continued between the IOC and the international federations as to who was to be responsible for the actual testing of athletes and what penalties were to be assessed for those who failed the test.

In any case, the debate turned out to be somewhat moot. Of the 86 athletes tested during the Grenoble Winter Games, none failed; among the 667 athletes tested at the Mexico City Summer Games, only one participant failed, pentathlon contestant Hans-Gunnar Liljenwall, who had ethanol in his blood. Table 2.1 shows the results of drug testing for other Olympic Games since testing originated in 1968.

Table 2.1   Results of Drug Testing in Olympic Games, 1972–2010

Summer Games

Year	Site	Number of Tests	Number of Positives	Percentage of Positives (%)
1972	Munich	2,079	7	0.34
1976	Montréal	786	11	1.40
1980	Moscow	645	0	0.00
1984	Los Angeles	1,507	12	0.80
1988	Seoul	1,598	10	0.63
1992	Barcelona	1,848	5	0.27
1996	Atlanta	1,923	2	0.10
2000	Sydney	2,359	11	0.47
2004	Athens	3,667	26[1]	0.74
2008	Beijing	4,770	20[2]	0.42

[1] Includes not only failed tests, but failures to comply with related rules, such as appearing on time for a test.
[2] Includes six horses which failed tests.

Winter Games

Year	Site	Number of Tests	Number of Positives	Percentage of Positives (%)
1972	Sapporo	211	1	0.47
1976	Innsbruck	390	2	0.51
1980	Lake Placid	440	0	0.00
1984	Sarajevo	424	1	0.24
1988	Calgary	492	1	0.20
1992	Albertville	522	0	0.00
1994	Lillehammer	529	0	0.00
1998	Nagano	621	0	0.00
2002	Salt Lake City	700	7	1.00
2006	Turn	1,219	7	0.57
2010	Vancouver	2,149	3[3]	0.14

[3] Introduction of the "wherever" program that allows testing of an athlete in a much wider range of circumstances.
Source: Adapted from International Olympic Committee. "Factsheet. The Fight Against Doping and Promotion of Athlete's Health." http://sportsanddrugs. procon.org/sourcefiles/IOCFactsheet2010.pdf. Accessed on June 16, 2012.

The considerable success of the testing program conducted by the Medical Commission at the Grenoble and Mexico City Games did not bring to an end the conflict among the three entities involved in this issue, the IOC, the international federations, and the national Olympic committees. Indeed, each of these three entities appeared to be eager to pass on the responsibility for testing, and only the Medical Commission was ready and willing to take on that challenge. The problem, of course, was that the Medical Commission was a division of the IOC, which was one of those groups eschewing the opportunity to run a testing program. (For a superb discussion of this history, see Hunt 2007, 45–51.)

The aura of confusion surrounding drug testing in the 1960s has not completely disappeared today. A number of different agencies are responsible for drug testing at various levels of competition in a great range of sports. For example, a runner who has qualified for the Olympic Games might expect to be tested by the United States Olympic Committee (USOC) through the United States Anti-Doping Agency (USADA); by USA Track and Field, the controlling body for the sport in the United States; by the IAAF, the controlling group for all amateur athletics worldwide; or by other local, regional, national, and international organizations that have interest in track and field at the national or international levels. Indeed, sorting out this maze of drugging regulations may demand the advice of someone trained in sports law (see, for example, Pilgrim and Betz 2012).

One of the most serious deficiencies in the 1967 actions by the IOC in Teheran was the omission of AS from the list of banned substances. Even when it was aware of the serious health consequences of taking AS, the IOC Board and Medical Commission weren't really quite sure what to do about the problem of their use in sports competitions. Testing issues were at the core of this uncertainty. One IOC official noted that tests conducted at the 1964 Olympics showed up a number of substances that were chemically similar to, but not identical to, substances on the banned list. The explanation for this observation is two-fold. In the first place, any substance that is ingested in the human body is not likely to remain in its original form throughout its period of time in the body. It is broken down, producing a number of so-called *metabolites*, the products of digestion. What drug tests must measure, then, is not only the banned substance itself, but also all possible metabolites of that substance. For many chemicals, that information simply was not available in the 1960s, so test analysts could not be certain whether they had really detected drug use or not.

The second problem is that chemists in many parts of the world were synthesizing new performance-enhancing drugs even as the Olympic committee was trying to develop foolproof methods for testing for the older products. As noted above, CIBA had already produced one such product, Dianabol, in the late 1950s, well in advance of the IOC's efforts to develop a drug testing program. From the time Dianabol was released in 1958 (and probably even earlier), weight lifters and other athletes around the world had access to an AS about which the IOC and other governing agencies knew relatively little and about which they could do even less. A similar story was being played out in the Soviet Union where researchers had developed a derivative of testosterone, nandrolone decanoate, sold commercially in the Soviet Bloc as Retabolil, and now available in the West as Deca Durabolin. And in East Germany, researchers had produced yet another testosterone derivative, 4-chlorodehydromethyltestosterone, marketed under the trade name of Oral Turinabol. Each of these new compounds found an eager and accepting market among competitive and amateur athletes (Baker 2012; Mantell 2012).

And this was just the beginning. One anonymous weight lifter who competed in the 1968 Games explained the challenge facing drug testers. When asked if he was concerned about the IOC ban on drugs, he responded with:

What ban? Everyone used a new one [performance-enhancing drug] from West Germany. They [the IOC] couldn't pick it up in the test they were using. When they get a test for that one, we'll find something else. It's like cops and robbers. (Gilbert 1969)

This "game" of back-and-forth between drug users and drug enforcers continues today, not only in the field of athletics and sports, but also in the everyday life of substance abusers around the world.

In spite of its concerns about the bad publicity that would almost certainly be associated with drug testing and the consequent banning of competitors, the IOC continued to find a way of adding AS to the list of prohibited substances first announced in 1967. For example, President Brundage wrote to Prince de Merode, chair of the Medical Commission, in 1971, asking if the committee had found any way of testing reliably for the presence of "hormones." De Merode responded that such testing was very difficult since all trace of hormones disappeared from the body within a matter of weeks, so it would be easy for an athlete to use drugs during training without hope of detection (Hunt 2012).

Even as this exchange of letters was taking place, researchers were making significant progress in finding ways to test efficiently for AS in the blood and urine. Between 1970 and 1975, researchers developed methods for using radioimmunoassay, gas chromatographic/mass spectrometric (GC/MS), and other methods for reliably detecting AS and their metabolites in body fluids (see, for example, Brooks, Firth, and Sumner 1975; Sumner 1974; Van Eenoo and Delbeke 2006; Ward, Shackleton, and Lawson 1975). And this progress prompted the IOC to consider adding AS to its list of prohibited substances. As a trial for the proposed policy, the new testing procedures for steroids were used at the Commonwealth Games held in Christchurch, New Zealand, in January 1974. At those games, nine competitors failed the initial immunoassay test, of whom seven also failed the confirmatory GC/MS test (Kicman and Gower 2003, 323).

This progress in testing technology was sufficient to convince the IOC Medical Commission that testing should be adopted for future Olympic events. It announced in April 1974 that random testing for AS would begin at the 1976 Games in Montréal. At its next meeting, in October 1974, the committee announced changes in Rule 26, the Eligibility Code for competitors in the Games. Those changes specified that

- The use of illegal substances was forbidden in Olympic competition, and the IOC would create a list of prohibited substances covered by this rule.
- Any competitor who refused to take a test or who failed a test was to be disqualified from competition.
- If the person who failed a drug test was a member of a team, the entire team was to be disqualified.
- Anyone who participates in a sport designated for women must be able to pass a gender test.
- Anyone who refuses to take a drug test or who fails such a test is to be withdrawn of any medals awarded.
- Any sanctions imposed by the IOC do not negate the possibility of additional sanctions from international sport federations (quoted in Wilson and Derse 2001, 72–73).

The new rules were implemented at the Montréal Games, and eight competitors tested positive, seven in the weight lifting competition and one in the track-and-field events. Those who failed the test were from five nations: Bulgaria (2), United States (2), Poland (2), Czechoslovakia (1), and Sweden (1). (Athletics at the 1976 Montréal Summer Games: Women's Discus Throw 2012; Chidlovski 2012). Two of the athletes who were disqualified were stripped of their gold medals, and one, of his silver medal, all in weight lifting.

The "cop and robbers" aspect of drug testing has not abated today. Pharmaceutical chemists continue to search for new AS that athletes can include in their training programs without violating existing doping rules. And athletic associations continue to keep an eye out for such substances and to include them in their latest list of prohibited performance-enhancing substances. The most recent such list, published by the World Anti-Doping Association (WADA) in 2012, provides a glimpse of that scope of the "cops and robbers" skirmish. That list of substances that are prohibited "at all times" contains 26 endogenous and 46 exogenous AS ranging from 1-androstenediol and 1-androstenedione to 19-norandrosterone and 19-noretiocholanolone. The list is actually much longer because it also includes, without naming them, "other substances with a similar chemical structure or similar biological effect(s)" for the list of exogenous steroids and all the metabolites and isomers of five basic endogenous steroids. In addition to this list, WADA provides two other lists of prohibited substances, those that are banned during a competition and those that are banned for specific sports (2012 List of Prohibited Substances and Methods 2012).

In addition to the lists of banned substances, WADA also provides a list of certain procedures that are not allowed. These procedures fall into three major categories: those that increase the concentration of oxygen available to a competitor; various forms of physical and chemical manipulation of body systems; and so-called gene doping, which involves altering a person's DNA, RNA, or genetic composition.

Testing Methodology

A critical feature to be noted from the preceding discussion is the absolute necessity of adequate testing procedures for detecting the presence of a prohibited substance in a person's body. This statement is especially true for AS among all banned substances because of the complexity of steroid chemistry. As one can see from the structural formulas for testosterone and other AS discussed earlier in this text, these substances have very complex molecular structures that make them difficult to detect, identify, and distinguish from other substances present in a sample. This may be the point in this text, therefore, for a review of the process by which antidoping tests are conducted.

The testing procedures for endogenous and exogenous AS are different. In the latter case, a laboratory can simply look for

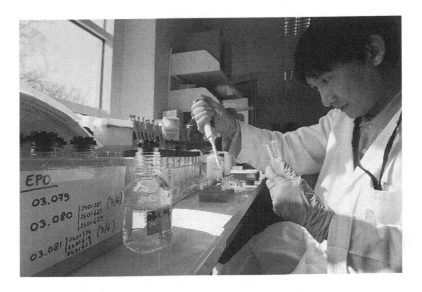

A lab technician performs tests for EPO (erythropoietin), a natural hormone and a blood booster, at the AFLD (French Anti-Doping Agency) laboratory on March 17, 2009. In this type of procedure, known as a "direct test," officials screen athletes' urine samples for the presence of banned substances such as EPO and other performance-enhancing substances. (AP Photo/Christophe Ena)

AS that do not occur normally in the human body (exogenous AS). If they are present in a person's urine, blood, or other bodily fluid, that person is probably guilty of having ingested the substance. The former case is more of a challenge. Suppose that a test shows that a male athlete has testosterone or its metabolites in his blood or urine. Well, of course they will be. All males have testosterone in their bodies, so it or its metabolites will occur naturally in their blood or urine. Some other technique is needed to decide if a person has ingested an endogenous anabolic hormone, such as having taken a "testosterone pill," for example, in order to boost his body's natural level of the hormone.

One basis for such a test might be to determine, first of all, the "normal" level of some AS, such as testosterone, in the male body. That research has already been done and a normal testosterone range can be given for most males. However, as with almost any human characteristic, that normal range varies from man to man and can vary significantly even for any one person. One solution to this problem is to measure a man's testosterone level over long periods of time so that a normal range for that person can be determined. But such a procedure is too expensive to be used in practice.

The most common method for solving this particular problem is to determine a person's T/E ratio, where the letter "T" stands for his serum testosterone level and the letter "E" stands for his serum epitestosterone level. Epitestosterone is an isomer of testosterone, that is, a form of testosterone with the same number of carbon, hydrogen, and oxygen atoms, but with a different arrangement of those atoms. When a person ingests testosterone, his testosterone serum level rises, as does the amount of testosterone metabolites in his urine. But the additional testosterone has no effect on the body's serum epitestosterone levels. So a person who is cheating by taking extra testosterone has a higher blood level of that steroid, but a normal level of epitestosterone. The current method of testing for testosterone use, then, is to take blood from an athlete and measure the amount of testosterone and the amount of epitestosterone present. If the ratio of testosterone (T) to epitestosterone (E), T/E, is *greater than* 4:1 (the normal ratio in a male), one can conclude that the person has been taking extra testosterone.

Some testing experts question that use of the 4:1 T/E ratio and have recommended other approaches to the testing for testosterone (see, for example, Sottas et al. 2008). And, as part of the "cops and robber" game between drug testers and athletes, the former are always trying to develop new and better methods for testing for the presence of banned substances. One of the more recent of these technologies has been the carbon-isotope ratio test. That test is based on the fact that the carbon atoms that occur everywhere in nature exist in two similar, but somewhat different, forms called *isotopes*. Isotopes are forms of an atom that have the same number of protons in their nuclei, but different numbers of neutrons. For example, by far the most common form of carbon in nature is carbon-12 (also written as ^{12}C), whose nucleus has six protons and six neutrons. A much less common form of carbon, however, is carbon-13 (^{13}C), which has six protons and seven neutrons. It is relatively easy to distinguish between ^{12}C and ^{13}C in the laboratory.

The important point about the carbon isotopes for testing is that exogenous AS contain a smaller fraction of ^{13}C than do endogenous AS. So the ratio of ^{13}C to ^{12}C will be lower in the blood of someone who has been taking exogenous testosterone than in someone who has not (again, the problem is to figure out what constitutes a normal ^{13}C to ^{12}C ratio for any particular person, but that problem can usually be solved) (de la Torre et al. 2001).

Testing for exogenous AS presents a somewhat different kind of challenge. The challenge here is to look for substances in blood, urine, sweat, and other bodily fluids for substances that are banned from use in athletic competitions. The fundamental steps involved in such tests were outlined in the 1970s and remain essentially the same today (see Beckett 1976). The technology involved in testing has, of course, evolved, but the chain of events involved in a test are essentially the same today as they were in 1976. The first step in that chain of events is the selection of the individual(s) to be tested. Various sporting groups and events have differing rules as to who will be tested and under what circumstances. In some cases, all athletes involved in a competition may be tested, while in other instances, only a random sample of athletes may be selected for testing. Testing may occur before, during, or after a competition on one occasion or more. One of the more recent elements of a testing program is the so-called *whereabouts* provision, in which an athlete must notify the testing agency where he or she can be found during one specific part of every day during the testing period. The agency may then appear unannounced during the whereabouts period and administer a drug test (The Athlete Drug Testing in Sport 2012; for an example in one sport, see A Look Inside the Whereabouts Program 2012).

An athlete to be tested will be asked to provide a sample of a bodily fluid. In theory, that fluid could be saliva, blood, urine, or some other fluid, although primarily for reasons of expense, urine testing is by far the most common type of procedure. An athlete is typically asked to provide about 100 milliliter (mL) of urine, which is then divided into two parts, known as Sample A and Sample B.

Although technically feasible, sample testing typically does not occur at the same place that a sample is collected. Instead, it is sealed and transmitted to a certified testing laboratory. Precautions in the sealing and transmittal of a specimen are critical, because chemical changes may occur within the sample that invalidated the test results. One of the most common objections raised by athletes to adverse testing results is that individuals in charge of the sample have not cared properly for the sample and the results reported for the specimen are not, therefore, accurate. Keeping a careful record of the location of a sample, the conditions under which it was held, the individuals responsible for the sample, and other relevant factors is known as the *chain of custody* for that sample.

Once the samples have reached a testing laboratory, the first sample (Sample A) is subjected to chemical analysis that may consist of two steps, the screen and the confirmatory test. In antidoping terminology, the term *screen* refers to the first test performed on a sample. That test is performed to decide whether the sample is a candidate for further testing. For example, the test might find the presence of no substance on the list of banned substances and, therefore, the athlete who supplied the specimen can be regarded as "clean." On the other hand, the screen might find the presence of one or more chemicals that suggest that a banned substance may be present. In such a case, a second screen test is usually performed on the sample to determine whether the first result was reliable or not.

If, after both screening tests, there is reason to believe that a banned substance may be present in the sample, a second test is performed. That test is called a *confirmatory test* because it is accurate enough to determine at a high stage of reliability that the sample does or does not contain the banned substance. If the banned substance is present, the person who has supplied the sample is assumed to have ingested a prohibited substance and is subject to penalties laid down in the sporting organization's guidelines (World Anti-Doping Agency 2012).

The most common screening test used for antidoping analyses today is called an immunoassay (IA) or radioimmunoassay (RIA) test. The term *immunoassay* provides a hint as to how such tests work. The test works, in general, the way the human body does when exposed to some foreign substance, such as pollen. When the pollen, called an *antigen*, enters the body, it is captured and inactivated by chemicals in the body called *antibodies*. This system protects the body from harmful attacks by foreign substances.

In preparing for an IA test, a laboratory prepares a "test" solution by producing one or more substances (call them "A," "B," and "C") against which can be made a second set of substances (call them "anti-A," "anti-B," and "anti-C") that combine with the first set of substances, "A" with "anti-A," "B with anti-B," and "C with anti-C." The testing solution consists of anti-A, anti-B, anti-C, and as many other "antibodies" as one might choose. When this solution is added to the urine sample taken from an athlete, any A present in the urine will bind to anti-A in the testing solution, any B will bind with the anti-B in the testing solution, and so on. Making the anti-A, anti-B, and anti-C in the testing solution radioactive simply makes the products formed during this reaction (anti-A/A, anti-B/B, and so on) easier to see because they give off radiation that can easily be detected.

An IA screen is quite good at detecting the presence of prohibited substances in a sample, but not good enough. A sample thought to contain a banned substance is then tested a second time. The usual procedure used in the confirmatory test is called gas chromatography-mass spectrometry (GC-MS). This procedure actually consists of two discrete operations. The first operation, gas chromatography, depends on the fact that different substances move through a medium at different rates of speed. Imagine, for example, that a piece of blotting paper is just barely placed into contact with a container that holds three different colors of ink. Under the proper circumstances, those three different colors will migrate upward through the blotting paper at different speeds.

That process is known as *liquid chromatography*. The only way in which gas chromatography is different is that the three colors of ink are caused to move upward through a column of gas, which is technically a bit more difficult, but not much.

In some chemical procedures, the liquid or gas chromatography procedure can be refined sufficiently so that different substances can be separated from each other quite well. But GC-MS adds a second procedure, mass spectrometry (MS). In MS, charged particles are caused to spin around the inside of a metal container, like the horses on a carousel. As these particles spin, they are flung outward toward the inner sides of the container. Where they end up on the container depends on how heavy they are, how fast they are moving, and other properties. What makes the MS test work is that scientists *know* where a testosterone molecule will end up in an MS machine when it is spun at a certain speed, where a methandrostenolone molecule will end up, and where any other AS molecule will end up under experimental conditions.

The GC-MS test, then, combines these two procedures. An athlete's urine is first subjected to a GC test, in which suspect molecules can be seen separating from other substances in the mixture. These suspect molecules can then be removed from the GC apparatus and injected into a mass spectrometer. When the MS test is performed, the test supervisor can determine whether the suspect molecules ended up in places where testosterone would have been expected, where methandrostenolone would have been expected, and so on. In other words, she or he would be able to say which substances were present in the sample being tested. (For a detailed technical description of these procedures, see Saugy et al. 2000.)

Problems Associated with Testing

The basic principles of drug testing, as outlined here, are relatively simple. But there are a number of circumstances under which important complications may arise. Two of the most important of those circumstances are so-called *false positive* and *false negative*. False positive tests are also known in statistics as Type 1 errors, and false negatives, as Type 2 errors. A false positive is a case in which a test appears to show that a sample contains a banned substance when, in fact, it does not. In such a case, an individual would probably be accused of having violated a regulation by having ingested a substance that was not permitted. That individual would be banned from competition and, if she or he had won any awards, those awards would be stripped from her or him. A false negative is a case in which an individual *has* taken an illegal substance, but the testing procedure fails to detect that substance. In such a case, the person "got away with it" by violating a drug test ban without getting caught.

False positives and false negatives can be caused by any number of factors, including human error, machine error, or a break in the chain of custody. The bottom line is that neither machines nor humans are perfect, so that some error is always a part of any testing procedure. Testing laboratories make every possible effort to reduce such errors to zero, but that goal is probably not completely possible.

Of course, the important point to note about false results is how much more serious a false positive result is than a false negative. A false negative means that someone may have recorded an achievement he or she did not deserve (a gold medal after using a banned substances), but a false positive means that someone will be accused of using illegal substances when they have not actually done so. That individual may eventually be cleared of the accusation, but achieving exoneration may be time-consuming and expensive, and members of the general public and that person's colleagues may never fully accept the "true" decision. It is for this reason that one observer has written that "[s]port authorities must ensure that the possibility of a false positive is virtually nonexistent" (Connolly 2006, 49).

According to one fairly sophisticated mathematical analysis of this problem, the rate of false positives in sports antidoping programs can be expected to range from 0.0 percent to 0.53 percent. While that number does seem very low, one needs to remember the number of athletes tested each year, 146,539 in this particular study. In such a case, one might expect to find 777 false positives, a fairly large number (WADA Statistics 2005 2012).

Another problem associated with the issue of false positives is the intentional or unintentional ingestion of products that may contain prohibited substances. In some cases, for example, athletes may have taken certain prescribed medications for the treatment of chronic or acute medical problems. (Chronic problems are those that continue for an extended period of time, such as cancer, while acute problems are those that last a relatively short period of time, such as the common cold.) All organizations responsible for the testing of athletes are aware of and sensitive to such problems and provide special conditions for the testing of such athletes. The World Anti-Doping Agency (WADA), for example, makes available certificates that athletes can fill out and return explaining why they need to take certain medications that might cause positive results in drug tests (Therapeutic Use Exceptions 2012). Some examples of medications that are eligible for consideration under the therapeutic use exception policy of the USADA are the analgesics/anti-inflammatories acetaminophen, aspirin, and codeine; the antacids Maalox, Myalanta, and Tums; the antianxiety/antidepressant agents Celera, Elavil, Valium, and Zoloft; the antidiarrheals atropine, Donnagel, Immodium, and Loperamide; the antifungals Cruex, Micatin, and Sporonox; the antinausea/antivertigos Antivert, Kytril, and Motion-aid; the antihistamines Allegra, Benadryl, and Claritin; the antiseizure medications Lyrcia, phenobarbital, and Topamax; and the cold medications Advil cold and sinus, Pepto Bismol, and Sudafed (Bowers 2007, 65–66).

"Beating the Game"

Dealing with the use of prohibited substances in athletic competitions would be much less of a problem (probably not a problem at all) if some athletes were not committed to finding a way to "get around" rules and regulations and actually use one or another of the drug that have been banned. There are a number of ways of achieving this objective. One of the most obvious approaches, of course, is to find out about any new AS that may recently have been discovered or developed by a reputable (or not-so-reputable) drug company. In such a case, an athlete might legally be able to use that substance unless and until antidoping agencies found out about the drug and decided to place it on its list of prohibited substances. For example, news began to leak out in the early 2010s about a newly developed compound with properties similar to those of AS, but with a somewhat different chemical structure. The substance had been developed by the pharmaceutical firm of Merck/Schering-Plough Pharma and its subsidiary Gtx and was given the temporary designation of MK-0773. Clinical trials on its effectiveness for the treatment of sarcopenia (loss of muscle mass) in women began in late 2007.

MK-0773 belongs to a category of compounds known as selective androgen receptor modulators (SARMs). Some SARMs have molecular structures similar to those of AS, but some have very different molecular structures. Compare the molecular structure of one experimental SARM, MK-2866, also known as Ostarine or Gtx-024, in Figure 2.1 with that of testosterone in Figure 1.1. The characteristic that all SARMs share is that they attach to androgen receptors, just as AS do. In some cases, they produce responses that are many times greater than those produced by AS themselves. MK-0773, for example, is said to initiate a response four times that of testosterone itself. One can assume that, once MK-0773 becomes available, either legally or illegally, some athletes will want to experiment with its use as a muscle-building supplement (see, for example, Merck's New Anabolic Steroid 2012).

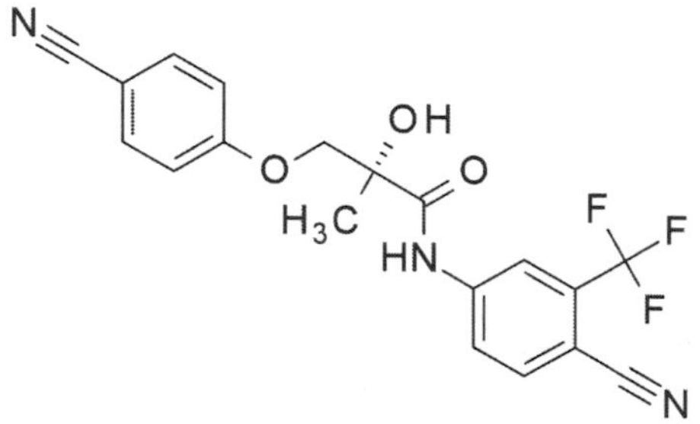

Figure 2.1   Ostarine

In some ways, the game of catching athletes who try to cheat on their drug tests is stacked against regulatory agencies in favor of those athletes. There are far more AS and other performance-enhancing drugs available to athletes than there are tests for those drugs. For example, one of the most knowledgeable experts on the use of AS in sports, William Llewellyn, has been quoted as saying that "There are more than 500 steroids in here [referring to a book in which he has collected all known anabolic steroids, legal and illegal, tested and untested]. All the drug tests in the world can maybe find 50" (Assael 2003, 40). An even more authoritative assessment of the problem comes from Don Catlin, Professor of Molecular and Medical Pharmacology at the University of California at Los Angeles Medical School and the Director of the UCLA Olympic Analytical Laboratory, the only lab in the U.S. accredited for sports doping control by the WADA. In testimony before the U.S. Senate Committee on Commerce, Science, and Transportation in May 2005, Catlin observed that "[a]thletes determined to cheat have little trouble beating the test . . . and there are legions of doctors telling them how to do it" (Hearing before the Committee on Commerce, Science, and Transportation 2005, 18).

Individuals concerned about not being able to pass a drug test have developed a number of imaginative techniques for avoiding a positive test. One technique involves the substitution of one's own urine (assumed to contain evidence of illegal drug use) with a "clean" product. A number of suggestions have been made as to how this objective can be achieved, such as collecting and substituting urine from a friend or using "synthetic" urine. A well-known example of the latter option is a kit called the Whizzinator, which consists of an artificial penis, dried urine, a syringe, and a heater pack to warm reconstituted urine to body temperature. As of late 2012, the product was still available and being advertised on the Internet as "Your Number One Choice for Synthetic Urine." A comparable product for women is sold under the name "Go Number One."

Another common approach to avoiding a positive drug test is with the use of some type of *masking agent* or *masking procedure*. The term *masking* refers to any substance or procedure used to prevent an antidoping agency from detecting the presence of a prohibited substance in a person's body. Some substances act as masking agents because they react chemically with the substance for which one is being tested. The chemical reaction converts the substance into a form that cannot be recognized by the testing process. Perhaps the most common form of masking is urine dilution. In this process, a person attempts to increase one's rate of urination as much as possible with the intent of "washing out" traces of any prohibited substance or its metabolites. One way to achieve this objective is with diuretics, substances that increase the loss of water and electrolytes through an increased rate of urination. A number of commonly available substances, including coffee and tea, are diuretics (Cadwallader et al. 2010).

Antidoping agencies now include diuretics and other types of masking agents among the substances for which they test in a typical drug screen. Among the 16 banned diuretics on the current USADA list of prohibited substances are bumetanide (Bumex), ethacrynic acid (Edecrin), mersalyl (Salyrgan), torsemide (Demadex), and triamterene (Dyazide, Maxzide). The USADA list of prohibited masking agents and procedures include adulterated forms of testosterone and epitestosterone, catheterization, sample substitution or tampering, and adulterating agents, such as commercially available agents, such as the Whizzinator or commercial detergents (Bowers 2007, Tables 3 and 4, 27–28).

The efforts to avoid drug detection described here are only the most common of all such procedures that have been tried by athletes in the past. A summary of other methods for avoiding detection is provided on the web page "Sports and Drugs," part of the ProCon.org website (What Are the 19 Known Methods of Cheating to Pass Performance Enhancing Drug Tests? 2012; as an example of the types of commercial products available for such purposes, also see PassYourDrugTest.com at http://www. passyourdrugtest.com/text.htm).

So, in the end, how effective are current antidoping programs at identifying athletes who have used performance-enhancing drugs? A great deal of dispute remains on this issue. On the one hand, many experts, including administrators of high-level antidoping programs, argue that these efforts have been very successful in the past and are likely to become even more successful in the future. In response to a series of questions about drug testing in sports, for example, Gary I. Walder, chair of the WADA Prohibited List and Methods Subcommittee, noted that

> The detection methods are accurate and reliable. They undergo rigorous validation prior to being introduced. . . . [WADA] has funded a number of studies in anticipation of the seeming inevitability of gene doping in the years ahead. . . . The I.O.C. [International Olympic Committee] retains ownership of the athlete's samples (blood and urine) for eight years following the Olympic Games . . . if

a technique is developed that would enable the detection of a prohibited substance . . . the stored specimen could be tested for that specific substance and the athlete would be held accountable. (Dr. Gary Wadler of the World Anti-Doping Agency Gives His Answers to Your Questions (Part I). 2008)

Other individuals are not so optimistic about the success of antidoping programs. In 2007, for example, WADA commissioned a literature review of a number of studies conducted on antidoping programs conducted in countries around the world. The report noted that about a third of all respondents in these studies offered the view that testing programs were not effective in achieving the goals for which they were designed. Indeed, researchers found that anywhere between 19 and 31 percent of the college athletes interviewed were aware of ways to "beat the system" for drug testing (Backhouse et al. 2007, 36).

Perhaps one of the most interesting themes that run through the debate over the effectiveness of antidoping programs is the notion that athletes are more or less successful in escaping detection in the use of banned substances based on their own knowledge of the drug testing process and their access to advice and resources from professionals in the field. One research team noted, for example, that athletes from economically less-developed nations at the 2004 Athens Olympic Games generally were less familiar with more recent developments in performance-enhancing drug technology and, therefore, tended to rely on older technologies, such as the use of the well-established AS stanozolol. Since that substance has been around for a very long time and tests for it are now well developed, athletes who used the drug were more easily detected than were those who used more recent substances. This result prompted the researchers to conclude that "doping tests are not effective if they lead merely to catching those athletes who do not have the best 'rogue' scientists working for them" (Kayser, Mauron, and Miah 2007, 3).

The 1970s: Doping Gone Wild

The 1970s can be remembered as a decade of great progress in the development of regulations against the use of AS in athletic events and the implementation of sophisticated testing programs for banned substances. But it was also a period that witnessed some of the most egregious uses of AS to gain unfair advantages in some of the most prestigious athletic competitions in the world. By most accounts, the worst offender in this regard was the German Democratic Republic (GDR; Deutsche Demokratische Republik, or DDR), more commonly known as East Germany. One piece of data often cited to reinforce this accusation is the improvement in the performance of East German Olympic competitors between 1968 and 1980. As Table 2.2 shows, the East Germans won a total of 25 medals in the 1968 games, the first year in which it competed as an entity distinct from West Germany. Over the next three Games, the East Germans quintupled the number of medals they received, vastly outdistancing their colleagues from West Germany. How did such a dramatic improvement take place in East German athletic skill?

Throughout the 1970s, athletes who competed against their East German colleagues often noted certain physical characteristics that made them wonder about the nature of the training program in which these individuals were engaged. They observed that women athletes, for example, often had physical traits more commonly associated with males than females,

Table 2.2   Olympic Medals Won by the United States, East Germany, and West Germany, 1968–1984

Nation	Total Number of Medals Won (Rank)				
	1968	1972	1976	1980	1984
United States	107 (1)	94 (2)	94 (2)	dnc	174 (1)
East Germany	25 (5)	66 (3)	90 (3)	126 (2)	dnc
West Germany	26 (4)	40 (4)	39 (4)	dnc	59 (2)

dnc = did not compete

Source: databaseOlympics.com. http://www.databaseolympics.com/. Accessed on June 16, 2012.

such as large muscle mass, deeper voices, and facial hair. One of the most outspoken of these observers was Brigitte Berendonk, who competed in the discus throw in the 1968 and 1972 Olympic Games. Berendonk had been born in Dankmarshausen, then part of the German Democratic Republic. At the age of 16, she defected from East Germany with her family and settled in West Germany, where she eventually joined the West German Olympic track-and-field team. On a number of occasions, she mentioned her doubts about East German athletes to her superiors and the press, who largely ignored or ridiculed her concerns (Ungerleider 2001, 10).

In fact, it was not until the fall of the Berlin Wall in 1989 that information about the East German doping program began to leak to the Western world. Over a period of years, documents about the program were slowly uncovered by a number of committed researchers until a final picture of the program eventually emerged (see especially Frank and Berendonk 1997). The East German doping program appears to have originated on a somewhat informal basis in the late 1960s as the GDR government attempted to improve its international image as a modern and powerful national state. One element in that effort was the development of a national athletic program that would achieve international recognition at events such as the Summer and Winter Olympic Games. Boys and girls who showed promise in one or another athletic field were diverted into special training programs aimed at developing their maximum potential. An important component of these training programs was the use of AS to improve muscle mass, strength, endurance, and other physical characteristics. The primary substance used for this purpose, as noted earlier in this chapter, was the chlorinated derivative of methandrostenolone sold commercially as Oral Turinabol. That substance had not yet been prohibited in the late 1960s when the East German got underway, although it was later listed as a banned substance by the IOC.

The East German program was expanded in the 1970s and formalized in 1974 with adoption of the so-called Research

Program 08, later called State Plan Research Theme 14.25, in 1974. The top secret legislation creating this program included a number of elements with regard to the use of AS:

- They would be an integral part of all training programs for international competitions.
- They would be under central control and subject to regular evaluation by sports physicians.
- They would be under direct control of the Sports Medical Service (Sportmedizinischer Dienst; SMD).
- An ongoing research program would develop and test the efficacy of new AS and new and improved methods of administration of the drugs.
- Information about their use would be taught in formal programs to coaches and sports physicians.
- The program for the use of AS would be highly classified and regarded as an Official State Secret (Franke and Berendonk 1997, 1267–1268).

Overall responsibility for security of the program was under the control of the notorious East German agency, the Ministry for State Security (Ministerium für Staatssicherheit, MfS, most commonly known as the Stasi). Director of the program was Manfred Ewald, minister of sport for the GDR from 1961 to 1988 and president of the GDR national Olympic committee from 1973 to 1990. His chief assistant was Dr. Manfred Höppner who, in 1977, issued a report to his Stasi superiors describing the success of State Plan 14.25. He wrote that

At present anabolic steroids are applied in all Olympic sporting events, with the exception of sailing and gymnastics (female) . . . and by all national teams. . . . The positive value of anabolic steroids for the development of a top performance is undoubted. [He then provides a few examples from track and field for both men and women to support his statement.] Remarkable rates of increase in performances were also noted in the swimming events of women. . . . From our experiences made so far it can be concluded that women have the greatest advantage from treatments with anabolic hormones with respect to their performance in sports. . . . Especially high is the performance-supporting effect following the first administration of anabolic hormones, especially with junior athletes. (quoted in Franke and Berendonke 1997, 1264)

The scope of the East German program was truly amazing. According to one source, more than 10,000 athletes received AS during the 1970s and 1980s, with as many as 1,500 full-time scientists and doctors and 8,000 trainers involved in the program at its height. During its final year of operation in 1989, the East German government budgeted 400 million marks (about 200 million U.S. dollars, at the official exchange rate) (Sport's Greatest Cover Up: Part One 2012; Gilbert et al. 2012).

As international sports organizations, such as the IOC, established stricter rules against the use of AS and as their tests became better able to detect prohibited substances, East German officials learned to become more adept at avoiding detection of their doping efforts. For example, they purchased the latest in drug testing hardware to use on the testing of their own athletes. Their objective was to make sure that East German athletes would not receive positive tests once they reached an international competition. Athletes who did score positive on the East German test would be withdrawn from competition with the explanation that they were "ill" or "injured" (Rosen 2008, 53).

East German athletes also became experts at the art of detection avoidance. Most of the techniques used today by dishonest athletes and described above, such as using synthetic urine, were part of the East German arsenal against detection. At the same time, East German researchers were strongly urged to develop new AS that could not yet be detected by existing technology (Franke and Berendonk 1997, 1272; Rosen 2008, 54).

The East German doping scandal has actually had two somewhat discrete parts, the first of which involved the two-decade history of the State Plan 14.25 program described here. The second part of that scandal involves the long-term effects of that program on the hundreds or thousands of athletes who were, to a large extent, innocent victims of an experiment of which they were unaware. (The steroids they were given were handed out in the form of small blue or pink pills described as vitamins or nutritional supplements.) The AS they were given over a period of many years, often during the formative years of their lives, have had long-term effects that their superiors neither anticipated nor probably much cared about.

As a consequence, many veterans of the GDR training programs have, since details of those programs have slowly come out, taken court action as a way of gaining partial restitution for their misuse by the East German government. One part of that action has involved criminal complaints against leaders of the GDR program. Beginning in 1998, a number of trials have been held in Germany that resulted in the conviction of trainers, doctors, and research scientists for their role in the State Plan 14.25 activities (Andrews 2012). The last of these trials, in 2000, resulted in the conviction of Ewald and Höppner for providing steroids to more than 140 young female athletes, some as young as 11 years of age. Ewald was sentenced to 22 months of probation, and Höppner, to 18 months of probation (Kettmann 2012; Moseley 2000). The controversy over the East German doping program may not completely have come to an end. In April 2009, five former coaches of East German athletic teams (long jump, discus, javelin, shot put, and heptathlon) admitted that they had knowingly been involved in the use of AS to improve the performance of athletes whose training they directed (Doping: Five German Coaches Admit to East German Doping Past 2012).

A second part of the reaction to news about the GDR doping program has been the effort to obtain monetary or other forms of restitution for athletes who were part of that program.

In 2002, two years after criminal trials had ended, the German government established a fund of US$2.5 million to compensate men and women who had been harmed by the East German doping program. By the deadline on which claims had to be filed, 311 athletes had submitted requests for the maximum $12,500 payment for which each person was eligible. One of those filing a claim was Andreas Krieger, formerly Heidi Krieger, who had undergone a sex change operation because steroids had already caused such severe masculinization that she/he could no longer live as a woman. Many of the victims applying for compensation appeared before the court with horrifying stories of the damage to their bodies and minds that had occurred as a result of long-term exposure to large doses of AS (Longman 2012b).

While by far the most extensive and best known example of steroid abuse, the East German State Plan 14.25 program was by no means the only situation in which elite athletes used AS during the 1970s. In cycling, for example, these substances gradually became more popular throughout the decade. As testing programs for amphetamines, previously the drug of choice among cyclists, became more efficient and widespread, competitors began turning to AS for the "extra push" they needed in their rides. Finally, in the 1978 Tour de France, the first rider tested positive for an illegal steroid. Belgian cyclist Michel Pollentier won the 13th stage of the tour and earned himself the yellow jersey as tour leader at that point. However, during the drug test that followed the day's race, Pollentier was found to be using a Whizzinator-like device filled with clean urine from a friend. He was disqualified from the race and banned from racing for a two-month period (Rosen 2008, 49–50).

The Great Breakthrough: The 1980s

By the early 1980s, the value of AS as performance-enhancing drugs was becoming widely known among both amateur and elite athletes. Among weight lifters and bodybuilders, this knowledge was hardly news, but the availability of a greater range of products soon made them an essential part of almost every participant's training schedule. Especially on the West Coast of the United States, a new business for the production, advertising, and sale of AS was developing, beginning in 1982 with the publication of the first handbook on AS, *Underground Steroid Handbook for Men and Women*, written by Dan Duchaine. Duchaine was a transplant from Maine to the Venice Beach, California, area, a center of weight lifting and bodybuilding in the United States. Duchaine's booklet provided a complete review of the 29 performance-enhancing drugs of which Duchaine knew, with detailed commentaries on each. The slim volume sold for $6 and was first advertised in *Muscle Builder & Power* magazine in early 1982. Duchaine was overwhelmed with orders and had sold 80,000 copies of the book with a profit of a half million dollars by the spring of 1982. (Copies of that publication are virtually impossible to find today.) The popularity of the work prompted Duchaine to produce a revised edition of the handbook two years later and then a larger and more complete version in 1988, *Underground Steroid Handbook II*, a publication that is still in print and available through many booksellers (Assael 2007, 5–8; Pietaro 2012).

After the first edition of the handbook came out, Duchaine rapidly became the "go to" man for information about steroids and for the steroids himself. Before long, he had earned the title of the Steroid Guru. He also realized that his new fame and notoriety held the potential for a lucrative career in dealing with steroids. In February 1986, he and his two friends, David Jenkins and William Dillon, made a deal with a Mexican entrepreneur, Juan Macklis, to manufacture and package steroids for exportation to the United States (Jenkins was a former silver medal winner in the 1972 Olympics and Dillon was a former Mr. Collegiate Illinois bodybuilding champion. Macklis owned a drug manufacturing plant, Laboratorios Milanos, near Tijuana and was regarded as one of the most powerful men in Mexico at the time) (Assael 2007, 16).

The Duchaine–Jenkins–Dillon operation quickly became a huge financial success, at one point bringing in so much money that "it was a struggle to spend it all" (Assael 2007, 17). The group's success did not long escape the notice of U.S. officials, however, and in early 1987, an investigator for the U.S. Food and Drug Administration (FDA) pounced on the operation. The principals were all arrested and later found guilty of a variety of charges including conspiracy, mislabeling of drugs, and distribution of illegal drugs. Duchaine was sentenced to a maximum of 3 years in prison and 5 years of probation; Jenkins was sentenced to 7 years in prison, but served only 9 months before being released; and Dillon was sentenced to 16 years in prison for his part in the affair (Cram 2012; Eisendrath 2012; Harrah 2012). After completing their prison terms, Duchaine and Jenkins joined efforts to create a legitimate nutritional supplement company, which survives today under the name of Next Nutrition. Jenkins became president of the company when Duchaine died in 2000 at the age of 47. By all accounts, Next Nutrition has no connection whatsoever with the steroids that formed such a large part of the lives of Duchaine, Jenkins, and Dillon more than two decades ago (Donati 2007).

While the use of AS continued to spread throughout the athletic community in the 1980s, attention was also increasingly being paid to other types of performance-enhancing substances, especially the process known as blood doping and the use of a new (to athletics) type of hormone, human growth hormone (hGh). The term *blood doping* refers to any technique or substance that increases the ability of the blood to transport oxygen to cells. Any such procedure increases an athlete's endurance and stamina. Three methods of blood doping are best known: blood transfusions, oxygen transport enhancement, and the use of erythropoietin (EPO). A blood transfusion is simply a way of increasing the total blood volume in a person's body, thus increasing the amount of oxygen the blood can carry. Oxygen-enhancement systems make use of synthetic materials that bind to oxygen in much the way hemoglobin does in normal blood, again increasing the amount of oxygen available to cells during exercise. EPO is a naturally occurring hormone that regulates the production of red blood cells in the body. If the hormone is supplied to the body artificially, the rate of red blood cell production increases, as does the amount of oxygen available to cells. EPO was apparently used as a performance-enhancing substance as early as the 1970s, and deaths among cyclists have been attributed to the use of the substance. The addition of exogenous EPO to the bloodstream can increase the density of blood, causing the heart to work harder, and increasing the risk of cardiac failure. Since EPO was not specifically banned until the early 1990s, insufficient information is available on its use prior to that time. That information is also difficult to find because a test for EPO was not developed and put into use until the early 2000s (Jenkins 2012; Robinson et al. 2006).

hGh also occurs naturally in the human body. It is produced in the anterior pituitary gland from which it travels to other parts of the body. In the liver and other organs, hGh stimulates the production of insulin-like growth factor (IGF-1). The primary function of IGF-1 is the stimulation of cells that produce new cartilage, thus contributing to the growth of new bone, muscles, and organs. Research indicates that the use of exogenous hGh can improve a person's athletic performance both directly and by acting synergistically with AS. The IOC banned the use of hGh in 1989, but that action was of little value since no test for the substance was then available. In fact, no athlete was disqualified for using hGh until after 2004, when the first blood test for the hormone was developed (The Researcher's Perspective 2007).

One of the factors that long limited the use of both EPO and hGh was the cost and difficulty of collecting these hormones. That problem was solved to a considerable extent when researchers developed methods for synthesizing both hormones by recombinant DNA (rDNA) technology in the late 1990s for EPO and in 1981 for hGh (Human Growth Hormone History 2012; Winearls 1998).

According to many observers, the signal event in the history of drug use in the 1980s was the rescinding of the gold medal in the 100-meter (m) dash at the 1988 Olympic Games in Seoul, Korea. The winner of that race, Canadian sprinter Benjamin Sinclair ("Ben") Johnson, had had a memorable decade in track and field, having won gold medals in the 100-m dash at the 1985 World Cup in Canberra, the 1985 World Indoor Championship in Paris, the 1986 Goodwill Games in Moscow, the 1986 Commonwealth Games in Edinburgh, and the 1984 bronze medal in the Los Angeles Summer Olympics. His contest in the 100-m dash with American sprinter Carl Lewis and a star-filled cast in the 1988 Games was expected to be the high point of the Seoul games.

In that race, Johnson defeated Lewis in the 100-m dash by 0.13 seconds (s). Johnson's time, 9.79 s, constituted a world record in that event. Three days later, however, the IOC announced that Johnson had tested positive for the AS stanozolol, and he was disqualified from the event. The gold medal was given, instead, to Lewis, whose 9.92 s was also recognized by the IOC as a new world record in that event.

Johnson's initial reaction to his disqualification was that he had never used illegal substances and that the IOC had made an improper decision. Over time, however, both he and his coach gradually changed their comments about the event. Johnson's coach, Charlie Francis, put forth the argument—first to Johnson and later to the general public—that using illegal substances was not cheating if everyone else was doing the same thing. In such a case, taking steroids was simply a matter of "keeping up with crowd," maintaining a level playing field for all competitors in an event. Johnson later said that he resisted Francis' idea at first, but gradually saw the logic in it. Finally, he said to Francis, "Charlie, I'm OK with it. Let's go" (McRae 2012).

Still, at Seoul, Johnson had argued that the case was not so clear. He had tested positive for stanozolol, but he had not taken that drug for some time because of the adverse effects it had produced in his body. Instead, he was taking a drug called furazabol. He hypothesized that some unknown "mystery man" had intentionally spiked one of his drinks with stanozolol, finally identifying the person as a "family friend" named Andre Jackson. Jackson had, Johnson later said, actually confessed to him that he had given Johnson the illegal steroid in a drink (Hurst 2012).

The complex and unpleasant story of Johnson's disqualification finally reached a measure of conclusion in 2010 when Johnson self-published his autobiography, *Seoul to Soul*, in which he presents his final explanation of the event. He still claims never to have taken the illegal substance for which he was banned, but does admit that he had used other illegal substances at other times in his career, all under the influence and recommendation of his coach. In any case, his once-promising track-and-field career came to an end in 1988 (Ben Johnson Takes Witness Stand 2012; Gatehouse 2012).

Johnson did try to make a comeback in 1991, but it was short-lived. At a meet held in Montréal in January 1993, he tested positive for an illegal substance once again, this time testosterone. His measured T/E ratio was 10.3:1 at a time when the highest permissible ratio was 6:1. Two other tests produced comparable results and the IAAF decided to ban Johnson from competition for life (Cohen 2012).

The 1990s: Steroid Use *Ne Plus Ultra*

In his excellent history of the use of performance-enhancing drugs in sports since the 19th century, Daniel M. Rosen devotes much of his chapter on the 1990s to a number of specific events in which elite athletes were found to have used illegal AS. These events include (all page citations from Rosen 2008):

- A number of performers in the World Wrestling Federation testified that they had regularly used illegal AS obtained from physician George T. Zaharian III and promoter Vincent McMahon (81–82).

- Professional football player Lyle Alzado died at the age of 43, possibly from the effects of long-term use of AS (82–84; also see Puma 2012).

- Rumors of an East-German-like program for the development of Chinese athletes percolated just below the surface through much of the decade. Among the confirmed results of antidoping tests was the discovery that a number of participants in the 1994 Asian Games had been using the banned steroid dihydrotestosterone (DHT) (85–89; see also Longman 2012a).

- Just prior to the 1998 Tour de France, a car driven by Willy Voet was stopped at the French-Belgian border and found to contain very large quantities of a number of performance-enhancing drugs. Voet was an assistant for the Festina cycling team, based at the time in France. As a result of later investigations, seven members of the team admitted to taking EPO and were banned from the race. The team doctor, Eric Rijkaert, was also arrested (100–102; also see Chronology of 1998 Tour de France Drug Scandal 2012).

The BALCO Scandal

The other event to which Rosen refers in his chapter on the 1990s was the appearance of the Bay Area Laboratory Cooperative (BALCO), an event that actually dates to the early 1980s. In 1983, Victor Conte, Jr., purchased rights to the use of a machine used for testing human blood for vitamin deficiencies. Conte had already had a distinguished career as a musician with a number of major musical groups, including most notably, Tower of Power. By the early 1980s, however, he decided to look for more mainstream employment and decided that he could use the blood-testing machine as a basis for advising men and women about the health of their blood, followed by selling them nutritional supplements that would improve their overall health. That scheme rapidly evolved into a somewhat different type of endeavor.

In 1984, Conte purchased a natural foods shop in Millbrae, California, and renamed it the Bay Area Laboratory Collective (BALCO). For more than a decade, Conte struggled to make a living with BALCO, eventually focusing on a nutritional supplement that featured the minerals zinc and magnesium, which he marketed as ZMA. Throughout the late 1980s and early 1990s, Conte began making a number of important connections among elite athletes, developing friendships, providing free tests, and then supplying complimentary samples of ZMA to his new friends.

Conte's work took a turn in the late 1990s, however, as he was introduced to a much broader range of "health products" that promised to provide profound performance enhancement. These products included EPO, hGh, an analeptic drug called modafinil, and a number of AS, including testosterone, tetrahydrogestrinone (also known as THG or "The Clear"), and norbolethone (Williams and Fainaru-Wada 2012). Before long, he was supplying this collection of illegal substances to a distinguished group of professional athletes that included track and field stars Kelli White, Christie Gaines, Dwayne Chambers, Tim Montgomery, and Marion Jones; National Football League stars Bill Romanowski, Chris Cooper, Barrett Robbins, and Dana Stubblefield; boxer Shane Mosley; cyclist Tammy Thomas; and baseball players Jason Giambi, Barry Bonds, and Gary Sheffield (a list that is almost certainly not complete) (BALCO Investigation Timeline 2012; Victor Conte: BALCO—The Straight Dope on Steroids 2012).

By the turn of the 21st century, major sporting organizations could no longer ignore the increasingly widespread understanding that illegal drug use was rampant in most sports. On October 1, 2000, the USADA was created to assume the testing responsibilities formerly carried out by individual sports organizations for Olympic, Pan American, and Paralympics events. Three years later, on September 3, 2003, a combined task force from the Internal Revenue Service and local law enforcement agencies raided the BALCO offices, collecting a mass of evidence to support a charge of distributing illegal substances. (For a detailed description of the BALCO scandal, see Assael 2007, Chapters 14–18.)

Over the next decade, the BALCO scandal and a number of other revelations revealed the width and depth of illegal AS use among amateur and professional athletes in the United States and the rest of the world. One after another, famous names from track and field, cycling, football, weight lifting, bodybuilding, wrestling, baseball, and other sports have come forward to admit their use of steroids, often with explanations of mitigating circumstances. ("I didn't know what I was taking"; "They were legal then anyway"; "Everyone else was using them, so why shouldn't I?"; "In today's world, taking drugs is the only way of remaining competitive"; and so on.) Perhaps hardest hit during this decade was major league baseball. A report prepared by former U.S. Senate Majority Leader George Mitchell in 2007 listed 86 current and previous baseball players who had admitted to or were reasonably suspected of having used steroids during their career. Some of the best known of these names remained in the public eye for years either because they spoke and wrote openly about their drug use (e.g., Jose Canseco) or were widely suspected of the practice (e.g., Barry Bonds) (Players Listed in the Mitchell Commission Report 2012).

Should Steroid Use Be Legal?

One can hardly read the first two chapters of this book without gaining the distinct impression that most organizations and individuals responsible for the administration of amateur and professional sports programs in all fields and at all levels tend to oppose—usually quite strongly—the use of AS in athletics. (A similar statement is true for other types of performance-enhancing drugs, such as EPO and hGh.) A key component of this argument is the adverse side effects that steroids have on the human body, including shrinking of the testicles, development of breasts in males, decreased sperm count with possible impotence, masculinization in females, development of acne, jaundice, loss of body hair, cardiac disorders, increased risk of liver disease, tendency of tendon ruptures and tears, increase in cholesterol levels, and a range of emotional and psychological problems that include increased tendencies toward rage, aggression, violence, and mood swings (Why Steroids Are Bad for You 2012). Reflecting this viewpoint, nearly every amateur and professional sport organization now has a ban on virtually all AS that are currently known to science (Performance-Enhancing Drugs 2012).

Another important component of this argument is fairness in athletics. Taking drugs is seen by most authorities as "cheating," a way by which an individual has an unfair advantage over her or his opponents. As Dr. Timothy Noakes, Discovery Health Professor of Exercise and Sports Science at the University of Cape Town, South Africa, has written:

> Sport is meant to be about honesty—what you see is all there is. Doping is part of an evil influence extending to match fixing and gambling that has always been a (hidden) part of professional sport, but which will likely ultimately destroy it. If we do not attempt to control this evil triad, professional sport finally distances itself from the mystical endeavour it is meant to be. Without the illusion that professional athletes are somewhat like ourselves, just better, their profession has no appeal. Rather, sport becomes no different from any other commercially driven activity. (Noakes 2006, as quoted in Should Performance Enhancing Drugs (Such as Steroids) Be Accepted in Sports? 2012)

Another argument for drug prohibitions in sports and athletics is even more direct. Such drugs are usually illegal in the general society. For example, in the United States, they are likely to be listed in Schedule II, III, or IV of the Controlled Substances Act of 1970. If such substances are illegal for the ordinary man or woman on the street to take, how can anyone argue that they should be permitted to athletes? In an e-mail to the ProCon.org, Joe Lindsey, a writer for *Bicycling* magazine asked the question, "Should people have the right to use a substance that is not legal for human use under ANY circumstances?" The answer to that question, he said, "cannot be anything other than 'No'" (Should Performance Enhancing Drugs (Such as Steroids) Be Accepted in Sports? 2012).

This argument for the banning of steroid use in athletics does not, however, have unanimous support from experts in the field. A number of writers have pointed out reasons that sports organizations should reconsider their long-held bans on certain types of performance-enhancing substances such as AS. One of the most outspoken of these critics is Norman Fost, professor of pediatrics and bioethics and director of the Program in Medical Ethics at the University of Wisconsin at Madison. Fost offers a number of reasons for, at the very least, raising questions about banning certain substances, such as AS, in athletic competitions. (He does agree that such bans are appropriate for children and adolescents whose bodies are still growing and who may, therefore, experience adverse events that would not be observed in older adults. See Collins 2012.)

One of Fost's primary arguments is that peer-reviewed scientific studies on the deleterious effects of steroids on human health are lacking. Supporters of bans on the use of steroids in athletics frequently offer a long list of problems that may develop from their use. But, he says, scientific evidence for these claims is never presented. As he says in one article, "Quick: name an athlete who died, or was diagnosed, with steroid-related cancer, heart disease, or stroke." He then refers to the case of Lyle Alzado, a professional football player who died in 1992 from circumstances that many observers attributed to his long use of AS. "What is missing," Fost goes on, "is a single article, or evidence, or even a quote from any authority on the topic to support any connection between steroids and Alzado's tumor" (Fost 2005).

Perhaps even more to the point, according to Fost, is that people who engage in athletic events do so usually knowing fully well what the possible physical consequences of their actions are likely to be. In an interview with sports attorney Rick Collins, Fost pointed out that for men who play professional football, it is "something that competent adults decide to do in exchange for the money, glory and pleasure that they get out of it. We don't think, in America, that people's liberty to take risks like that should be interfered with, just so long as they are not harming anyone else" (Collins 2012). Surveys of people who engage in dangerous sports appear to confirm this position. On a website devoted to choosing the world's ten most dangerous sports, for example, a reader is struck by the number of respondents who describe the terrible risks they took in horseback riding, gymnastics, football, hockey, and other sports, often pointing out, however, that they would do it all over again if they could and that they had taken part in a sport because they loved it so much (Most Dangerous Sports 2012).

Fost is also one of many observers who point out that it is difficult to complain about steroids giving one athlete a "special advantage" over another athlete, when sports competitions are filled with special advantages. What do observers think that special swimsuits, specially designed golf clubs and tennis rackets, specially fitted and built running shoes, high-altitude training, availability of the best coaches and trainers, and other "perks" used by athletes to reach their maximum potential are? Do spectators at professional football games complain about "drugging" when players are given pain killers that allow them to go back onto the field after an injury? Even more fundamentally, Fost argues, who ever said that "enhancing performance" is unfair? If that were the case, he says, "we should ban coaching and training" (Fost 2005).

Some critics also dispute the notion that AS give athletes an extra "boost" of which they are otherwise not capable. For example, Lincoln Allison, founding director of the Study of Sport in Society at England's Warwick University, has written that "[a] sportsman or woman who seeks an advantage from drugs just moves up to the level appropriate to his or her underlying ability." He goes on to point out that

> There are no drugs to enhance the human characteristics of judgment and leadership. If there were, would we not want the prime minister to take them? And if there were drugs for hand-eye coordination, would we not pay more to see a performer who had taken them than one who had not? (Faster, Stronger, Higher 2012)

Proponents and opponents of steroid prohibition also argue over the importance of records in sports: most home runs in a season, most completed passes for touchdowns, fastest 100-m dash, and so on. When Mark McGwire was found to have used illegal substances in setting new home run records in professional baseball, a number of critics suggested adding an asterisk to the new record in the official books of statistics. As one observer has written, "[s]ports that revere records and historical comparisons (think of baseball and home runs) would become unmoored by drug-aided athletes obliterating old standards" (Murray 2012). A writer with a different view, Scott Long, has responded to that argument, however, that "[p]ersonally, I don't have a big problem with some of baseball's greatest records being broken by athletes who are under suspicion as cheaters." Think of all the changes that have taken place in professional baseball over the past century or more: baseballs that are more or less "lively," changes in bat manufacturing, closer or more distance outfield fences, better overall nutrition and conditioning, more or less aggressive play on the bases, changes in the size of the strike zone, more or fewer and better or less-qualified umpires, and a host of other factors. Why should steroid use not be considered as just one more factor that might affect the numbers that eventually make their way into the record books? Long concludes by asking "[a]re you telling me that the Ty Cobb Tigers or the Gas House Gang Cardinals wouldn't have taken anything they thought that gave them a chance to perform better?" (Scott 2012).

So perhaps the argument is not entirely settled. For the better part of two centuries, organized sports has battled to keep itself clean from performance-enhancing substances it has claimed would introduce dangerous and unsafe practices into athletics. Now that organizations have succeeded to some extent in achieving that goal, the question has arisen whether all that battle was really worth the effort.

References

"The 1936 Wrestling Team of Germany During Nazi Rule." http://www.usawrestlingnation.com/phpBB3/viewtopic. php?f=10&t=13113. Accessed on June 13, 2012.

"2012 List of Prohibited Substances and Methods." *World Anti-Doping Agency.* http://list.wada-ama.org/prohibited-all-times/prohibited-substances/. Accessed on June 21, 2012.

Andrews, Edmund L. August 21, 1998. "Swimming: 3 Guilty of Giving Drugs to East German Athletes." *New York Times.* Available online at http://www.nytimes.com/1998/08/21/sports/swimming-3-guilty-of-giving-drugs-to-east-german-athletes.html. Accessed on June 23, 2012.

Assael, Shaun. 2003. "Cut and Run." *ESPN The Magazine* (July 7, 2003): 40–49.

Assael, Shaun. 2007. *Steroid Nation.* New York: ESPN Books.

"The Athlete. Drug Testing in Sport." *The Athlete.org.* http://www.theathlete.org/Drug-Testing-In-Sports.html. Accessed on June 21, 2012.

"Athletics at the 1976 Montréal Summer Games: Women's Discus Throw." *SR/Olympic Sports.* http://www.sports-reference.com/olympics/summer/1976/ATH/womens-discus-throw.html. Accessed on June 17, 2012.

Backhouse, Susan, et al. January 2007. *International Literature Review: Attitudes, Behaviours, Knowledge and*

Education—Drugs in Sport: Past, Present and Future. [n.p.]: World Anti-Doping Agency.

Baker, Millard. "The History of Anabolic Steroids in Sports." http://thinksteroids.com/articles/history-anabolic-steroids-sports/. Accessed on June 17, 2012.

"BALCO Investigation Timeline." *USA Today.* Available online at http://www.usatoday.com/sports/balco-timeline.htm. Accessed on June 25, 2012.

Beamish, Rob. 2011. *Steroids: A New Look at Performance-enhancing Drugs.* Santa Barbara, CA: Praeger.

Beamish, Rob, and Ian Ritchie. 2005. "The Spectre of Steroids: Nazi Propaganda, Cold War Anxiety and Patriarchal Paternalism." *The International Journal of the History of Sport.* 22(5): 777–795.

Beckett, Arnold H. 1976. "Problems of Anabolic Steroids in Sports." *Olympic Review.* 109–110: 591–598. Available online at http://www.la84foundation.org/OlympicInformationCenter/OlympicReview/1976/ore109/ore109l.pdf. Accessed on June 21, 2012.

"Ben Johnson Takes Witness Stand, Confesses that He Used Steroids." June 13, 1989. *Toronto Observer-Reporter.* Available online at http://news.google.com/newspapers?nid=2519&dat=19890613&id=985dAAAAIBAJ&sjid=UV0NAAAAIBAJ&pg=3832,3949573. Accessed on June 24, 2012.

de Borbon, Daniel. "Anabolic Steroids—Everything You Wanted to Know." *Yahoo! Voices.* http://voices.yahoo.com/anabolic-steroids-everything-wanted-know-1718681.html. Accessed on June 13, 2012.

Bowers, Larry D., Sr. ed. 2007. *2008 Guide to Prohibited Substances and Prohibited Methods of Doping.* Colorado Springs, CO: United States Anti-Doping Agency.

Brooks, R. V., R. G. Firth, and N. A. Sumner. 1975. "Detection of Anabolic Steroids by Radioimmunoassay." *British Journal of Sports Medicine.* 9(2): 89–92.

Cadwallader, Amy B., et al. 2010. "The Abuse of Diuretics as Performance-enhancing Drugs and Masking Agents in Sport Doping: Pharmacology, Toxicology and Analysis." *British Journal of Pharmacology.* 161(1): 1–16.

Chidlovski, Arthur. "The Eraser: History of Disqualifications at the Men's Olympic Weightlifting Tournaments." http://www.chidlovski.net/liftup/l_disqualifications_olympics.asp#eraser. Accessed on June 17, 2012.

"Chronology of 1998 Tour de France Drug Scandal." *CNN Sports Illustrated.* http://sportsillustrated.cnn.com/cycling/1998/tourdefrance/news/1998/08/02/drug_chronology/. Accessed on June 24, 2012.

Cohen, Roger. March 6, 1993. "Johnson Is Banned for Life after Testing Positive for Drugs a 2d Time." *New York Times.* Available online at http://www.nytimes.com/1993/03/06/sports/track-field-johnson-banned-for-life-after-testing-positive-for-drugs-2d-time.html. Accessed on June 24, 2012.

Collins, Rick. "Steroids and Sports: A Provocative Interview with Norm Fost, M.D." http://www.steroidlaw.com/steroid-law-45.html. Accessed on June 25, 2012.

Connolly, Ryan. 2006. "Balancing the Justices in Anti-Doping Law: The Need to Ensure Fair Athletic Competition Through Effective Anti-Doping Programs vs. the Protection of Rights of Accused Athletes." *Virginia Sports and Entertainment Law Journal.* 5(2): 41–80.

Cowart, Virginia. 1987. "Steroids in Sports: After Four Decades, Time to Return These Genies to Bottle?" *JAMA.* 257(4): 421–427.

Cram, Steve. "Jenkins Shows Jones that Cheats Can Prosper." *The Guardian.* The Sport Blog. http://www.guardian.co.uk/sport/2008/jan/15/athletics.sport2. Accessed on June 24, 2012.

de la Torre, Xavier, et al. 2001. "13C/12C Isotope Ratio MS Analysis of Testosterone, in Chemicals and

Pharmaceutical Preparations." *Journal of Pharmaceutical and Biomedical Analysis.* 24(4): 645–650.

Donati, Alessandro. *World Traffic in Doping Substances.* World Anti-Doping Agency, February 2007. http://www. wada-ama.org/rtecontent/document/Donati_Report_ Trafficking_2007-03_06.pdf. Accessed on June 24, 2012.

"Doping: Five German Coaches Admit East German Doping Past." Reuters. http://uk.reuters.com/article/2009/04/06/ doping-germany-coaches-idUKL616969920090406. Accessed on June 23, 2012.

"Dr. Gary Wadler of the World Anti-Doping Agency Gives His Answers to Your Questions (Part I)." 2008. *New York Times* (June 26, 2008). Available online at http:// beijing2008.blogs.nytimes.com/2008/06/26/dr-gary- wadler-of-the-world-anti-doping-agency-gives- his-answers-to-your-questions-part-I/. Accessed on June 22, 2012.

"Drugs in Sports." [IAAF] http://www.iaaf.org/mm/ Document/imported/42026.pdf. Accessed on June 15, 2012.

Dvorchak, Robert. 2005. "Never Enough/Steroids in Sports: Experiment Turns Epidemic 46 Years after Steroids Were Injected into Sports, There Is a Frenzy to Get Rid of Them." *Pittsburgh Post-Gazette* (October 2, 2005). Available online at http://www.ergogenics.org/123.html. Accessed on June 14, 2012.

Eisendrath, John. "Confessions of a Steroid Smuggler: When the Quest for Big Muscles Turns into a Passion for Big Money." *Los Angeles Times* (April 24, 1988). Available online at http://articles.latimes.com/1988-04-24/magazine/ tm-2306_1_william-dillon. Accessed on June 24, 2012.

"The Elixir of Life." HubPages. http://leahlefler.hubpages. com/hub/The-Elixir-of-Life-A-Brief-History-of- Testosterone. Accessed on June 13, 2012.

Eyquem, Marie-Thérèse. February 1961. "Women Sports and the Olympic Games." *Bulletin du Comité International*

Olympique: 48–50. Available online at http://www.aafla. org/OlympicInformationCenter/OlympicReview/1961/ BDCE73/BDCE73k.pdf. Accessed on June 15, 2012.

Fair, John D. 1993. "Isometrics or Steroids? Exploring New Frontiers of Strength in the Early 1960s." *Journal of Sport History*. 20(1): 1–24.

"Faster, Stonger, Higher." *The Guardian*. Available online at http://www.guardian.co.uk/sport/2004/aug/09/ athensolympics2004.olympicgames. Accessed on June 25, 2012

Fost, Norman. 2005. "Steroid Hysteria: Unpacking the Claims." *Virtual Mentor*. 7(11). [no pages]. Available online at http://virtualmentor.ama-assn.org/2005/11/oped2-0511. html. Accessed on June 25, 2012.

Franke, Werner W., and Brigitte Berendonk. 1997. "Hormonal Doping and Androgenization of Athletes: A Secret Program of the German Democratic Republic Government." *Clinical Chemistry*. 43(7): 1262–1279.

Gale, 2008. "Performance-enhancing Drugs." *Sports in America: Recreation, Business, Education, and Controversy*, Chapter 9. Available online at http://www.encyclopedia. com/topic/Performance-Enhancing_Drugs.aspx. Accessed on June 25, 2012.

Gatehouse, Jonathan. "Ben Johnson: From Seoul to Soul." http://www2.macleans.ca/2010/10/26/from-seoul-to-soul/. Accessed on June 24, 2012.

Gilbert, Bil. June 23, 1969. "Problems in a Turned-on World." *Sports Illustrated*. Available online at http:// sportsillustrated.cnn.com/vault/article/magazine/ MAG1082543/index.htm. Accessed on June 17, 2012.

Gilbert, Cathrin, et al. "The Doping Legacy." *Der Spiegel*. http://www.presseurop.eu/en/content/article/80561- doping-legacy. Accessed on June 23, 2012.

Goldman, Denie, and Robert Goldman. April 1980. "Father of Dianabol." *Muscle Training Illustrated*. 75:5.

Harrah, Scott. "Dan Duchaine Unchained: The "Guru" Breaks the Silence on Steroids." *Elite Fitness*. http://www.elitefitness.com/articledata/dan-duchaine-interview.html. Accessed on June 24, 2012.

Hearing before the Committee on Commerce, Science, and Transportation. United States Senate. One Hundred Ninth Congress, First Session, May 24, 2005. Available online at http://bulk.resource.org/gpo.gov/hearings/109s/24722.pdf. Accessed on June 22, 2012.

Hoberman, John M. 1992. *Mortal Engines: The Science of Performance and the Dehumanization of Sport*. New York: Free Press.

"Human Growth Hormone History." Somatropin. http://www.somatropin.net/hgh-history.htm. Accessed on June 24, 2012.

Hunt, Thomas M. 2011. *Drug Games: The International Olympic Committee and the Politics of Doping, 1960–2008*. Austin: University of Texas Press.

Hunt, Thomas M. "Sport, Drugs, and the Cold War: The Conundrum of Olympic Doping Policy, 1970–1979." http://www.la84foundation.org/SportsLibrary/Olympika/Olympika_2007/olympika1601d.pdf. Accessed on June 17, 2012.

Hunt, Thomas Mitchell. "Drug Games: The International Politics of Doping and the Olympic Movement, 1960–2007." Doctoral thesis. University of Texas at Austin, August 2007. Available online at http://repositories.lib.utexas.edu/bitstream/handle/2152/3255/huntt51425.pdf?sequence=2. Accessed on June 16, 2012.

Hurst, Mike. December 25, 2009. "Johnson Finds His Drink Spiker." *The Telegraph*. . Available online at http://www.dailytelegraph.com.au/sport/

more-sports/johnson-finds-his-drink-spiker/story-e6frey6i-1225813659234. Accessed on June 24, 2012.

Jenkins, Mark. "Erythropoietin." http://www.rice.edu/˜jenky/sports/epo.html. Accessed on June 24, 2012.

Kayser, Bengt, Alexandre Mauron, and Andy Miah. 2007. "Current Anti-doping Policy: A Critical Appraisal." *BMJ Medical Ethics*. 8(2). Available online at http://www.biomedcentral.com/content/pdf/1472-6939-8-2.pdf. Accessed on June 22, 2012.

Kettmann, Steve. "E. German Olympic Dopers Guilty." *Wired*. Available online at http://www.wired.com/politics/law/news/2000/07/37631. Accessed on June 23, 2012.

Kicman, Andrew T., and D. B. Gower. 2003. "Anabolic Steroids in Sport: Biochemical, Clinical and Analytical Perspectives." *Annals of Clinical Biochemistry*. 40(Pt. 4): 321–356.

Long, Scott. "The Happy Hypocrite Takes on Jason Grimsely." http://thejuice.baseballtoaster.com/archives/398606.html. Accessed on June 25, 2012.

Longman, Jere. 2012a. "Drug Sleuths' Surprise Produces a Breakthrough." *New York Times*. (December 18, 1994). Available online at http://www.nytimes.com/1994/12/18/sports/olympics-drug-sleuths-surprise-produces-a-breakthrough.html?pagewanted=all&src=pm. Accessed on June 24, 2012.

Longman, Jere. 2012b. "East German Steroids' Toll: 'They Killed Heidi'." *New York Times*. (January 26, 2004). Available online at http://www.nytimes.com/2004/01/26/sports/drug-testing-east-german-steroids-toll-they-killed-heidi.html?pagewanted=all&src=pm. Accessed on June 23, 2012.

"A Look Inside the Whereabouts Program." *Cycling Tips*. http://www.cyclingtips.com.au/2012/02/living-with-the-whereabouts/. Accessed on June 21, 2012.

Mantell, Gregory. "Doping and the Global Fight Against Doping in Sport: Nandrolone." http://minebuilding.org. ua/. Accessed on June 17, 2012.

McRae, Donald. "Ben Johnson: 'My Revelations Will Shock the Sporting World'." *The Guardian*. Available online at http://www.guardian.co.uk/sport/2010/oct/05/ben-johnson-drugs-olympics. Accessed on June 24, 2012.

"Merck's New Anabolic Steroid: MK-0773." ergo-log.com. http://www.ergo-log.com/newsteroidmk0773.html. Accessed on June 22, 2012.

Moseley, Ray. September 4, 2000. "E. Germany's Doping Leaves Athletes Suffering." *Chicago Tribune*. Available online at http://articles.chicagotribune.com/2000-09-04/news/0009040025_1_east-germany-manfred-ewald-doping. Accessed on June 23, 2012.

"Most Dangerous Sports." *The Top Tens*. http://www.the-top-tens.com/lists/most-dangerous-sports.asp. Accessed on June 25, 2012.

Mullegg, Gaston, and Henry Montandon. July 1951. "The Danish Oarsman Who Took Part in the European Championships at Milan in 1950; Were They Drugged?" *Bulletin du Comité International Olympique*, 25–26. Available online at http://www.la84foundation.org/OlympicInformationCenter/OlympicReview/1951/BDCE28/BDCE28l.pdf. Accessed on June 14, 2012.

Murray, Thomas H. "Sports Enhancement." The Hastings Center. http://www.thehastingscenter.org/Publications/BriefingBook/Detail.aspx?id=2206. Accessed on June 25, 2012.

Noakes, Timothy D. 2006. "Should We Allow Performance-enhancing Drugs in Sport? A Rebuttal to the Article by Savulescu and Colleagues." *International Journal of Sports Science and Coaching*. 1(4): 289–316.

Pietaro, Joe. "27 Years Later: Duchaine's 'Underground Steroid Handbook' Still Speaks Volumes." http://www.

musclesportmag.com/2008/05/29/27-years-later-
duchaine%E2%80%99s-%E2%80%9Cush%E2%80%
9D-still-speaks-volumes/. Accessed on June 23, 2012.

Pilgrim, Jill, and Kim Betz. "A Journey Through Olympic
Drug Testing Rules: A Practitioner's Guide to Understanding
Drug Testing Within the Olympic Movement." http://
www.thesportjournal.org/article/journey-through-olympic-
drug-testing-rules-practitioners-guide-understanding-drug-
testing-wi. Accessed on June 16, 2012.

"Players Listed in the Mitchell Commission Report."
ESPN MLB. http://sports.espn.go.com/mlb/news/
story?id=3153646. Accessed on June 25, 2012.

Puma, Mike. "Not the Size of the Dog in the Fight." *ESPN
Classic.* http://espn.go.com/classic/biography/s/Alzado_
Lyle.html. Accessed on June 24, 2012.

Quinn, T. J. "Pumped-up Pioneers: The '63 Chargers." *ESPN
Outside the Lines.* http://sports.espn.go.com/espn/otl/news/
story?id=3866837. Accessed on June 15, 2012.

"The Researcher's Perspective." 2007. *Play True.* 2: 15–18.
Available online at http://www.wada-ama.org/Documents/
Resources/Questions_and_Answers/PlayTrue2007_Summer
Research_En_15-18.pdf. Accessed on June 24, 2012.

Riordan, Jim. "The Rise and Fall of Soviet Olympic
Champions." http://www.aafla.org/SportsLibrary/
Olympika/Olympika_1993/olympika0201c.pdf. Accessed
on June 14, 2012.

Robinson, N., et al. 2006. "Erythropoietin and Blood Doping."
British Journal of Sports Medicine. 40(Suppl 1): 30–34.

Rosen, Daniel M. 2008. *Dope: A History of Performance
Enhancement in Sports from the Nineteenth Century to Today.*
Westport, CT: Praeger.

Saugy, Martial, et al. 2000. "Test Methods: Anabolics."
*Baillière's Best Practice & Research. Clinical Endocrinology
and Metabolism.* 14(1): 111–133.

Schudel, Matt. "Harold Connolly, Olympic Gold Medalist in Hammer Throw, Dies at 79." *The Washington Post*. http://www.washingtonpost.com/wp-dyn/content/article/2010/08/21/AR2010082102538.html. Accessed on June 15, 2012.

Scott, Jack. October 17, 1971. "It's Not How You Play the Game, But What Pill You Take." *New York Times*: 40–41. Available online at http://query.nytimes.com/mem/archive/pdf?res=F00D1FF63D5E127A93C5A8178BD95F4587 85F9. Accessed on June 15, 2012.

Sottas, Pierre-Edouard, et al. 2008. "From Population- to Subject-based Limits of T/E Ratio to Detect Testosterone Abuse in Elite Sports." *Forensic Science International*. 174(2–3): 166–172.

"Sport's Greatest Cover Up: Part One." *BBC World Service*. http://www.bbc.co.uk/worldservice/science/2009/08/090805_discovery_sports_cover_up_one. shtml. Accessed on June 16, 2012.

"Should Performance Enhancing Drugs (Such as Steroids) Be Accepted in Sports?" *ProCon.org*. http://sportsanddrugs. procon.org/view.answers.php?questionID=001200. Accessed on June 25, 2012.

Sumner, N.A. 1974. "Measurement of Anabolic Steroids by Radioimmunoassay." *Journal of Steroid Biochemistry*. 5(4): 307.

Taylor, William N. 1982. *Anabolic Steroids and the Athlete*. Jefferson, NC: McFarland.

Taylor, William N. 1991. *Macho Medicine: A History of the Anabolic Steroid Epidemic*. Jefferson, NC: McFarland.

"Therapeutic Use Exceptions." *World Anti-Doping Agency*. http://www.wada-ama.org/en/Science-Medicine/TUE/. Accessed on June 21, 2012.

Todd, Jan, and Terry Todd. 2001. "Significant Events in the History of Drug Testing and the Olympic Movement." In

Wayne Wilson and Ed Derse, eds. *Doping in Elite Sport: The Politics of Drugs in the Olympic Movement.* Champaign, IL: Human Kinetics, 65–104.

Todd, Terry. 1965. "The Jovial Genius of Dr. John Zeigler." *Strength & Health.* 33: 44–45.

"Transgender and Intersex Olympians." http://www.h2g2. com/entry/A87724588. Accessed on June 15, 2012.

Ungerleider, Steven. 2001. *Faust's Gold: Inside the East German Doping Machine.* New York: Thomas Dunne Books/St. Martin's Press.

Union Cycliste Internationale. "The UCI and the Fight Against Doping." http://www.uci.ch/Modules/ ENews/ENewsDetails.asp?id=MjMz&MenuId=MT YxNw&BackLink=/Templates/UCI/UCI5/layout. asp?MenuID=MTYxNw. Accessed on June 15, 2012.

Van Eenoo, P., and F. T. Delbeke. 2006. "Metabolism and Excretion of Anabolic Steroids in Doping Control–New Steroids and New Insights." *Steroid Biochemistry and Molecular Biology.* 101(4–5): 161–178.

"Victor Conte: BALCO—The Straight Dope on Steroids." *Diet, Health & Fitness News.* http://www.diethealthand fitnessnews.com/balco-book-victor-conte.html. Accessed on June 25, 2012.

"WADA Statistics 2005." *Now THAT's Amateur.* http://now-thats-amateur.blogspot.com/2006/04/wada-statistics-2005. html. Accessed on June 22, 2012.

Wagner, Ulrik. 2010. "The International Cycling Union under Siege–Anti-doping and the Biological Passport as a Mission Impossible?" *European Sport Management Quarterly.* 10(3): 321–342.

Ward, R. J., C. H. Shackleton, and A.M. Lawson. 1975. "Gas Chromatographic-Mass Spectrometric Methods for the Detection and Identification of Anabolic Steroid Drugs." *British Journal of Sports Medicine.* 9: 93–97.

"What Are the 19 Known Methods of Cheating to Pass Performance Enhancing Drug Tests?" ProCon. org. http://sportsanddrugs.procon.org/view.resource. php?resourceID=002706. Accessed on June 22, 2012.

"Why Steroids Are Bad for You." WebMD. http://www. webmd.com/fitness-exercise/news/20050316/why-steroids-are-bad-for-you. Accessed on June 25, 2012.

Williams, Lance, and Mark Fainaru-Wada. "An Unlikely Cast of Characters at Center of Doping Scandal." SFGate. http://www.sfgate.com/sports/article/An-unlikely-cast-of-characters-at-center-of-2796932.php#page-1. Accessed on June 25, 2012.

Wilson, Wayne, and Ed Derse. 2001. *Doping in Elite Sport: The Politics of Drugs in the Olympic Movement.* Champaign, IL: Human Kinetics.

Winearls, Christopher G. 1998. "Recombinant Human Erythropoietin: 10 Years of Clinical Experience." *Nephrology, Dialysis, Transplantation.* 13(Suppl 2): 3–8.

World Anti-Doping Agency. "The World Anti-Doping Code International Standard: Laboratories," January 2012. http://www.wada-ama.org/Documents/World_Anti-Doping_Program/WADP-IS-Laboratories/ISL/WADA_Int_Standard_Laboratories_2012_EN.pdf. Accessed on June 21, 2012.

Yesalis, Charles E., and Michael S. Bahrke. 2002. "History of Doping in Sports." In Michael S. Bahrke and Charles Yesalis, eds. *Performance-enhancing Substances in Sport and Exercise.* Champaign, IL: Human Kinetics, 42–76.

Yesalis, Charles E., et al. 1990. "Incidence of the Nonmedical Use of Anabolic-androgenic Steroids." *National Institute on Drug Abuse Research Monographs.* 102: 97–112. Available online at http://archives.drugabuse.gov/pdf/monographs/102.pdf. Accessed on June 14, 2012.

Opposition to the use of performance-enhancing substances and practices has been widespread in the sports and athletics communities over the past century or more. Most groups that control the operation of sporting activities have now written detailed rules and regulations for the control of these substances and activities, accompanied by an intensive program of testing. As these efforts have gone forward, however, some opposition has developed to this trend, with a number of individuals arguing that the use of anabolic steroids (AS) and other performance-enhancing drugs is not necessarily a practice that needs to be banned. This chapter presents a variety of viewpoints on this topic. The case for permitting the use of AS in sports and other settings is presented by Bennett Foddy and Julian Savulescu, at the Institute for Science and Ethics at the University of Oxford; Lewis Kurlantzick, Zephaniah Swift Professor of Law at the University of Connecticut School of Law; Dave Steen, at Muscle Space. Some cautions about the use of AS are offered by Mark Fuerst, and the chapter concludes with two essays on the less-discussed topics of the use of AS for gender reassignment and for the treatment of homosexual

---

Press clamors around Lance Armstrong during Stage 17 of the Tour de France on July 22, 2010. The American cyclist at the center of the sport's biggest doping scandal came clean in January 2013 about his use of performance-enhancing drugs. While expressing remorse for the lies, Armstrong made clear that he does not consider doping, in a sport filled with athletes using all means to find that competitive edge, to be cheating—a controversial perspective that is nonetheless shared by many in the sports world. (Alexander Gordeyev/Dreamstime)

behavior. These two essays provide useful information about the use of AS for purposes other than sports and exercise.

USING STEROIDS ETHICALLY
Bennett Foddy and Julian Savulescu

Three arguments are commonly given in favor of prohibiting the use of any performance-enhancing drug in sporting competition: (1) the drug is too unsafe; (2) it perverts the nature and spirit of the sporting competition; (3) we should ban the drug simply because it enhances performance.

The last of the three ought to be dismissed out of hand every time it appears. Modern athletic sport is entirely focused on finding new ways to break the old records, and most of the effective methods are legal. Hypoxic training tents, which simulate the effect of training at high altitude by allowing the blood to carry more oxygen, are legal. Caffeine, which improves reaction time and fights fatigue, is legal. So are advanced dietary regimes, which maximize the amount of energy available to the athlete's muscles on the day of competition. Dietary supplements, such as creatine, are legal. And through most of human history, people used various substances in an attempt to enhance their performance.

The other two arguments, by contrast, provide us with good reason for banning certain drugs in certain situations. Some drugs do change the nature of a given sport, so that it changes into a less interesting or less valuable pursuit. For example, we tend to think that one of the most interesting things about boxing is that boxers need to overcome their fear of being hit to perform well. If they took a drug that entirely eliminated their ability to feel fear, or pain, this valuable aspect of the performance would be eliminated from the sport. Similarly, when archers or professional pistol shooters use beta-blocker drugs to steady their hands, that removes one of the most interesting aspects of those sports: the challenge of controlling one's nerves.

Do AS make cycling and athletic sports like running less interesting? It is hard to see why this would be the case. Steroids enhance performance by allowing athletes to train longer and recover more quickly. They enhance the effect of training. Athletes on steroids still have to train hard; in fact, they still have to overcome every challenge faced by their nondoping peers. If every Olympic sprinter or cyclist were using steroids, it would still be the same sport, just slightly faster. And athletes could recover better and more quickly from injuries which are inevitable given the grueling training required by modern competitive sport.

Finally, there is the argument that drugs need to be banned because they are too dangerous. In the history of competitive sport, several exceedingly dangerous drugs have been used to enhance performance. In the third modern Olympic Games, the winner of the men's marathon was given strychnine (a lethal poison) during the race as a stimulant. More recently, drugs that allow athletes to modify their genes to increase the performance of their muscles have been discovered but these drugs are nowhere near safe enough for humans, and their side effects are not well understood. It makes sense to ban drugs like these.

However, the dangers of any performance-enhancer need to be put in context. Nothing in life is completely safe, not even drinking water or going for a morning stroll. Athletic sport is especially dangerous—it causes more deaths, both in training and competition, than steroids do, and it produces millions of crippling injuries every year. Rugby, horse riding, and American football are associated with spinal cord injury that can render the victim quadriplegic and dependent on a ventilator for life, like "Superman" Christopher Reeves. Boxing and soccer are associated with chronic brain damage. If a performance-enhancing drug is significantly less dangerous than the training for that sport, or than competing in it, then the dangers of the drug may be so low as to make them relatively insignificant. In the case of cycling, the dangers of cycling at speeds in excess of 60 kilometers per hour (km/hr) vastly outweigh the risks of use of steroids, when administered by a medical professional.

AS are nothing more than the synthetic form of the natural hormone, testosterone. To receive a benefit in sporting performance, ordinary athletes need to take a dose of the hormone that would be very unusual in an unenhanced body. But testosterone is not a poisonous substance like strychnine. In its naturally occurring form, it is a natural by-product of heavy training, and many of its worst side effects—immune deficiency, enlarged ventricles in the heart, and depression—are also common symptoms of overtraining. In this context, steroids are still dangerous, but perhaps not much more dangerous than hard training and professional full-contact sport.

We have good reason to ban certain kinds of performance-enhancing drugs. Boxers should not be allowed to take strong painkillers during competition, and no athlete should be allowed to take truly dangerous or untested drugs like the new genetic medicines. But the case against steroids is much weaker.

The biggest problem with AS is that they are obtained illegally, and then self-administered in secret by athletes who are not trained to identify overuse or to scale their dose appropriately. Like many behind-the-counter drugs, steroids can be taken safely but it is not safe enough to take them on your own. It would be much safer to take steroids for performance enhancement if they could be administered and monitored by a doctor. Such sports doctors could be held responsible for their athlete's health.

For these reasons, we suggest that the legal shackles be removed from steroid use, and put in the hands of the medical and prescription system. Athletes would be able to obtain steroids from their doctor on request. However, the moral and legal responsibility for the athlete's health would be passed from the athlete, who after all is no expert on modern medicine, to the doctor. Any doctor who overprescribed steroids, or who prescribed any unreasonably dangerous drug, would be struck off the medical register.

We can preserve the nature and spirit of competitive sport as well as the health of athletes, and we can do it within the existing structures of the medical drug schedule and prescription system. Perhaps there is no need for an antidoping program at all.

Would such a regime remove the human element from sporting performance and place it in the hands of pharmaceutical companies and scientists? In some cases, such as radical genetic re-engineering, it might. But in the case of steroids, it doesn't. Steroids merely enhance what is normal, and which varies from individual to individual, and still requires predominantly human physical and psychological input to train and perform. Enhancing human performance is different from dehumanizing sporting performance.

Julian Savulescu is Uehiro Chair in Practical Ethics and Director of the Institute for Science and Ethics at the University of Oxford. Bennett Foddy is Deputy Director of the Institute for Science and Ethics and Senior James Martin Research Fellow at the University of Oxford.

THE PROBLEMATIC CHARACTER OF THE CASE FOR REGULATION OF STEROIDS
Lewis Kurlantzick

The seemingly simple question of the proper treatment of steroid use in professional athletics is, in fact, highly complicated. That complexity reflects a mix of controverted justifications, enforcement mechanisms that implicate privacy interests and feature an inverse relationship between expense and reliability, and historically untrustworthy national and international enforcement authorities.

At the core of the debate, though, is the matter of rationale. What are the justifications proffered for a ban on steroid use? Probably most common is the "unnatural" performance-enhancing quality of these substances. This rationale, apparently simple, is, in fact, hardly free of difficulty. The problem is that over time the ingestion by athletes of a large range of supplements and "restorative" substances, the use of novel training methods and diets, and, of course, advances in equipment have all "enhanced" performance (Fost 1986, 5–6; Murray 1987, 11, 13). A difficulty lies in articulating a convincing distinction between these enhancers and steroids. If the claimed difference is rooted in a notion of naturalness, we presently have no convincing explanation of why some substances, including synthetic vitamins, are considered "natural" and others, including naturally occurring hormones, are considered unnatural. This task of differentiation may be not only difficult but also impossible, as the debates on this topic among philosophers of sport suggest that composition of a satisfying distinction between permissible and impermissible substances may be beyond our powers of conception and articulation (Carr 2008, 193, 194; Simon 2004, 72, 80). There appears to be no moral distinction between the various natural and unnatural assists to performance. And the absence of such a distinction underlines the ambiguity of a moral evaluation of drug use and of the meaning of our cultural notion that the "right" way to obtain success is through hard work.

A second justification for disapproval rests on a concern for the athlete's health. Yet, assuming that accurate information is available and therefore ignorance of any physical risk of steroid use is not present, this rationale is problematic, at least for competent adults. Athletes are in a position to make a decision about what behavior is in their best interest, to weigh the risks and benefits according to their own values. And a paternalistic rule that attempts to prevent the athlete from harming himself runs counter to the important values of independence and personal choice. Moreover, it is likely that the feared harm is neither life-threatening nor irreversible. Presumably, under this health rationale, if performance is enhanced by substances that cause neither short-term nor long-term harm to the athlete, these substances should not be banned.

A third justification, though more intricate and less often voiced, is more promising. This justification is rooted in a concern for a form of "coercion" in the athlete's decision making and his inability to coordinate a response without outside intervention. If one person is perceived to have an advantage in using a drug, others may feel compelled to use it in an effort to try to stay even. That use decision is not necessarily troubling, any more than the initial decision to engage in a risky sport. After all, the athlete can choose to forego the opportunity and any attendant risks. However, if a large percentage of participants in a particular sport would choose not to use steroids if left to their own independent decisions, but feel pressured to use them in order to remain competitive with users, a case can be made for intervention in the form of a rule banning (or limiting) use. In light of the large number of potential users, the costs of individuals contractually establishing an advanced arrangement that would serve the collective interest of assurance of nonuse would be prohibitive. Thus, a rule here could be seen as a response to a problem of coordination that the interested parties cannot resolve themselves. Under this justification, the athletes' situation can be seen as analogous to that of the fishermen who will "overfish" and excessively deplete the stock in the absence of a legal rule limiting the permitted catch. The coordination function, though, need not be effected by public intervention. Indeed, in the case of all major professional sports leagues, a private mechanism, the players' union, exists to effectuate the players' interests, and the union and management can adopt a rule by contract. But, of course, even if this coordination justification is theoretically persuasive, there remains the empirical question of whether the assumption about participant attitudes is accurate.

A decision by owners and players to ban or limit the use of steroids might proceed from a quite different perspective, that of entertainment. That is, the parties are engaged in the joint sale of an entertainment product and consequently the views of their consumers are of critical concern to them. Hence, if present and potential fans are likely to change their preferences with respect to consumption of the sport in the absence of league action against steroid use, it would make sense simply as a matter of sound commercial judgment to take action to avoid this customer alienation. League action would be rooted in a practical concern about the financial implications of athletes with bad images. This rationale for response, though, has nothing to do with concern for athletes' health, preservation of an "even" playing field, or a distinction between natural and unnatural substances. Rather the decision to condition employment on abstention from use of steroids derives from a judgment about the marketing of the product.

There is good reason to question the prevailing view in the sports community that performance-enhancing drugs are bad and that their use should be banned. Cogent criticisms of the arguments for prohibiting steroid use exist. Recognition of the incoherence of many of these claims and, more generally, that the moral foundations of drug testing in sports are suspect should inform decisions and beget caution about both establishment of testing schemes and the design and implementation of such schemes. Robert Simon has suggested that, assuming the lines of argument for and against the view that steroid use is immoral are inconclusive, sports authorities have reasonable grounds to impose a ban, and their decisions, if reached pursuant to a proper process, have normative force (Simon 2004, 86–88, 90). While this perspective has some merit, its persuasiveness is weakened in the not-uncommon situations where—unlike professional sports leagues—the athletes have no representation in the policy-making process that formulates (and executes) governing rules. The NCAA and the IOC are examples of this kind of structure.

References

Carr, Craig L. 2008. "Fairness and Performance Enhancement in Sport." *Journal of the Philosophy of Sport.* 35(2): 193–207.

Fost, Norman. 1986. "Banning Drugs in Sports: A Skeptical View." Hastings Center Report (August 1986).

Murray, Thomas H. 1987. "The Ethics of Drugs in Sport." In Richard H. Strauss, ed. *Drugs & Performance in Sports.* Philadelphia: W. B. Saunders.

Simon, Robert. 2004. *Fair Play: The Ethics of Sport,* 2nd ed. Boulder, CO: Westview Press.

Lewis Kurlantzick is the Zephaniah Swift Professor of Law at the University of Connecticut School of Law. A 1965 graduate of Wesleyan University, Professor Kurlantzick received his law degree in 1968 from Harvard where he was a member of the Board of Editors of The Harvard Law Review. *He regularly teaches a seminar on Sports and the Law and writes on copyright and sports law issues for both popular and legal newspapers and journals.*

DENIAL AND DISHONESTY
Adrianne Blue

Banning them has not stopped the use of AS. Instead, it has turned champions and their coaches into liars and cheats. It has also put high school and college athletes and ordinary guys at the gym at risk. So it is high time we made steroids and other banned performance-enhancing drugs legal in sports.

As long as we demand new world records and greater and flashier skills, sports doping won't go away. If we remove the bans on performance-enhancing drugs, they can be regulated and athletes on the way up—whose entourages do not yet include savvy physiotherapists and doctors—won't overdose and do themselves damage. Legalizing steroids would do away with the hypocrisy as well as the dangers to self-medicators at the local gym.

Anyone who reports on top-level sports or who participates in them knows that the use of AS and other performance-enhancing drugs is widespread. Insiders know that many—perhaps most—world-ranked sportsmen and sportswomen take banned drugs. The trainers, sports doctors, nutritionists, physiotherapists, and managers of the big names make sure that banned substances are taken at the safest and most efficient levels, and when they can, the governing bodies look the other way.

Few sports stars even feel guilty about using steroids because so many people they know do it, and anyway these drugs don't give you a free ride. You have to put in the work. What more than one champion has told me off the record is essentially this: "I doped so I could train harder and more frequently. So I don't feel guilty. I earned my medal."

Other state-of-the-art chemicals such as vitamins, minerals, special diets, and anti-inflammatory creams aren't against the rules. So are performance-enhancing surgery and injections of pain relieving corticosteroids. Why draw the line at AS?, athletes say. But they say it in private. In public these same world-ranked champions deny everything. Sports administrators and sponsors, and many sports writers also decry drugs in sport and express apparent surprise when a champion is found out. Surely they cannot be more ignorant than I am of the prevalence of drug use. Are they in denial, or are they merely pretending to be?

When, at the infamous 1988 Seoul Olympics, Ben Johnson, who finished first in the 100 meters (m), was shown to have taken AS, insiders were not surprised that he had taken them; they were surprised that he had been dosed so badly he was caught. There is now no doubt he doped regularly as part of his training routine, but as his great rival Carl Lewis hinted in his autobiography (Lewis and Marx 1990, 161–162), Johnson may have been found out because he was sabotaged by one of Lewis's friends. Ben Johnson's career was ruined, but other convicted 100 m sprinters have made comebacks. When the British sprinter Dwain Chambers returned from his ban, the performance director of UK Athletics told the press (Blue 2006), "We are not making ethical statements. We are picking a team to do the best we can." The disgraced American world and Olympic champion Justin Gatlin was applauded when he won a bronze medal in the 100 m dash and a gold medal in the 4 × 100 m relay at the 2012 Olympics after serving his four-year ban.

Both champions and the sports establishment profess to hate sport doping while, at the same time, they protect many doped-up superstars. Huge amounts of money is spent on drug testing which does catch a few users but whose main function, intentionally or not, is to maintain the illusion that the sports family is trying to end doping. The phoney denial I mention is a cynical, image-protecting strategy. Not a conspiracy of silence, rather, it is a double bluff. What happens is this: Doping is widely denied and said to be abhorred even by dopers, and wherever possible when a top practitioner is caught, the doping is portrayed by athletes, administrators, sponsors, and many in the media as a flawed individual's wrong-doing—not the world sports network's. It may even be portrayed as a medication taken by accident, that is, an honest mistake.

Interestingly six of the eight 100 m finalists at those long ago 1988 Seoul Olympics—these were the fastest men on the planet—have over the years been found to have taken banned drugs (Cooper 2012). More recently, the biggest stars of the world's top endurance event, the Tour de France cycle race, have been implicated in doping scandals. Floyd Landis, who has admitted to testosterone boosting, and Lance Armstrong, who denies it, are in very good company. Baseball, cricket, football, tennis, and speed skating too have had revelations involving performance-enhancing drugs, and of course, so has athletics. You name it, someone takes it if they think it will help. Tales of sport doping go back to ancient Egypt, where the hoof of an Abyssinian ass ground up and boiled in oil was prescribed to improve performance.

Today, sport's dirty little secret is doping. Instead of turning a blind eye or pretending to condemn doping, we should legalize AS and other performance-enhancing drugs so they can be properly regulated. This is what will clean up sports, protect both the weekend warrior and the up-and-coming star, and restore dignity to champions who now have little option but to live a lie.

References

Blue, Adrianne. 2006. "It's the Real Dope: Drugs in Sport." *New Statesman*. Available online at http://www.newstatesman. com/node/153965?quicktabs_most_read=1. Accessed on August 8, 2012.

Cooper, Chris. 2012. *Run, Swim, Throw, Cheat: The Science behind Drugs in Sport*. New York: Oxford University Press.

Lewis, Carl, and Jeffrey Marx. 1990. *Inside Track*. London: Pelham Books, pp. 161–162.

Adrianne Blue was among the first in Britain to speak out in favor of legalizing drugs in sport. A former London Times *and* Sunday Times *correspondent and sports columnist of the* New Statesman, *she is the author of six books published in 21 languages. Dr. Blue is a Senior Honorary Fellow at the City University of London.*

ANABOLIC STEROIDS SHOULD BE LEGALIZED
Dave Steen

The sales and use of anabolic steroids (AS) in the United States are governed by the Controlled Substances Act, as amended by the Anabolic Steroid Control Act of 1990 and later by Anabolic Steroid Control Act of 2004.

It should be noted that the Controlled Substances Act is the main U.S. antinarcotics piece of legislation, and since 1990 it classifies AS among the most dangerous illegal drugs.

But is it reasonable to put AS in one basket with cocaine and LSD lysergic acid diethylamide (LSD)? Do they really cause so much damage? Are AS (or anabolic androgenic steroids, AAS, as they are more often referred to) really such a social evil—toxic, addictive, and socially dangerous?

Let's examine such claims one by one:

1. AS are not addictive in their nature. Therefore both the U.S. Drug Enforcement Administration (DEA) and Food and Drug Administration (FDA) did not initially approve of their inclusion in the list of scheduled substances. True, some scientists were trying hard to find some opiate-like properties in AAS and at least one scientific study claims to have found them. However, one should not forget that

many commonly sold substances like coffee, wheat (gluten exorphins, type of opioid peptides), and cow milk (caso-morphin peptides) contain much stronger opioids.

2. Most AS are not toxic. While some AAS are severely liver-toxic (e.g., oxymetholone and fluoxymesterone), several others show no toxicity beyond that of other prescription drugs.

3. The use of AAS isn't more prevalent in countries where they are legal. Outlawing the AAS doesn't lead to reduction in their use.

I'm of the opinion that education, regulation, and controlled application would help our society more than criminalization and persecution.

There is a serious debate about legalizing some drugs. Legalizing AAS should be a much less controversial issue.

Ethical Questions

Use of AAS is a form of doping. Some people claim that any form of doping is simply not ethical and should be eradicated from sports. Maybe. But who shall decide for us what is and what is not doping? Where is the border between permitted and forbidden? Creatine is a potent muscle-growth stimulator and it's legal. Banning the AAS from official sports is one thing and treating them like narcotics is a completely different thing.

We live in a very liberal society. How often did you hear that "a woman has the right to make decisions about her body"? Yes, it refers to abortion, a question of life and death. How many females undergo sex-changing surgery every year? They are destined for testosterone-replacement therapy (in other words steroid use) till the end of their days.

How many senior men undergo testosterone-replacement therapy, a treatment that is essentially going against nature?

So we preach freedom of decision in all those very controversial cases but we deny this freedom to (mostly) men with a very natural wish: to grow bigger muscle.

Comparison with Legal Drugs

Prescription drugs can be dangerous. They must be used only where prescribed and in proper dosage. Therefore the unauthorized sales of prescription drugs are illegal and punishable by law in all civilized countries.

Even if used properly, prescription drugs can cause serious side effects and sometimes death. One would think that the danger of death is the inevitable price we pay for life-saving medicines but the annoying truth is that it just happens with such nonessential drugs as Viagra.

This drug claimed 522 lives during first two years of use in the United States alone. According to a study conducted at the Cedars-Sinai Medical Center, "the majority of deaths were associated with standard Viagra dosages . . . were due to cardiovascular causes and appeared to be clustered around the time of dosing. . . . The majority of deaths occurred in patients who were less than 65 years of age, and who had no reported cardiac risk factors" (Levine 2012).

I beg you to notice that the citation speaks of legitimate use, not of the illegally sold Viagra.

Now—can someone give me number of deaths caused by testosterone and its derivatives? Hardly so. Even the very few isolated cases of death associated with AAS use didn't show any direct link between the two.

What really is dangerous is the unsupervised use of AAS. Let's face it—people didn't stop using steroids when they became illegal. Guidance, observation, and supervision can only help lowering any morbidity associated with these substances.

Comparison with Tobacco and Alcohol

According to the Centers for Disease Control and Prevention (CDC), "More deaths are caused each year by tobacco use than by all deaths from human immunodeficiency virus (HIV), illegal drug use, alcohol use, motor vehicle injuries, suicides, and murders combined" (Tobacco-Related Morality 2012).

Unlike testosterone, which is a natural hormone with many health benefits (for instance, protection against diabetes and heart disease), tobacco is clearly bad for your health while being strongly addictive just like narcotics.

Alcohol is directly responsible for at least 150,000 deaths in the United States every year, not including alcohol-related accidents.

Both alcoholic beverages and tobacco products are readily available to the wide public.

The Consequences of Anti-AAS Legislation

There are a number of consequences resulting from past legislation that has criminalized the use of AAS:

- The number of steroid users didn't decrease.
- A whole billion-dollar industry went underground.
- Underground laboratories mushroomed and replaced legitimate pharmaceutical producers.

Such laboratories are not controlled by anyone. Their products are not sterile (most AAS are injectables). People running the laboratories have no way of controlling the active substances from China (about 90 percent of raw material is thought to originate in that country) they are using and they are usually being sold inferior materials.

- Millions of AAS users became criminals overnight.
- Millions of (mostly young) people are using powerful drugs under no medical guidance.
- Not only are countries losing millions of dollars on the taxes every year, their antidrug agencies are also busy chasing body-builders instead of drug dealers, all financed by taxpayers.

References

Levine, Jeff. "Viagra Linked to 522 Deaths." WebMD. http://www.webmd.com/erectile-dysfunction/news/20000314/viagra-linked-to-522-deaths. Accessed on July 30, 2012.

"Tobacco-Related Morality." Centers for Disease Control and
Prevention. http://www.cdc.gov/tobacco/data_statistics/
fact_sheets/health_effects/tobacco_related_mortality/.
Accessed on July 30, 2012.

*Dr. David Steen was born in Amsterdam, Netherlands, and
studied Biology at the Charles University of Prague. He spe-
cializes in performance enhancement in sports and is currently
employed at Muscle Space, online fitness and bodybuilding
media.*

STEROID ABUSE AND THE ARTIFICIAL MAN
Mark Fuerst

We live in an era of drug abuse with a widespread problem
among high school and college athletes—extensive use of AS.
Teens nationwide are taking these drugs under the misconcep-
tion they will enhance strength, speed, and looks.

Hundreds of thousands of teens have used steroids. A study
in the January 2008 issue of *Medicine & Science in Sports &
Exercise* shows that most teens who take steroids look upon
professional athletes as role models (Hoffman et al. 2008).
More than half of 3,200 8th–12th graders in 12 states sur-
veyed said they would take drugs to excel even if it shortened
their lives, and about two-thirds say they'd take drugs, including dietary supplements, to guarantee athletic success even if it
harmed their health.

Most steroids users are boys who want to bulk up, but some
girls use steroids for body shaping as well. The 2011 "Monitoring the Future Survey" by The University of Michigan, an ongoing study of the behaviors, attitudes, and values of American
secondary school students, college students, and young adults,
found that a little more than 1 percent of high school seniors
reported they had tried steroids at least once in their lifetime,
which is down from a high of 2.4 percent in the early- to mid-
2000s (Monitoring the Future 2012). The majority of teenage

steroid abusers are male athletes who want to perform better in sports, to be more competitive in gaining an athletic scholarship, or simply to look better. The most common reason for teenage girls to use steroids is for aesthetic purposes. Shockingly, both males and females report they have tried steroids as early as age 11.

Kids' interest in steroids may begin with the use of vitamins, supplements, and protein powders from the health-food store. If athletes happen to perform well while taking supplements, they may look for something stronger to become even better.

When I was researching the book *Sports Injury Handbook* (John Wiley & Sons, Inc. 1993) with Allan Levy, MD, who was then team physician for the National Football League (NFL)'s New York Giants, he told me that steroids are the single most dangerous group of legal prescription drugs besides the poisonous chemicals used to treat cancer. "These drugs are widely available through an underground black market, mostly through weight lifting gyms. But even in suburban health clubs, the guys in the weight room often know where to find steroids," we wrote in the book (Levy and Fuerst 1993, 38).

Whether they are called "juice" or "roids," taken in pill form or by injection, steroids have become a major problem among high school and college football players. Dr. Levy, who had a regular sports medicine practice in Westwood, NJ, before he retired, said that during football season he spotted one or two high school players a week who were taking steroids while he examined them for other injuries. Most of these players said they used steroids to improve athletic performance.

But Dr. Levy has some strong opinions on whether this use of steroids is ethical. "It is not fair for an athlete to compete against another one who is artificially built up," he says. "Just as baseball bats can't contain cork and boxing gloves can't contain lead, athletes shouldn't contain any performance enhancing drugs."

Young athletes would tell him that they had to take steroids because they perceived their larger opponents were taking them. So the smaller player would use steroids to keep up and "get bigger." Then the player who was bigger believed he had to get bigger still. The end result is that both athletes have had their bodies ravaged by steroids.

One reason steroids have become so widespread is that they fit in with society's attitude of self-gratification. Some high school and college athletes will do whatever it takes to get ahead. Even after doctors explain all of the dangers of steroid use, most of these athletes still plan to use the drugs because that's the only way they can see to achieve their goals.

Even when doctors talk about the side effects of steroids with teens, they often believe they won't suffer the consequences. This feeling of invincibility is known by medical experts as the "Superman Syndrome," that is, they believe they are immune to the affects. "I think the only way to keep teens clean is to make sure that they understand all of the dangers and that there is no way of avoiding them," says Dr. Levy. "They have to understand that they are as mortal as anyone else."

Luckily, if the steroid use is not too prolonged, some of the side effects are reversible when the user stops taking the drugs. However, many of them are not reversible, such as hair loss and heart problems. At the moment, no one can predict for any one person whether the side effects of steroid abuse will be reversible.

Parents need to be educated about steroids as well. Dr. Levy remembers one mother of a teenage son who was into body-building. "She asked me to prescribe the proper dose of steroids so he wouldn't get into trouble. I told her that I don't prescribe or deal in steroids, and attempted to talk her out of finding steroids for her son," he says.

The No. 1 reason teens seek out performance-enhancers is the pressure to perform. Parents need to emphasize the lessons their kids learn from sports—teamwork, being healthy, gaining self-confidence, and having fun—besides winning. Let them play sports, cleanly, for the right reasons.

References

Hoffman, J. R., et al. 2008. "Nutritional Supplementation and Anabolic Steroid Use in Adolescents." *Medicine and Science in Sports and Exercise.* 40(1): 15–24.

Levy, A. L., and M. L. Fuerst. 1993. *Sports Injury Handbook.* New York: John Wiley & Sons, Inc..

"Monitoring the Future." http://www.monitoringthefuture. org/pubs/monographs/mtf-overview2011.pdf. Accessed on August 1, 2012.

Mark L. Fuerst is a freelance health and medical writer based in Brooklyn (www.marklfuerst.com). He holds a graduate degree in journalism from the University of Missouri. He has written hundreds of articles for major women's and health magazines and is the coauthor of 10 books for consumers, including the Sports Injury Handbook *and* Tennis Injury Handbook, *and is the coauthor of the upcoming* Harvard Medical School Guide to Tai Chi, *to be published in March 2013.*

LEGALIZING STEROIDS—A PERSPECTIVE
Dean A. Haycock

Perhaps there was a time when sporting events were exercises in fair play, honest competition, wholesome entertainment, and the development of character. The situation is a bit murkier now.

Today, "Sports" is an industry with a profit motive bigger than a line of 300-pound, steroid-filled linebackers. It can be characterized by the word "excess." Some teams spy on each other to gain any advantage they can on their competition. Some coaches and players conspire to identify and exploit performance-enhancing drugs that don't yet show up in drug tests.

Doping is a problem wherever the best athletes meet, including the Olympic Games. "Games" might not be the right word to describe the competition, however. Recall that officials at the 2012 Olympics needed a $31 million, state-of-the-art, dope-detecting lab to test half of the competing athletes in London. And despite the massive effort, there is a good chance they didn't find every cheater. The expensive new lab could not detect a banned compound called growth-hormone releasing peptide, for example, according to a report in *The Wall Street Journal* (Wang 2012, D7).

In this atmosphere, calls to legalize steroids might seem sensible, especially in light of claims by many adult athletes that they use AS without serious consequences (if you consider breast development, shrinking testicles, and other side effects in nearly a third of users as being "not serious").

It is naïve, however, to think that legalizing steroids will solve the problem of doping in sports. The motive to cheat will not disappear with legal AS prescriptions. Desperate competitors will continue to search for new substances they can swallow and inject into themselves when the opposing team is full of legalized steroids.

Will these new compounds be made legal too? When? After testing for their safety? Does anyone believe win-at-all-costs competitors will wait for those tests? It's likely some will wait only as long as it takes to empty a syringe into their already unnaturally enlarged muscles.

The search for new advantages has already raised the possibility that gene manipulation, "gene doping," will one day be used to improve performance.

Scientists have shown that genetic variations give some lucky competitors tremendous advantages. In fact, researchers have identified 220 genes that are believed to play a role in determining how a person will perform in different athletic endeavors (Wenner 2008).

"It's obviously going to become more and more evident that what we call talent is really genetic variation," physiologist H. Lee Sweeney of the University of Pennsylvania School of Medicine told the producers of the 2008 documentary "Bigger,

Stronger, Faster." Sweeney is known to athletes interested in his research as the "gene doping expert" because he introduced genes into mice that greatly increased their muscle mass. "There is genetic enhancement available that might be able to give you what nature didn't," Sweeney added. He warned, however, that no one knows how to do it safely yet. He routinely turns down athletes who want to receive the same treatment his mice did despite the unknown risks (Enriquez and Gullans 2012; Greenemeier 2012).

At this time gene doping is illegal. Even if AS become legal, some competitors will move to gene doping as soon as they can. Do we then legalize gene doping? Will we inadvertently encourage an "arms race" of performance enhancements after steroids are approved? What will come next? Implants? Surgeries? New stimulants? Anything to increase chances of victory?

Even if you don't mind watching physically, biochemically, and genetically altered humans competing for victory and its financial rewards, there is another reason to draw the line at legalizing steroids and other performance-enhancing drugs. It may further encourage kids to abuse them.

Research by Jay R. Hoffman from The College of New Jersey, and others suggest that some kids are influenced in a negative way when top-ranked athletes are caught using banned substances. He and his colleagues conclude that "a professional athlete or celebrity caught using an illegal supplement may contribute to such use among adolescents who are attempting to emulate them" (Hoffman et al. 2008).

If illegal use inspires some kids to use steroids, imagine how much legal use will inspire them to grab a syringe or a handful of pills to be like their role models. Use of performance-enhancing substances, including AS, by young people should be discouraged because of proven and unknown consequences of such use, according to the American Academy of Pediatrics (Committee on Sports Medicine and Fitness 2005).

As quixotic as it might sound, it might be noble to draw the line at steroids and accept the fact that sports police will be doomed forever to chasing down cheaters and the new ways they find to cheat. It may send a message to some young athletes that they should not emulate the baseball players who routinely use banned substances to knock out more home runs, the football players who shoot up steroids to turn themselves into human tanks, and the runners who stimulate themselves to become cheetahs.

Maintaining the ban on AS won't stop cheating, but it might slow down the progression of the excessive win-at-any-cost mentality that pervades sports today.

References

Committee on Sports Medicine and Fitness, 2005. "Use of Performance-Enhancing Substances." *Pediatrics*. 115(4): 1103–1106.

Enriquez, J., and S. Gullans, 2012. "Olympics: Genetically Enhanced Olympics Are Coming." *Nature*. 487(7407): 297.

Greenemeier, L. July 12, 2012. "Unnatural Selection: Muscles, Genes and Genetic Cheats." *Scientific American*. Available online at http://www.scientificamerican.com/ article.cfm?id=muscles-genes-cheats-2012-olympics-london&page=2. Accessed on August 1, 2012.

Hoffman, J. R., et al. 2008. "Nutritional Supplementation and Anabolic Steroid Use in Adolescents." *Medicine & Science in Sports & Exercise*. 40(1): 15–24.

Wang, S. S. 2012. "London Aims to Be Doping Waterloo." *The Wall Street Journal*. July 25: D7.

Wenner, M. 2008. "How to Be Popular During the Olympics: Be H. Lee Sweeney, Gene Doping Expert. *Scientific American*. August 15, 2008. Available online at http://www.scientificamerican.com/article.cfm?id=olympics-gene-doping-expert. Accessed on August 1, 2012.

Dean A. Haycock, PhD, is a medical and science writer located in Salem, New York.

ANABOLIC STEROIDS IN THE TREATMENT OF HOMOSEXUALITY

Romeo Vitelli

One of the less well-known uses of AS is in the treatment of homosexuality. Dealing with "the homosexual problem" was a long-standing concern for almost all legal systems throughout the world until well into the 20th century. Lengthy prison sentences were typically handed out to thousands of men (and, less frequently, women) found guilty of the various "crime against nature" laws that were rigidly enforced by most courts. With the growing influence of psychiatrists in the legal system and the prospect of "curing" or otherwise controlling homosexual behavior, a rash of experimental (and often involuntary) medical procedures became increasingly common during the 1940s and 1950s. Often in conjunction with Freudian or other forms of psychoanalysis, convicted homosexual men were forced to undergo radical treatments including castration, lobotomies, and electroconvulsive therapy (ECT).

With the rise of the fledgling field of endocrinology and the development of synthetic sex hormones such as androgens and estrogen, researchers began examining the hormone levels of homosexuals to determine whether there was a biological cause. One early team of endocrinologists working in Los Angeles reported finding reduced androgen and elevated estrogen levels in homosexual males as compared to control subjects. Although the researchers had been dismayed to find a considerable overlap in sex hormone levels between homosexual and heterosexual males, they justified their findings by suggesting that low androgen heterosexual males were likely "latent homosexuals." They also suggested that hormone assays could be used to distinguish between "acquired, latent, and congenital types" of homosexual men (Glass 1940).

Based on the hypothesis that homosexuality was caused by a sex hormone imbalance, the same team of researchers carried out the first known experiment involving hormonal treatment of homosexual men in 1940. The prospect of using synthetic sex hormones to "cure" homosexuality was exciting both for the researchers and the pharmaceutical company that provided the sex hormones free of charge for the study. According to the lead researcher, S. J. Glass, "Obviously, if a biologic etiology were established, this would lead to investigation of therapeutic possibilities from a much wider perspective than now exists." Although many of the subjects in the study were treated voluntarily, all 17 of them had been arrested for homosexual conduct and were likely under pressure to cooperate (three of the subjects were underage boys whose parents had given permission for the treatment to be used and one adult was forced to participate by court order).

Dr. Glass and his fellow researchers were dismayed to find that the sex hormones actually led to an "intensification of the homosexual drive" in at least five of the subjects while only three felt that the increased androgen helped them suppress their homosexual urges. If androgen therapy for homosexual men was a dead end, an alternative approach was suggested by the research of Christopher W. Dunn, who, in a research project conducted that same year (Dunn 1940), found that large doses of estrogen completely suppressed sexual desire in males. Despite the continuing use of physical castration in dealing with convicted sex offenders (including homosexuals convicted of repeat offenses), it was not a popular option despite at least 11 U.S. states carrying laws allowing for castration and more than 50,000 cases on record. Since physical castration failed to suppress sexual desire completely, the prospect of a chemical alternative that was more effective spurred the adoption of "chemical castration" to control unwanted sexual behaviors. Compulsory hormonal treatment for convicted sex offenders became popular on both sides of the Atlantic.

The first British paper dealing with hormonal treatment of sexual offenders appeared in 1949 (Golla and Hodge 1949). F. J. Golla, then director of Bristol's Burden Neurological Institute carried out hormonal research on 13 homosexual men and concluded that "libido could be abolished within a month" with sufficiently large doses. Although physical castration was not allowed under British law, the new chemical castration approach was considered sufficiently promising for widespread use in dealing with the thousands of men convicted under Britain's antihomosexual statutes.

While actual statistics on the number of men who were forced to undergo hormonal treatment as an alternative to prison are relatively scarce, the most famous case, involving British mathematician Alan Turing provides a useful case history of how such treatment was actually used. Following Turing's conviction for Gross Indecency in 1952, he decided to take the hormones voluntarily to avoid jail and to be allowed to continue his research. Despite the considerable adverse publicity, Dr. Turing remained on the hormones for one year (as specified in the probation order laid down at his trial). Although he was distressed at the adverse side effects, which included breast enlargement (gynecomastia), reduced libido, mood changes, and general "feminization," he continued to be active professionally. It is still unclear whether the hormonal treatments had any role in his suicide on June 7, 1954. Despite the prominence of Alan Turing's case, he was only one of the thousands of men and women whose lives were adversely affected by mandatory hormonal treatment for homosexual behavior.

With increasing acceptance and the decriminalization of homosexuality in many jurisdictions (but not all), compulsory treatment was eventually phased out. After homosexuality was formally delisted as a psychiatric disorder by the American Psychiatric Association in 1973, the treatment emphasis shifted from providing a cure to helping homosexual men and women learn to accept their sexual orientation. Although medications such as medroxyprogesterone acetate (Depo-Provera), cyproterone acetate (Androcur), and more recently leuprolide acetate (Lupron) are still widely used to suppress sexual urges in convicted sex offenders, the chemical castration focus has shifted toward sexual disorders such as pedophilia and sexual sadism. Despite ongoing research investigating hormonal and genetic differences between homosexuals and heterosexuals, the results remain controversial.

References

Dunn, Christopher W. 1940. "Stilbestrol Induced Gynecomastia in the Male." *Journal of the American Medical Association.* 115(26): 2263–2264.

Glass, S. J., H. J. Deuel, and C. A. Wright. 1940. "Sex Hormone Studies in Male Homosexuality." *Endocrinology.* 26(4): 590–594.

Golla, F. J., and R. Sessions Hodge. 1949. "Hormone Treatment of the Sexual Offender." *The Lancet.* 253(6563): 1006–1007.

Romeo Vitelli received his doctorate in Psychology from York University in Toronto, Ontario, in 1987. He spent 15 years as a staff psychologist in Millbrook Correctional Centre, a maximum-security prison run by the Ontario government. In 2003, he left prison work and went into full-time private practice. He is a disaster management volunteer with the Red Cross and an active blogger. Check out his blog Providentia.

A BRIEF OVERVIEW OF HORMONE REPLACEMENT THERAPY FOR TRANSSEXUAL PATIENTS
Jessica Sideways

Few people in our modern society truly understand the process of transsexual transition, including the social, legal, and medical aspects. The purpose of this article is to discuss one of the medical aspects of transition, known as hormone replacement therapy (or HRT). There are several benefits of HRT, allowing the patient to settle more easily into his or her target gender role. This process is achieved through simple medication that is already in use either for the hormone replacement therapy of cissexual (people who identify with the gender that they were assumed to be by way of their birth sex) patients or for other purposes. There are three ways that most transsexual people begin HRT. Two of these involve a primary care physician and one does not, that last one is obviously not recommended due to the high risk to the patient.

The question why people change their sex is often asked, but the answer is not clear cut. There is insufficient medical research as of yet to show that transsexualism is a neurological abnormality that occurs in utero thanks to a hormonal flush that influences the brain's development. However, what we do know is that people choose to change their sex when they feel that they cannot live comfortably or genuinely as a member of their birth sex. They do this because they feel frustrated that they are not being seen as who they see themselves as and understand that in order to live a more genuine life, they must transition. While many people over the last few decades have transitioned later in life, we are now seeing more people transition at younger ages and parents supporting their child's wishes to transition. HRT is one of the first steps to start on the path of medical transition and can be done at a younger age, unlike more serious medical interventions such as facial feminization surgery (FFS) or sex reassignment surgery (SRS).

The benefits of HRT are a calmer state of mind and the development of secondary sex characteristics. While it may limit the development of secondary sex characteristics that are associated with the patient's birth sex, it cannot reverse the development of secondary sex characteristics. The secondary sex characteristics that are often developed include facial hair, breast development, and elongation of vocal chords (thus creating a deeper voice). Some other characteristics can be changed such as emotions, body hair, fertility, sexual function, and physical strength/endurance. However, HRT can also cause a number of side effects, such as sensitivity to sun burns, dehydration, osteoporosis, stroke, blood clots, and cancer (breast and colon). This is the reason that persons interested in HRT should consult a physician, so that such side effects can be prevented or minimized.

HRT often involves hormones that are associated with the target gender. This would be estrogen (and possibly progesterone) for transsexual women and testosterone for transsexual men. Additionally, preoperative (or preop, meaning prior to SRS) patients will receive a chemical way to block their natural hormones until they can have sufficient SRS to block the natural hormone production (vaginoplasty or orchiectomy for transsexual women, hysterectomy for transsexual men) and, in the case of teenage patients, puberty blockers.

The first way someone can begin HRT is with a physician's prescription following an extreme form of psychotherapy. This extreme form is codified in the World Professional Association for Transsexual Health's Standards of Care (SOC). The SOC can be interpreted in a number of ways by a variety of psychotherapists and psychiatrists and allows the therapist to retract their recommendation for whatever reason. In my years of advising people on how to get HRT, I have heard horror stories of therapists abusing this privilege to coerce people to continue to see them. It is for this reason that I do not recommend this path because it exercises a great deal of control over people who do not need it. However, I definitely do recommend this path for those who may not be mentally stable enough to realize the gravity of such a decision.

The second way is a physician's prescription following light psychotherapy or counseling. There are modalities by which one can get hormone therapy with little to no psychotherapy. However, formal consent and education about the potential problems and effects of the treatments are undertaken so that physician liability is limited while making hormone therapy to be more accessible to the public. This is what I recommend for most people because it allows people who may not have an urgent need for psychotherapy to put the appropriate focus on their medical care. This path is often found in free/low-income medical clinics, and there are treatment modalities developed for this purpose, such as the Tom Waddell Health Clinic Protocols for Hormonal Reassignment of Gender, used by the staff at the Tom Waddell clinic in San Francisco, along with other clinics across the country. Additionally, this path is almost exclusively used even by physicians who would require the SOC in other cases if the patient has had SRS.

The third way is often called "self-medicating." This is achieved either by purchasing or stealing either proper hormone replacement therapy or other off-label methods of hormone replacement therapy. Off-label vehicles for hormone replacement therapy are either natural phytoestrogens (which are estrogens that naturally occur in plants, including breast enhancement tablets that have little to no lasting effects) or birth control. Self-medicating can also be achieved by ordering hormone therapy through online retailers abroad. In recent years, however, U.S. Customs and Border Protection have been putting the squeeze on anyone who has ordered from overseas pharmacies by intercepting packages from these pharmacies.

The reasons why self-medicating must be discouraged are varied. The first is that operating outside the care of a primary care physician means that the patient may not be getting a dose that is right for the patient. Furthermore, the patient is not being properly monitored with blood tests in order to catch and treat the side effects in a timely manner. The second is the illegality of it, as ordering from overseas pharmacies is illegal, even more so for female-to-male transsexual persons, whose hormone therapy often involves drugs that are considered a controlled substance (many forms of testosterone are listed as a Schedule III controlled substance, per the U.S. DEA). The third is that, by using off-label or natural means for HRT, they may not be as effective. There are many physicians and low-income/free clinics who, in an effort to help people avoid the risks of self-medication, allow people who are self-medicating to get under the care of a physician and have their hormone replacement therapy monitored and moderated by a physician.

So, hormone replacement therapy for transsexual patients is a very complex situation and it is my hope that this article has helped you to gain some understanding of the reasons why people transition from one gender to another, the effects of hormone replacement therapy, and the ways by which one can receive hormone replacement therapy.

Jessica Sideways is a 23-year-old postoperative transsexual woman currently attending Metropolitan State College of Denver. She writes extensively on topics related to gender transformation.

KEEPING AN EYE ON STEROID ABUSE
Nicholas A. Ratamess

AAS use/abuse in athletes has been a topic of debate for many years. Historically, strength and power athletes primarily consumed AAS. Since, AAS use/abuse has increased dramatically and has spread to a multitude of male and female sports including those that require maximal muscle endurance. The rampant use of AAS has generated a number of opinions and responses with pros (ergogenic effects) and cons (health risks, illegality, ethics, and violation of fair competition). Questions of how to control or minimize abuse in athletes to whether or not AAS should be legal have arisen. Arguments on both sides have been made convincingly. However, it is clear from analysis over the last 60 years that AAS use: (1) has been effective in enhancing performance and led to numerous athletic records, (2) is widespread in many sports, (3) embodied athletes to seek information from many individuals, coaches, and fellow athletes with limited input from medical and scientific communities, and (4) will continue in a widespread manner despite attempts to curtail use.

Synthetic testosterone and AAS have many ergogenic effects on athletic performance (Hoffman and Ratamess 2006; Hoffman et al. 2009; Ratamess 2006), such as increased muscle strength, power, hypertrophy, endurance, and decreased body fat. Although some early reports suggested AAS had limited or no positive effects on performance, these reports have been strongly discredited and currently most experts widely accept the fact that AAS use (coupled with appropriate training) comprehensively increases performance beyond natural improvement. The effects are dose related, where the number of drugs and the amounts consumed has a quantitative influence. Some anecdotal reports from athletes indicate large strength, hypertrophy, and power increases from AAS use in as little as one month. These reports have prompted other athletes to experiment with AAS.

The use of AAS without a prescription is illegal and governing bodies have attempted to curtail use by incorporating drug testing policies and punishments for violations. Sports governing bodies have conveyed to the public they have controlled AAS use via stringent testing procedures and through lengthy suspensions/bans for athletes who fail drug tests. Others have publicly stated testing has rid their sport of drug use. In fact, several Major League Baseball (MLB) analysts have erroneously referred to modern-day baseball as the "poststeroids era" despite several players' testing positive for performance-enhancement drugs (PEDs), anecdotal reports of high use, and player statistics on the rise. The reality is drug testing has been largely ineffective in limiting AAS use. Although relatively few athletes have been suspended/banned in recent years, anecdotal reports from former and/or current players and coaches indicate that use in strength and power sports far exceeds that perceived by the public and the number of users are estimated to increase at higher competition levels. It has been estimated in some professional sports that more than 90 percent of the players used (in the past) or currently use at least one PED.

Limitations in drug testing methodology exist. Anecdotal reports indicate that many athletes are affluent in "beating a test" using a variety of methods. Thus, AAS use is higher than imagined as athletes have become more educated on escaping detection. The fear of repercussions, breaking the law, suspension from sport, and public scrutiny is far outweighed by performance gains and potential for success (athletic scholarships, improved records, championships, and lucrative contracts or endorsement deals for professional athletes), thereby making it very difficult, if not impossible, for governing bodies to effectively control AAS abuse.

A dilemma exists for sports governing bodies. On one hand, they readily appreciate the performance gains from AAS use. NFL players who weigh more than 250 pounds and run at fast speeds and MLB players who can hit many home runs increase the sport's popularity and revenues. On the other hand, sports governing bodies must publicly appear as if they care about athletes' health, rules enforcement, and fair play. Thus, testing has been adopted but many argue it has been ineffective because of a lack of impetus by governing bodies to stop AAS use, for example, benefits to the sport may be greater when athletes use AAS. A sport could be severely damaged if many prominent athletes test positive. For example, more than a hundred MLB players failed exploratory drug tests several years ago (before the current drug policy was implemented). Suspensions of this many athletes simultaneously could ruin an entire season. Thus, some believe that the selected suspension of only few athletes is a way of appeasing public outrage to the ongoing battle against AAS abuse. The public must be aware that the problem is much more widespread than these statistics reflect.

AAS abuse is associated with several unhealthy side effects (Hoffman and Ratamess 2006; Hoffman et al. 2009; Ratamess 2006). These side effects have been well documented and discussed in other chapters in this text. The majority of these side effects are reversible upon cessation. It should be noted AAS have been used medicinally, that is, to preserve and increase lean tissue mass, increase recovery/healing, and improve daily function in various patient populations. Nevertheless, differences in the side effects associated with AAS use (with medical supervision) versus abuse are noted with abuse posing a greater risk to athletes.

In addition, the poly-pharmacy approach (consuming multiple drugs along with AAS such as human growth hormone, diuretics, thyroid hormones, insulin, antiestrogens, and recreational drugs) dangers are poorly understood. Long-term studies examining AAS use in athletes are rare, leaving much speculation on the potential dangers imposed. The medical and scientific communities have underscored AAS efficacy and focused on side effects in order to dissuade AAS use. Any attempt to dissuade AAS use should be applauded. However, an unintended consequence was that it may have caused some athletes to lose trust in their physician's knowledge of AAS and seek advice from friends, other athletes, Internet sites, books, or drug suppliers.

The issue of fair competition is significant. Some have argued AAS use should remain illegal to maintain fair competition. However, many athletes have attested that AAS use will continue despite drug testing policies. Some athletes have publicly stated that "beating tests is easy" and athletes will still readily use drugs despite their illegality to maintain a competitive advantage. Some have argued AAS use should be legalized because of the failures of current testing procedures. However, legalizing drugs does not accomplish fair competition per se. Studies show a dose–response relationship and athletes who are willing to abuse AAS with high doses or multiple drugs may still gain a competitive advantage over athletes who will not. In addition, conscientious athletes who otherwise would not use drugs could be forced to use AAS to remain competitive.

In lieu of the inadequacies of testing, coaches, team doctors, therapists, and trainers can play a vital role in preventing AAS use. Some signs and symptoms of AAS use are visible to the human eye. Naivety or using a "blind eye" approach will not curtail AAS use especially among young athletes. Although signs and symptoms have been discussed in other chapters, the following are some critical factors to look for:

- A substantial increase in muscle mass and strength seen in a relatively short period of time

- Development of acne or a rash
- Gynecomastia (breast development)
- A change in temperament, mood swings, and aggressive behavior
- Increased muscle mass that appears disproportionate with body structure in young athletes
- Masculinization, bloating in the face, and appearance of aggression in facial expression
- Signs of AAS use (e.g., steroid-related information, needles, vials, pill bottles) and associations with known AAS users or distributors

References

Hoffman, J. R., and N. A. Ratamess. 2006. "Medical Issues Associated with Anabolic Steroid Use: Are They Exaggerated?" *Journal of Sports Science and Medicine.* 5: 182–193.

Hoffman, J. R., et al. 2009. "Position Stand on Androgen and Human Growth Hormone Use." *Journal of Strength Conditioning Research.* 23: S1–S59.

Ratamess, N. A. 2006. *Coaches Guide to Performance-Enhancing Supplements.* Monterey, CA: Coaches Choice Books.

Dr. Nicholas A. Ratamess, PhD, CSCS*D, FNSCA, is Associate Professor in the Department of Health and Exercise Science at The College of New Jersey. His major research interests are physiological adaptations to resistance training and sport supplementation. He has authored/coauthored more than 130 scientific and educational pub-lications including Coaches Guide to Performance-Enhancing Supplements *in 2006 and the "NSCA's Position Stand on Andro-gen and Human Growth Hormone Use" in 2009.*

This chapter contains brief sketches of individuals and organizations who are important in understanding the history of performance-enhancing drugs in the United States and around the world. The number of such individuals and organizations is legion, and only some especially significant organizations and individuals, or those typical of other organizations and individuals, are included.

Patrick Arnold (1966–)

Arnold is an organic chemist best known for his synthesis of a number of synthetic anabolic steroids, including tetrahydrogestrinone (THG; also known as "The Clear"), norbolethone, and desoxymethyltestosterone (DMT). He also introduced to the United States and the sports world other testosterone-like steroids with strong anabolic effects: androstenedione, 1-androstenediol, and methylhexanamine. At the time, the chemicals that Arnold invented and popularized were not on the list of substances prohibited for use by athletes by any major sports organization. Those substances were, however, later added to such lists. During the 1990s, he collaborated with the drug "guru," Dan Duchaine, to promote the use of

San Francisco Giants' Barry Bonds smiles and sticks his tongue out as he rounds the bases after hitting his record-breaking 73rd home before a home team crowd on October 7, 2001. A central player in baseball's steroids scandals, Bonds was convicted in 2011 for perjury and obstruction of justice for lying to the grand jury about illegal steroid use during an investigation of BALCO. (Bay Area Laboratory Cooperative) (AP Photo/Eric Risberg) these drugs among bodybuilders, weight lifters, and amateur and professional athletes from many sports. He was also very much involved in the invention, production, and distribution of testosterone analogs through the Bay Area Laboratory Co-operative (BALCO). In 2006, Arnold was convicted of conspiracy to distribute illegal anabolic steroids and sentenced to three months in prison and three months of house arrest. At his sentencing, U.S. District Judge Susan Illston told Arnold, "It's a really destructive path you've been on, and a very serious crime you've committed." Arnold responded, "I'm very regretful for what I've done and especially what it has precipitated in sports and society. Now, more than ever, I'm very much against sports doping. I do believe there should be a level playing field, and this whole thing needs to be addressed."

Patrick Arnold was born in 1966 in Guilford, Connecticut, into a middle-class home. His mother was a high school teacher, and his father, a professor of industrial engineering who was active in Democratic politics. He became interested in bodybuilding at the age of 11 when his grandfather gave him a set of weights, with which he started working out. He was introduced to anabolic steroids when he received a shot as treatment for his attention deficit disorder condition that had caused him to drop out of the University of New Haven (UNH) after his freshman year. He found that he quickly added substantial muscle to his body, an important benefit in the construction job that he had taken after leaving UNH. Intrigued by the potential benefits of these chemicals, Arnold decided to return to UNH, from which he eventually received his BS degree in chemistry in 1990.

After completing his college degree, Arnold took a number of jobs, none of which seemed to suit his background and expectations. He maintained his interest in steroids, however, taking classes at the University of Connecticut and Montclair State College (now Montclair State University). During this time, he also became a regular contributor to an Internet news group called misc.fitness.weights, through which he came to know Dan Duchaine, then known as the Guru of Steroids. Duchaine helped connect Arnold with others interested in the development and sale of anabolic androgenic steroids (AAS), including Bill Phillips, at EAS (Experimental and Applied Sciences) and Stan Antosh, founder and owner of Osmo Therapeutics, in San Francisco. The connection between Arnold and Phillips went nowhere, but Antosh offered Arnold a job with Osmo with the provision that any discovery Arnold made would be shared with the company for development and distribution. Antosh also convinced Arnold to do his research at a small pharmaceutical company, Bar North America, in Seymour, Illinois. The rural setting provided the privacy and solitude that Arnold needed to do the literature searches and laboratory experiments needed to uncover and develop a variety of new testosterone-like compounds.

Arnold made his first breakthrough in 1996, when he came across a scientific paper on androstenedione, a steroid that had proved to have excellent anabolic properties, but had never been developed commercially. (Androstenedione eventually became popular under the common name of "Andro.") He obtained samples of the substance from a manufacturer in China and presented his discovery to Antosh. The product soon proved its value when St. Louis Cardinals star Mark McGwire began using the product. Five years later, Arnold came through with another successful product, 1-androstenediol. Both androstenedione and 1-androstenediol are prohormones, compounds that are not hormones themselves, but that are converted in the body to testosterone or a testosterone-like hormone.

The focus of Arnold's research changed in 2005 when all of the prohormones that he had introduced and developed were added to the prohibited list under amendments to the Controlled Substances Act (CSA) of 1970. Instead, he began to search for new substances that were not included under the CSA prohibited list and, most important, could not be detected by existing drug tests. The most important of those new discoveries were the drugs norbolethone and THG, which he provided to BALCO for retail sales. It was largely his involvement with BALCO that eventually led to his arrest and conviction for the distribution of illegal substances in 2006.

After becoming settled in Seymour in 1996, Arnold arranged to establish a new company, LPJ Research, in conjunction with the owner of Bar North America, Ramlakhan Boodram. In 2003, the owners changed the name of the company to Proviant Technologies. The company markets nutritional supplements under the name of ErgoPharm. In 2009, Arnold left Proviant to create his own company, which supplies AAS-type products under the names of E-Pharm (http://epharmnutrition.com/) and Prototype Nutrition (http://www.prototypenutrition.com/default.asp). On the Prototype Nutrition website, Arnold summarizes his career in the development of performance-enhancing drugs, and concludes with the observation that "[h]e continues to be perhaps the number one driving force in the advancement of performance enhancing nutritional supplementation."

Joe Biden (1942–)

Joe Biden was coauthor (with Sen. Strom Thurmond [R-S.C.]) of the Crime Control Act of 1990, Title XIX of which was the Anabolic Steroids Control Act of 1990. That act placed anabolic steroids on Schedule III of the CSA, meaning that they could be prescribed, dispensed, and distributed for therapeutic purposes only. The act essentially outlawed the use of anabolic steroids for many of the purposes for which they have become so popular among bodybuilders, weight lifters, and other amateur and professional athletes. A decade later, Biden coauthored (with Sen. Orin Hatch [R-Utah]) an extension of the 1990 act, the Anabolic Steroids Control Act of 2004 that extended the listing of prohormones and other synthetic AAS under Schedule III of the CSA.

Both pieces of legislation were very popular in both houses of Congress and among the general public. They were each proposed at times when news of the use of AAS by amateur and professional athletes had become major stories that resulted in the downfall in the public esteem of stars such as Marion Jones and Ben Johnson in track and field, Lyle Alzado and Bill Romanowski in professional football, Floyd Landis in professional cycling, and Mark McGwire and Barry Bonds in professional baseball. Most observers at the time and since have argued that no politician (or very few politicians) could have taken a strong stand against steroid-legislation at the time it was proposed by Biden and his colleagues. Indeed, some observers have suggested that Biden undertook the campaign against steroid use at least in part because of failed campaign for nominee for president of the United States with the Democratic Party in 1988. Some measure of Biden's failure in that campaign is said to have come about as a result of his having plagiarized a speech originally given by British Labour Party leader Neil Kinnock in 1987.

Joseph Robinette Biden, Jr., was born in Scranton, Pennsylvania, on November 20, 1942. He was the first of four children born to Joseph R. Biden, Sr., and Catherine Eugenia Finnegan Biden. A 2008 *New York Times* article described Joseph, Sr., as someone who had "had it all" in 1920s, "sailing yachts off the New England coast, riding to the hounds, driving fast cars, flying airplanes." As a result of "drunken, faithless bosses and a thieving partner," the senior Biden eventually found himself out of work and virtually destitute. When Joseph, Jr., was 10, his family moved to Claymont, Delaware, where his father found work as a used car salesman. There he attended Archmere Academy, from which he graduated in 1961. He then matriculated at the University of Delaware, in Newark, where he majored in history and political science. He then continued his education at the Syracuse University College of Law, where he received his JD degree in 1968. He is reputed not to have been a particularly remarkable student at either institution, finishing 506th in his class of 688 at Delaware and 76th out of 85 at Syracuse.

After graduating from Syracuse, Biden returned to Delaware where he worked first as a public defender before organizing his own law firm, Biden and Walsh, in 1969. In a relatively short period of time, Biden found that he was more interested in politics than in the legal profession, and he ran for the New Castle County Council in 1970. He was elected and served for two years on the council, while still retaining his law practice. In 1972, Biden decided to run against sitting U.S. Sen. J. Caleb Boggs, a long-serving Republican from Delaware. He started his campaign with virtually no name-recognition, funding, or staff. At one point in the campaign, the 29-year-old Biden trailed the popular Boggs by more than 30 points. He continued to work for his election, however, and in November of 1972 won a startling upset victory with 116,006 votes (50.48 percent of the total) to Boggs' 112,844 votes (49.10 percent).

Less than six weeks after his reelection, Biden's wife and one-year-old daughter were killed in an automobile accident in Hockessin, Delaware. His two young sons were also critically injured in the accident. This terrible event caused Biden to reconsider his potential career in the U.S. Senate, but was eventually dissuaded from resigning his seat by Senate Majority Leader Mike Mansfield.

Biden was reelected six more times to the U.S. Senate, in 1978, 1984, 1990, 1996, 2002, and 2008. His two primary interests in the Senate have been the Judiciary Committee, of which he was chairman from 1987 until 1995, and ranking minority member from 1981 until 1987, and from 1995 until 1997; and the Foreign Relations Committee, which he chaired from 2001 until 2003 and again from 2007 until 2008. In mid-2008, Biden was chosen by Democratic Presidential nominee Barack Obama to serve as his vice-presidential candidate. The Obama–Biden slate won the 2008 election and won re-election to a second term in 2012.

Barry Bonds (1964–)

Bonds is widely regarded as one of the finest baseball players in the history of the sport. He holds many number of records, including the most home runs in a lifetime (762) and the most home runs in a single year (73 in 2001). He also holds the record for the most walks (2,558) and the most intentional walks (688) in a career. His skills have been recognized by selection as the Most Valuable Player in Major League Baseball a record seven times and receiving the Golden Glove award (for being the best defensive player at his position) on eight occasions. He was selected to play in Major League Baseball's All-Star Game on 14 occasions. His lifetime batting average was .298 and stole 514 bases in his career. His career statistics have been somewhat diminished by his arrest and conviction in 2011 on charges of obstruction of justice in connection with the illegal use of anabolic steroids reputedly provided by the BALCO drug testing laboratory in San Francisco.

Barry Lamar Bonds was born on July 24, 1964, in Riverside, California, to Bobby Lee Bonds, a renowned professional baseball player in his own right, and Patricia Howard Bonds. He grew up in San Carlos, California, and attended Junipero Serra High School, where he excelled in three sports, football, basketball, and baseball. After graduating from high school, Bonds was drafted by the San Francisco Giants professional baseball team, but he was unable to come to terms with the team and decided to go to college instead. He matriculated at Arizona State University (ASU) in 1983, planning to major in physical education. He continued to star in baseball at ASU, with a three-year batting average of .347 and a number of honors for his play in the PAC-10 conference, the College World Series, and other venues. In 1985, the Pittsburgh Pirates major league baseball team drafted Bonds again. This time he agreed to terms offered by the Pirates, and he joined the team in 1986 for his first season in major league baseball. Bonds played for seven seasons with the Pirates, winning his first Most Valuable Player award in 1990, followed by repeats in 1992 and 1993. Bonds became a free agent in 1993, and signed a six-year, $43.75 million contract with the San Francisco Giants, with whom he remained until he retired from professional baseball in 2007. He set most of his major league baseball records with the Giants, including a record-setting string of four Most Valuable Player awards in 2001–2004.

Allegations that Bonds might have used anabolic steroids to improve his body muscle mass and strength began to appear in 2003. His trainer since 2000, Greg Anderson, worked out of a gym that was two blocks from the offices of BALCO in Burlingame, California. When agents of the U.S. Food and Drug Administration (FDA) raided BALCO's offices in September 2003, questions were raised as to the possible involvement of Anderson and Bonds in the use of anabolic steroids. An important basis for those questions was the significant increase in Bonds' physical appearance during the previous decade, when he had increased his weight from 185 pounds in 1991 to 228 pounds in 2001. Bonds claimed that his improvement in body size and strength were the result of conditioning and improved nutrition, but a number of observers suspected that other factors might also have been involved, including drug use.

In a testimony before a grand jury in December 2003, Bonds admitted to using nutritional supplements supplied to him by Anderson, but said that they were only natural treatments for his arthritis. The cases against four individuals involved in the BALCO investigation brought by the grand jury were eventually dismissed in early 2005 in an action that included provisions for keeping private the names of any sports figures who may have used drugs supplied by the company. In April 2006, Bonds was in the news again when federal investigators announced that they were going to prosecute him for lying in his grand jury testimony of December 2003. That effort reached its climax in November 2007 when a federal grand jury indicted Bonds for lying in that testimony. Bonds pleaded not guilty to these charges, and, after a number of delays, a trial was held on the matter on March 21, 2011. Three weeks later, a jury found Bonds guilty of obstruction of justice. On December 15, 2011, U.S. District Judge Susan Illston sentenced Bonds to 30 days of house arrest, two years of probation, and 250 hours of community service. On May 3, 2012, Bonds' attorney filed a brief asking the 9th U.S. Circuit Court of Appeals to vacate Justice Illston's sentence based on the fact that Bonds' original testimony was "rambling and irrelevant," even if "truthful" to the grand jury. As of early 2013, Bonds' appeal in this case has still not been resolved.

In 2012, Bonds announced to the press that he was interested in returning to major league baseball again, perhaps in the role of batting coach for the Giants. Observers met that announcement with mixed emotions, acknowledging that Bonds had a great deal of knowledge and experience to share with young players, but that he still had a cloud of doubt about drug use lying over his long and very successful career.

Charles Brown-Séquard (1817–1894)

Brown-Séquard was a physiologist and neurologist who is perhaps best known today for his research on the nervous system and his discovery of the function of the adrenal glands. His name remains a part of the medical literature in the medical condition known as Brown-Séquard syndrome, also called Brown-Séquard's hemiplegia or Brown-Séquard's paralysis. The condition occurs as the result of damage to the spinal cord that results in a loss of sensation and motor function in the extremities.

In the history of anabolic steroids, Brown-Séquard is also known for a series of experiments that he conducted rather late in life to determine whether he could restore some of the normal bodily functions that he had lost as a result of the process of aging. In these experiments, he injected himself with extracts taken from the testicles of guinea pigs and dogs. He discovered that this treatment produced a "radical change" that renewed his body strength and intellectual vigor. Some historians doubt that Brown-Séquard actually conducted the experiments that he described, that the observed effects actually occurred, or that the effects were the result of the injections. In any case, word of Brown-Séquard's experiments rapidly spread through the medical world and was put to practical use on behalf of many aging men around the world who were seeking a "remedy" for the old age that was robbing them of their physical and intellectual powers. Materials like those produced by Brown-Séquard became commonly known as the Elixir of Life. Countless numbers of charlatans, as well as many well-meaning medical men, made small fortunes in selling these materials to their patients and customers.

Charles-Édouard Brown-Séquard (also Charles Edward Brown-Séquard) was born in Port Louis, Mauritius, on April 8, 1817. His father, Charles Edward Brown, was an American naval officer from Philadelphia of Irish heritage, and his mother was Charlotte Séquard, of French birth and a native of the island of Mauritius. Captain Brown lost his life at sea shortly after his son's birth. He was in command of a ship delivering provisions to Mauritius, which was undergoing famine at the time. Under the circumstances, young Charles grew up under his mother's care under modest circumstances. He obtained his early education at a private school in Port Louis where he was also in charge of two small circulating libraries. In 1838, he traveled to Paris with hopes of becoming a writer. When he made little progress in that direction, he turned his attention to medicine, a field in which he earned his bachelor of letters diploma in 1838 and his bachelor of science diploma in 1839 from the University of France, and his medical degree in 1846 from the medical faculty of the University of France. While studying for his medical degree, he also taught natural history, chemistry, natural philosophy, and physiology.

The topic of Brown-Séquard's doctoral thesis was "Vital Properties and Functions of the Spinal Cord," a topic that was to occupy his interest for many years following his graduation. He soon discovered that medical research was of at least as much interest to him as was patient care, and he attached himself to some of the best researchers in the field then working in Paris. In the years following his graduation, he published a series of papers describing the Brown-Séquard syndrome for which he is now best known, outlining the consequences of severing the spinal cord at various locations on sensory function at various parts of the body.

Brown-Séquard's living and working conditions in Paris were far more satisfactory. He is said to have carried out most of his experiments in his own small and cramped apartment, where he also kept his experimental animals. Finally, in 1852, he decided that he could not make a living in France, and he left for the United States. There he survived by teaching French, giving lectures, and, according to one biographer, "delivering babies at cut-rate prices." Even an appointment at the Medical College of Virginia (which lasted only four months) was not enough to keep him in the United States, however. With his new wife, Ellen, he returned to Paris, and then traveled on to Port Louis when conditions in France were no better than they had ever been.

In fact, Brown-Séquard spent most of the rest of his life traveling from place to place, trying to find a site at which he could settle down and focus on his medical research. He always seemed to end up in Paris, where he lived and worked from 1847 to 1850, in 1855, from 1857 to 1859, in 1865, from 1869 to 1873, and, finally, from 1878 to his death in 1894. Sandwiched in between these stays in France, he also taught at the Royal College of Surgeons in London in 1858 and worked as a physician at the National Hospital for the Paralysed and Epileptics, in London, from 1860 to 1863. In 1864 he was offered the chair of physiology and pathology in the Harvard Medical School, an appointment he held until 1867. In 1873 he moved from Paris to New York, where he established a private practice. Finally, in 1878, Brown-Séquard received a job offer with the promise of a permanent position to his liking, the post of professor of experimental medicine at the Collège de France, in Paris. In that post, he replaced one of the world's greatest medical experimentalists of the time, Claude Bernard. Brown-Séquard held that appointment until his death on April 2, 1894, in Sceaux, France.

Brown-Séquard received awards from the French Academy of Science on five separate occasions and twice from the British government. He was elected to the National Academy of

Sciences in 1868 and to the Royal College of Physicians of London in 1860. He was the founder and editor of three important journals in medicine, *Journal de la physiologie de l'homme et des animaux*, *Archives de physiologie normale et pathologique*, and *Archives of Scientific and Practical Medicine*.

Adolf Butenandt (1903–1995)

"One can say that he was always a 'first.'" That accolade was suggested by one of Butenandt's good friends and coworkers upon his death in 1995. He was the first person to isolate a number of sex hormones; the first person to discover the action of genes in the production of hormones; the first person to isolate an insect hormone; and the first person to isolate and study a pheromone. He was awarded a share of the 1939 Nobel Prize in Chemistry for the first of these achievements and for his work on sex hormones in general.

Adolf Friedrich Johann Butenandt was born in the town of Lehe, a section of Bremerhaven, Germany, on March 24, 1903. He was the second son of Otto Louis Max Butenandt, a businessman, and his wife, Wilhelmina Thomfohrde Butenandt. He attended the Bremerton Oberrealschule for his secondary education before enrolling at the University of Marburg in 1921, where he majored in biology and chemistry. Before graduating, he transferred to the University of Göttingen, where his most influential teacher was Adolf Windhaus, who had won the 1928 Nobel Prize in Chemistry for his research on sterols. Sterols are a family of organic compounds that consist of a characteristic four-ring structure to which is attached at least one hydroxyl (-OH) group. Butenandt was awarded his PhD in biochemistry in 1927 for research on a compound found in insecticides.

After earning his degree, Butenandt remained at Göttingen to complete his habilitation. (Habilitation is a characteristic European type of study that involves original research and writing of a thesis beyond the level normally presented for awarding of the doctoral degree.) He then took the post of professor of organic chemistry at Danzig Institute of Technology, where he remained until 1936. Butenandt left Danzig in 1936 to become director of the Kaiser Wilhelm Institute for Biochemistry (later the Max Planck Institute for Biochemistry) in Berlin. When the institute was moved to Tübingen in 1945 because of air raids on Berlin, he also assumed the post of professor of physiological chemistry at the University of Tübingen and, when the institute was moved once again in 1956 to Münich, he also was named professor of physiological chemistry at the University of Münich. He retired from his post at Münich in 1971. For an extended period of time, from 1960 to 1972, Butenandt also served as president of the Max Planck Society for the Advancement of Science, the most powerful and famous research institution in Germany.

Butenandt's first scientific breakthrough came in 1929 when he announced the discovery of the female sex hormone estrone (also, oestrone). He followed up that discovery with the announcement of a comparable male sex hormone, androsterone, in 1931 and another female sex hormone, progesterone, in 1934. He and Leopold Ružička, cowinner of the 1939 Nobel Prize in Chemistry, independently isolated the primary male sex hormone, testosterone, in 1935, after which they were successful in synthesizing both estrogen and testosterone. After the war, Butenandt continued his work on hormones, isolating the first insect hormone, ecdysone, in 1954. Ecdysone is the hormone responsible for the transformation of a caterpillar into a butterfly. In 1959, Butenandt also discovered the first hormone used by insects as a sexual attractant, a substance known as a pheromone. He named that substance bombykol.

Prior to and during the war, Butenandt was a member of the Nazi party, an affiliation for which he was severely criticized by many colleagues outside of (and some within) Germany. His membership in the party did not allow him, however, to travel to Stockholm to receive his Nobel Prize in 1938, nor to accept an earlier invitation from Harvard University to join its faculty in 1935. He did, however, use his membership to justify and support requests for funding for some wartime research projects that he defended as being critical to the war's success. Butenandt died in Münich on January 18, 1995.

Butenandt received many honors and awards throughout his lifetime. In addition to the Nobel Prize, he was awarded the Gold Cross for Federal Services of West Germany and the gold and silver Adolf von Harnack medals of the Max Planck Association for the Advancement of Science. In addition, he was awarded honorary doctoral degrees by the universities of Graz, Leeds, Madrid, Münich, and Tübingen, as well as Cambridge University. He was also elected as a corresponding or honorary member of corresponding member of the Academy of Sciences at Göttingen, Royal Society of London, New York Academy of Sciences, Japanese Biochemical Society, Deutsche Akademie der Naturforscher Leopoldina at Halle, and Austrian Academy of Sciences. In his honor, the University of Münich named its molecular biology unit the Adolf-Butenandt-Institut Molekularbiologie. In 1969, Butenandt was also named a commander of the Legion of Honor of France.

Jose Canseco (1964–)

Canseco was a major league baseball player from 1985 to 2001, during which time he set a number of records and won many accolades as one of the leading players of his time. He was chosen American League Rookie of the Year in 1986, American League Most Valuable Player in 1988, and American League Comeback Player of the Year in 1994. He was named to the All Star game on six occasions and played for seven different major league teams during his career, the Oakland Athletics, Texas Rangers, Boston Red Sox, Toronto Blue Jays, Tampa Bay Devil Rays, New York Yankees, and Chicago White Sox. In 2005, he published his autobiography, *Juiced: Wild Times, Rampant 'Roids, Smash Hits & How Baseball Got Big*, in which he described his own use of anabolic steroids and suggested that as many as 85 percent of all major league baseball players had also used AAS at some time in their career. Among the players he named as steroid-users were stars such as Jason Giambi, Juan González, Mark McGwire, Rafael Palmeiro, and Iván Rodríguez. Over time, some of the individuals named by Canseco admitted to steroid use, while others have continued to deny that they were ever involved in drug use.

José Canseco Capas, Jr., and his twin brother, Osvaldo (Ozzie), were born on July 2, 1964, in Havana, Cuba, to José Canseco, an oil company executive, and his wife, Barbara. In 1965, the Cansecos received permission to leave Cuba and moved to Opa-Locka, Florida. There the Canseco boys attended Coral Park High School, where they both played baseball. After completing high school, both Canseco boys were drafted by major league baseball teams, Ozzie by the New York Yankees, and José by the Oakland Athletics. He made his major league debut at the end of the 1985 season in a game against the Baltimore Orioles, and by the next year had improved to the point of being named the American League Rookie of the Year. His peak year came in 1988 when he batted .307, hit 42 home runs, had 124 runs batted in, and stole 40 bases, the first major league baseball player in history to register a "40–40" year.

In 1992 he was traded to the Texas Rangers, where he played three years, before moving on to a number of other teams, with whom he never stayed more than two years (Boston). He spent the 2000 season with Tampa Bay and the Yankees, before completing his major league career with Chicago in 2001. Since leaving major league baseball, Canseco has pursued a number of athletic careers, including a single mixed martial arts contest (which he lost), a brief prize fighting career, and short stints with six minor league baseball teams. Among the most recent of those contracts was with the Quintana Roo Tigers of the Mexican League in 2012, which ended when Canseco declined to take a drug test for testosterone. In 2007, the first year he was eligible, Canseco received six votes for Baseball's Hall of Fame, disqualifying him from being listed on the Hall of Fame ballot vote by sportscasters for future years. (He could still be elected by the Hall's Committee of Baseball Veterans.)

Canseco has always been an outgoing individual, somewhat interested in promoting himself to the general public. He has appeared on a variety of television and radio programs, including *The Simpsons, 60 Minutes, The Late Show with David Letterman, The Howard Stern Show*, and *The Celebrity Appearance*. He has also been troubled by a number of run-ins with the law, including an arrest for reckless driving in 1989, an arrest for carrying a loaded handgun in his car in 1989, a charge of aggravated battery for a dispute with his then-wife in 1992, an arrest for battery on a second wife in 1997, an arrest for violating his parole agreement for using steroids in 2003, and an arrest for bringing an illegal drug into the United States from Mexico in 2008.

As of mid-2012, Canseco had signed with the Massachusetts's Worcester Tornadoes, according to one observer who blogs about Canseco, "a ragtag bunch of dead-enders."

Don Catlin (1938–)

Catlin has sometimes been called the Father of Drug Testing in Sports. In 1981, the International Olympic Committee (IOC) asked Catlin to be in charge of drug testing for the 1984 Olympic Games to be held in Los Angeles. At the time, Catlin was a member of the faculty at the University of California at Los Angeles (UCLA) School of Medicine. He had spent most of his professional career on issues related to drug abuse, so he seemed the ideal candidate for the job. At first, he declined the IOC offer, but later changed his mind when he realized that the university would be allowed to keep the drug testing equipment. He continued his affiliation with the IOC for two decades while retaining his academic position in the UCLA Department of Molecular and Medical Pharmacology. He left UCLA and resigned from his IOC position in 2005 to open his own business, Anti-Doping Research, Inc. (ADRI), in Los Angeles.

Don Hardt Catlin was born on June 4, 1938, in New Haven, Connecticut, to Kenneth Catlin, an insurance executive, and Hilda Catlin, a homemaker. He attended Yale University, from which he received his bachelor's degree in psychology and statistics in 1960. He then continued his studies at the University of Rochester Medical School, from which he received his MD in 1965. After completing his residency and internship, Catlin enlisted in the U.S. Army and was assigned to the Walter Reed Army Medical Center, in Washington, D.C. He very soon became interested in the problem of drug addiction, to a large extent because of the problem posed by military men and women returning from duty in Vietnam who had become addicted to one or another illegal substance. He later said that he had a running battle with superior officers who preferred simply to imprison such individuals rather than offering them medical care, as Catlin preferred and continued to recommend.

In 1972, Catlin resigned his commission in the army and accepted a position as assistant professor at the UCLA School of Medicine in the department of pharmacology. He was later promoted associate professor and full professor at UCLA. After his retirement from UCLA, Catlin was named Professor Emeritus of Molecular and Medical Pharmacology at UCLA.

When Catlin accepted the IOC's offer to conduct drug tests for the 1982 Olympics, the whole course of his professional career was changed. He spent the better part of the next two decades carrying out drug tests, not only for the IOC but also for the groups such as the U.S. Olympic Committee (USOC; since 1985); the National Collegiate Athletic Association (NCAA; since 1986); National Football League (NFL; since 1990); National Center for Drug Free Sport, which runs the drug testing program for the NCAA (since 1999); U.S. Anti-Doping Agency, which runs the USOC antidoping program (since 2000); and Minor League Baseball (since 2004). His team's responsibilities include both testing for illicit drugs and providing education to athletes, coaches, sporting organizations, and other groups about the risks of illegal substances.

Over the years, an increasingly important part of Catlin's work has been the isolation and identification of "designer" drugs. Designer drugs are analogs of natural and/or known synthetic drugs that are synthesized to produce comparable results as those drugs, but that are difficult or impossible to detect by conventional analytical techniques. Among the substances that Catlin has identified are the steroids norbolethone, THG, and madol, as well as the blood enhancer darbepoetin and the aromatase inhibitor 4-androstene-3,6,17-trione (popularly known as 6-OXO). He has also developed new technologies for the identification of prohibited substances, perhaps the most important of which is the carbon isotope ratio (CIR) test, which allows the differentiation between natural testosterone in the body and exogenous forms of the hormone. One of his team's most recent accomplishment was the development in 2009 of a test for the drug methoxy polyethylene glycol-epoetin beta, originally developed for the treatment of anemia, but sometimes used illegally to improve blood volume (and, thus, racing performance) in race horses.

Catlin founded ADRI as a nonprofit organization whose goal is to conduct research on illegal substances used in sport, as well as to develop new technology for the detection of such materials. The company's major project at the current time is the development of a test for human growth hormone (hGH), a substance believed to be in wide use among athletes at all levels of sport, but for which no reliable test yet exists. In addition to his work at ADRI and UCLA, Catlin currently serves as chairman of the Equine Drug Research Institute's Scientific Advisory Committee, member of the Federation Equestre Internationale Commission on Equine Anti-Doping and Medication, and member of the IOC Medical Commission. He is the author or coauthor of more than 100 peer-reviewed scientific papers on drugs and drug technology.

Victor Conte (1950–)

Conte is perhaps best known as the founder and president of BALCO. Conte founded the business in 1984, officially for the purpose of conducting blood and urine tests and for providing food supplements to the general public. In fact, the primary function of the laboratory was to supply performance-enhancing drugs, primarily to professional athletes. In 1988, he established a close working relationship with a number of U.S. Olympic competitors by offering them free blood and urine tests. His connections to the sports world grew rapidly after that point and eventually became associated with leading performers in Major League Baseball, the NFL, U.S. Track and Field, and other major sports. Because of his role in the spread of anabolic steroids and other drugs among professional athletes, he eventually earned the nickname of "The Darth Vader of Sports."

Victor Conte was born in Death Valley, California, on July 10, 1950. His father owned a gas station adjacent to a restaurant owned by his aunt. At the age of four, Conte's family moved to Lake Tahoe, California, where his father had taken a job in construction. The family later moved back to Southern California and settled in Fresno, where Victor attended McLane High School. He participated in track at McLane, but his real passion was for music. While still in high school, he formed a band with two cousins, but set his musical ambitions aside briefly to attend Fresno City College. His track skills were good enough to earn him an athletic scholarship to Fresno State College, but he decided to pursue a career in music instead. Over the next 15 years, he played with a number of bands, including the Tower of Power, Pure Food and Drug Act, the Jump Street Band, Common Ground, and Herbie Hancock's Monster Band. Overall, he was involved in the production of more than 15 albums.

By the end of the 1970s, Conte had achieved considerable success in the field of music. Interestingly, as he has pointed out, he was one of the few professional musicians who was not involved in the use of drugs. His interest in that field came about when he was introduced to the field of holistic medicine. In 1980, he decided to open a small business in Millbrae, California, that sold vitamins. He called the business the Millbrae Holistic Health Center. As his interest in medical products grew, he expanded his business to include blood and urine testing and renamed his business the Bay Area Laboratory Cooperative, later more commonly known as BALCO. During the period between 1984 and 1995, Conte gradually expanded the number of his contacts in amateur and professional sports until some of the most famous names in athletics had become customers of his. A federal investigation of BALCO records in 2003 found evidence connecting Conte to a long list of athletes that included major league baseball players Barry Bonds, Benito Santiago, Jeremy Giambi, Bobby Estalella, and Armando Rios; hammer thrower John McEwen; shot putters Kevin Toth and C. J. Hunter; sprinters Dwain Chambers, Marion Jones, Tim Montgomery, Raymond J. Smith, Zhanna Block, and Kelli White; middle-distance runner Regina Jacobs; boxer Shane Mosley; and cyclist Tammy Thomas.

Based on evidence collected in 2003, U.S. Attorney General John Ashcroft announced a 42-count indictment against Conte and three other men for a variety of offenses, including conspiracy to distribute and possess with intent to distribute anabolic steroids, conspiracy to defraud through misbranded drugs, and money laundering. On July 15, 2005, Conte pleaded guilty to two charges, steroid distribution and money laundering, and was sentenced to four months in prison. He served that sentence at the end of 2005 and the beginning of 2006, and was released on March 30, 2006.

Since his release from prison, Conte has returned to his work with nutritional supplements for athletes, but now in a more carefully focused and controlled manner. He has chosen to work primarily with prize fighters, helping them to develop a nutritional program that will allow them to achieve the maximum potential possible with the bodies they have. He lists as his clients Shane Mosley, Zab Judah, Andre Berto, Karim Mayfield, Brandon Gonzales, and Nonito Donnaire. He says he has turned down some of the best-known names in boxing because he suspects that they use performance-enhancing drugs, and he does not care to become involved in that field again. What he does focus on is his athletes' blood chemistry, nutrition, and training schedules to help them achieve their goals. Many of the people who now work with Conte in the field of prize fighting believe that he has really changed. They also say that his background may offer a huge benefit to the sport, which many argue is among the "dirtiest" (in terms of performance-enhancing drug use) of all forms of competition. As one colleague has said, "he is somebody who understands the problem. If you can't listen to someone like that, you're really doing the athletes a disservice."

Daniel Duchaine (1952–2000)

Duchaine is widely regarded as the person most responsible for making the potential of anabolic steroids in improving body strength and muscle mass known to the world of bodybuilding and weightlifting. He was often referred to as the "Guru of Steroids" for this contribution to athletics and sports. In 1982, he and his partner of the time, Michael Zumpano, published one of the most memorable books on AAS ever written, an 18-page pamphlet entitled *Underground Steroid Handbook for Men and Women* (sometimes referred to as *The Original Underground Steroid Handbook*) listing the steroids available and outlining them for weight lifters and bodybuilders. The book sold for $6 and almost immediately became enormously popular worldwide. Within the first year of publication, the pamphlet sold more than 80,000 copies and produced an income of more than half a million dollars for Duchaine and Zumpano. Copies of Duchaine's original book are extremely rare today. He later produced an updated version, *The Underground Steroid Handbook*, in 1983, and a third version, *Underground Body Opus: Militant Weight Loss & Recomposition* (XIPE Press) in 1996. These two books are both generally available.

Daniel Duchaine was born on a date not generally available in 1952 in Connecticut. His mother, whom he barely knew, was a single mother who was later admitted to a psychiatric hospital for a personality disorder. (The admitting physician wrote that she was "without personality.") Duchaine was taken in by a childless pair of mill workers in Westbrook, Maine, who soon died—the adoptive mother when Duchaine was 10, and his adoptive father, two years later. After that time, Duchaine essentially raised himself, living on his own in his adoptive parents' cottage outside of town. Those with a memory of his early days have noted that Duchaine's dress and behavior made him stand out in the quite rural community. Perhaps in keeping with this image, Duchaine attended Boston University, where he majored in theater arts and earned his bachelor of arts degree in 1975. He then returned to Maine, where he worked at a bicycle shop for two years.

By this time, Duchaine had become interested in bodybuilding, perhaps as a way of improving his own self-image. He persuaded his personal physician to prescribe steroids to improve his body mass, strength, and endurance, and rapidly experienced a significant improvement in all of these areas. He became convinced that, used in moderation, steroids could be a powerful and safe way of improving one's performance in weight lifting and bodybuilding.

In 1978, he decided that Maine was not the most appropriate location for him to pursue his interests in steroids and bodybuilding, so he moved to Venice, California, where he quickly became a regular member of the local gym culture. He later said that his own experience with steroids made him the resident expert on performance-enhancing drugs "by default." He appeared to know more about the subject than anyone with whom he came into contact. In a short biographical sketch he wrote toward the end of his life, Duchaine noted the following major accomplishments during this period:

1983—Introduced Ultimate Orange as the first MRP (meal-replacement product) using maltodextrins and MCTs (minimum chain triglycerides).

1984—Started the first mail-order steroid business, the John Siegler Fan Club, that delivered steroids via UPS C.O.D.

1985—Cofounded Laboratories Milano, the largest black-market steroid-manufacturing plant in Tijuana, Mexico.

The U.S. government soon became interested in Duchaine's activities, and the next item on his biographical list was arrest for conspiracy and mislabeling of drugs produced in his Tijuana factory. He pled guilty and was sentenced to three years in jail, although he served only months. In 1991, while he was still on probation for his first conviction, Duchaine was picked up by agents of the U.S. FDA and arrested again, this time for trading in a restricted substance, gamma-hydroxybutyrate (GHB). This time he was sentenced to the full three-year term. Duchaine's final entry in his short autobiography, dated 1997, notes that he was the first person to introduce the steroid androstenedione to the bodybuilding world.

Dan Duchaine died on January 12, 2000, at the age of 47. The cause of death was polycystic kidney disease, a hereditary condition about which he had learned from a long-lost sister he first met in 1987. Until the end of his life, Duchaine never stopped speaking out about the value of anabolic steroids, when used in moderation. In 1988, *The New York Times* featured a story on Duchaine, briefly outlining his career with steroids. In the article, he described himself as "a guiding light" for the use of AAS in weightlifting, bodybuilding, and other sports. He also appeared on a number of radio and television programs, including "60 Minutes" and "20/20," promoting his views on steroids.

I Won't Cheat Foundation

165 W. Canyon Crest Rd., #350
Alpine, UT 84004
Phone: (801) 310-3200
URL: http://www.iWontCheat.com
E-mail: http://www.iwontcheat.com/contact-us

The I Won't Cheat Foundation was established in 2005 by former major league baseball player Dale Murphy, arguably one of the finest players of the last two decades of the 20th century. Murphy played for 15 seasons with the Atlantic Braves, from

1976 to 1989 and again in 1991. He finished his career with the Philadelphia Phillies (1990–1992) and Colorado Rockies (1993). He was Most Valuable Player of the National League in 1982 and 1983 and hit a career total of 398 home runs. From 1982 to 1985, he played every game of the season for the Braves. He was selected for the Major League All-Star Game on seven occasions between 1980 and 1987, missing being selected only in 1981. He won Golden Glove awards for being the best fielder at his position in 1982 through 1986 and was awarded the Lou Gehrig Memorial Award in 1985 and the Roberto Clemente Award in 1988. Observers have credited the success of I Won't Cheat to a considerable extent to Murphy's own personal character. He is a Mormon with a strong reputation and a decent and honorable person highly respected and well regarded by his peers in professional baseball and by members of the general public with whom he has interacted.

The first decade of the 21st century was a tumultuous one for major league baseball in particular and professional sports in general as revelations about the widespread use of anabolic steroids became generally known. By that time, Murphy had been retired from professional baseball for more than a decade, but he was concerned about the damage done to professional baseball by the steroid news. He was particularly concerned about the potential effects that such revelations were likely to have on young boys and girls who might want to pursue a career in professional sports at some later time in their lives. As a reflection of these concerns, he formed the I Won't Cheat Foundation as a 501(c)3 nonprofit public charity with the motto, "Injecting Ethics into America's Future."

The Foundation's primary function is to provide a character education program to elementary, middle, and high schools; summer camps; and organized leagues, such as Little League, Pop Warner, Youth Soccer, and Pony League. The purpose of the program is "to confront the growing epidemic of dishonesty that permeates society." At the conclusion of the program, participants take a pledge not to cheat in sports or in life, and they receive a certificate acknowledging their commitment to this goal. The Foundation reports that more than 10 million boys and girls have taken part in such programs and taken the I Won't Cheat pledge since August 2008. The Foundation achieved a significant breakthrough in 2010 when Little League Baseball agreed to a collaboration with I Won't Cheat and allowed its Little League World Series players to wear "I Won't Cheat" emblems on their uniforms. Little League opened a press release to parents about the new policy with the statement that "Using steroids equals cheating." League officials also noted that steroid abuse was not really a problem for the under-12-year-olds in their primary program, so cooperation with I Won't Cheat is largely symbolic and motivational. It would, at least in theory, also make players and coaches think about other ways in which young players could cheat, such as using illegal equipment or allowing unqualified individuals to join a team.

The I Won't Cheat Foundation also sponsors an annual essay contest on the topic "Why Does Character Matter Most?" although no information about the contest is provided on the foundation's website. (That information is currently available on the Little League website at http://www.littleleague.org/Assets/forms_pubs/IWC_Scholarship_Flyer.pdf.) The website also provides a page on which individuals can sign and submit the I Won't Cheat pledge.

Probably the most useful part of the organization's website is the media center, which offers a number of magazine and newspaper articles, videos, and Internet sites that provide more details about the foundation's activities. Dale Murphy is featured in many of these references, explaining the basis of his organization and the functions that it performs.

International Association of Athletics Foundation
17 Rue Princesse Florestine
BP 359
MC98007 Monaco
Phone: +377 93 10 8888

Fax: +377 93 15 9515
URL: http://www.iaaf.org/
E-mail: http://www.iaaf.org/about-iaaf/contact-us

The International Association of Athletics Foundation (IAAF) is the international governing organization for the sport of athletics. The term *athletics* refers to a number of sports involving running, walking, jumping, and throwing. Included among these sports are track-and-field events, cross country, road running, and race walking. The IAAF was founded in 1912 when 17 national sporting organizations joined together to form an international association through which the sport of athletics could standardize the approach to equipment, record keeping, and other activities essential to the sport. The organization was originally called the International Amateur Athletics Federation as a way of emphasizing its commitment to athletic competition among individuals who participated not because of the hope of financial or other awards, but for the love of the sport. Over time, the demands of commercialization became more pronounced in athletics, and the IAAF changed its name to its present title in 2001. The association has had its headquarters in Stockholm (1912–1946), London (1946–1993), and, most recently, Monaco (1993–present).

The IAAF currently has 212 national member federations organized into six so-called area associations—Asian Athletics Association in Asia (AAA), Confédération Africaine D'athlétisme in Africa (CAA), Confederación Sudamericana de Atletismo in South America (CONSUDATLE), European Athletic Association in Europe (EAA), North American, Central American and Caribbean Athletic Association in North America (NACACAA), and Oceania Athletics Association in Australia and Oceania (Australasia) (OAA). One of the primary responsibilities of the IAAF is record keeping. Records in every athletics event for men and women can be found on the association's website at http://www.iaaf.org/statistics/recbycat/index.html. The organization also sponsors and operates a number of world championships in various fields of athletics including the World Championships in Athletics, World Indoor Championships in Athletics, World Cross Country Championships, World Half Marathon Championships, World Junior Championships in Athletics, World Youth Championships in Athletics, World Race Walking Cup, World Marathon Cup, and the IAAF Continental Cup (involving team, rather than individual, competitions). All of these events are held biennially except for the Continental Cup, which is held every four years.

The IAAF was the first sports organization to adopt a policy prohibiting the use of performance-enhancing substances in athletic competitions. In 1982, it added a section to its Handbook that said:

> Doping is the use of any stimulant not normally employed to increase the poser of action in athletic competition above the average. Any person knowingly acting or assisting as explained above shall be excluded from any place where these rules are in force or, if he is a competitor, be suspended for a time or otherwise from further participation in amateur athletics under the jurisdiction of this Federation.

That statement was largely symbolic because tests were not yet available for most of the substances that athletes had been using—or would begin to use in the near future—to improve their athletic performance.

Since its original statement, the IAAF has tended to work closely with the World Anti-Doping Agency (WADA) and the IOC in achieving most of its antidoping objectives. In 1979, for example, the IAAF Council accepted the rules for accreditation of testing laboratories developed by the IOC and, in 1981, designated the first laboratories approved for this purpose. Since the creation of WADA in 1999, the IAAF has followed that organization's lead in defining substances to be prohibited from athletic competition, policies for testing, and other issues relating to the ban of performance-enhancing drugs in athletic competitions. At its 44th Congress held in Paris in 2003, the IAAF voted to accept the World Anti-Doping Code as its own statement of antidoping principles. Like other national organizations however, the IAAF has the right to adjust the WADA prohibited list to correspond with its own individual objectives and policies. For example, the IAAF does not list alcohol and beta-blockers on its list of prohibited substances although both substances do occur on the WADA list.

IAAF antidoping policies are set by the IAAF Council, the chief administration group of the organization. Those policies are then implemented by a troika of three divisions, the Medical and Anti-Doping Commission, the Doping Review Board, and the IAAF Anti-Doping Administrator. The Medical and Anti-Doping Commission is responsible for constantly reviewing the IAAF antidoping rules and guidelines and making suggestions for changes that may be needed. As its name suggests, the Doping Review Board is responsible for considering the legal and regulatory status of specific cases of suspected doping and deciding by what means such cases are to be resolved. Finally, the Anti-Doping Administrator is responsible for the day-to-day operation of the IAAF antidoping program. Specifically, he or she is responsible for reviewing the results of drug tests and determining what sanctions, if any, shall be assessed for positive results of such tests.

Publications available from the IAAF are somewhat limited in scope. They include guidelines and regulations for competition under IAAF sponsorship and regulations, as well as comprehensive lists of winners and record holders in athletic events worldwide. The association's web page on antidoping activities contains many news stories of events relating to the topic. Some recent examples include stories on the first doping violation resulting from the Athlete Biological Passport program, the most recent meeting of the IAAF Medical and Anti-Doping Commission, the release of a new educational program on the evils of doping in athletics, and sanctions taken against athletes who failed the IAAF testing program in one sport or other.

Charles Kochakian (1908–1999)

Kochakian has been called the Father of Anabolic Steroids because of his extensive research and important discoveries on the members of this family of biochemical compounds. Probably his most notable work was completed very early in his career, when he was still a graduate student in endocrinology at the University of Rochester. He arrived at Rochester, he wrote in his autobiography, *How It Was: Anabolic Action of Steroids and Remembrances*, knowing almost nothing about the subject of endocrinology. But he registered to take a course in the subject and was soon excelling in his studies. In fact, his instructor told him that he no longer had to take exams in the course, but suggested, instead, that he become involved in some original research being conducted in the department.

The focus of this research was the relationship between certain components of male urine and basal metabolic rate (MBR), the minimum amount of energy an organism needs to maintain basic bodily functions such as respiration, digestion, and circulation. Early studies had suggested that extracts prepared from male human urine increased the BMR in castrated dogs. The hypothesis Kochakian set out to test, then, was whether in fact there is a positive correlation—and, perhaps, cause and effect relationship—between the extract and BMR in dogs and maybe even humans.

Kochakian's own experiments failed to confirm the earlier results, even after they had been modified and repeated a number of times. What he did discover, however, was that the urine extract significantly affected the nitrogen balance in the castrated dogs. It appeared that injection of the extract increased the amount of nitrogen used up during the dog's metabolism, suggesting the element was being used to synthesize new body tissue. Indeed, he found that both castrated dogs in the study gained body weight in response to additional injections of the urine extract.

These experiments were going on at just the time that researchers in other laboratories were beginning to identify the essential elements of male urine that produce primary and secondary male sex characteristics. The first sex hormone, estrone, had been discovered in 1929 and the first sex hormone to be synthesized artificially, androsterone, was produced in 1934. The key to the whole process of masculinization, the hormone testosterone, was itself first discovered only a year later, in 1935. By the time Kochakian was well into his research, samples of synthetic testosterone, androsterone, and some of their analogs were commercially available. Kochakian began to make use of these commercial products to continue his tests on the castrated dogs. Kochakian devoted the rest of his productive professional career on the synthesis, characterization, and study of dozens of anabolic hormones, the precursors, and metabolites.

Charles Daniel Kochakian was born in Haverhill, Massachusetts, on November 18, 1908. His parents were immigrants from Armenia, his father in 1900 and his mother in 1904. He has written that, like many immigrants, his parents had only a meager elementary school education themselves, but were insistent that their children would receive the most extensive and best education possible. His mother hoped, in particular, that her son would pursue a career in dentistry, an ambition that young Charles did not himself share. Upon graduation from high school, he matriculated at Boston University (BU), from which he received his AB in chemistry in 1930. He then continued his studies at BU, earning his AM in organic chemistry a year later.

The early 1930s were a difficult time for a young man to be seeking work, even with a master's degree in organic chemistry. His applications for work produced no results until September 1933, when he was offered a position in the graduate school at the University of Rochester in the field of endocrinology. The offer was accompanied by a modest scholarship that was, he later wrote, adequate only for a "bare living." It was at Rochester that he began his work on anabolic steroids that was to occupy his professional career for the next half century. He was awarded his PhD in physiological chemistry by Rochester in 1936.

After completing his graduate work, Kochakian remained at Rochester as an instructor (1936–1940), associate professor (1940–1944), and assistant professor (1947–1951) in the Department of Physiology and Vital Economics (a somewhat unusual division in which teaching and research was focused on hygiene and human nutrition). In 1951, Kochakian accepted an appointment as head of biochemistry and endocrinology at the Oklahoma Medical Research Foundation in Oklahoma City, where he also served as associated director, coordinator of research, and professor of research biochemistry until 1957. In 1957, he left Oklahoma to become professor of physiology at the University of Alabama at Birmingham (UAB), where he spent the remainder of his academic career. While there, he held the titles of Professor and Director of Experimental Endocrinology (1961–1979), Professor of Biochemistry (1961–1979), and Professor of Physiology and Biophysics (1964–1975). In 1979, he was named Professor Emeritus at UAB.

Among his honors, Kochakian was awarded the Claude Bernal Medal of the University of Montreal in 1950 and the Osaka Endocrine Society Medal in 1962. Kochakian was particularly proud of his religious involvement, listing a number of church-related activities in his curriculum vitae. These activities included secretary of the Men's Club at the Centre Congregational Church in Haverhill; Chair of the Christian Education Committee at the Brighton Presbyterian Church in Rochester; Member of the Building Committee of the Westminster Presbyterian Church in Oklahoma City; and Active Elder of the Southminster Presbyterian Church in Birmingham. He was listed in a number of "who's who" books, including *Who's Who in American History*, *Who's Who in America*, *Who's Who in American Education*, *Who's Who in the South and Southwest*, *Who's Who in the World*, *International Who's Who in Community Service*, *Notable Americans*, and *American Men of Science*. Kochakian died in Birmingham on February 12, 1999.

Floyd Landis (1975–)

Landis is an American cyclist racer best known for his remarkable victory in the 2006 Tour de France, the premier cycling event in the world. A two-day period in the race that will forever be a part of cycling history began on July 16 during the 182-km face from Bourg-d'Oisans to La Toussuire. Landis had a miserable day and trailed the stage leader Michael Rasmussen by more than 10 minutes. On the next day, however, Landis made one of the most amazing comebacks in racing history, winning the 201-km run from St.-Jean-de-Maurienne to Morzine by nearly six minutes. The stage was notable for an especially difficult 18.3-km climb up the Alps. Only a few days after the race had been completed, antidoping officials notified Landis' manager that he had failed a drug test conducted just prior to the historic St. Jean de Maurienne to Morzine stage. The test had shown that Landis' testosterone to the hormone epitestosterone (T/E) ratio, a common doping test, was 11 to 1. The normal ratio for someone who is not taking steroid supplements is 4 to 1.

These test results set into motion the normal series of events leading to a consideration of voiding Landis' eventual triumph in the Tour de France. Less than a month after Landis had been declared winner on the 2006 Tour de France, the United States Anti-Doping Agency (USADA) confirmed Landis' test results and was disqualified from the race. Spanish cyclist Óscar Pereiro was declared winner of the event. Landis appealed the USADA decision, but an appeals board confirmed that decision on September 20, 2007, and Landis was banned from professional cycling for two years. Landis appealed again, this time to the Court of Arbitration for Sport (CAS), an international tribunal to hear disputes having to do with athletic competitions. On June 30, 2008, the CAS announced its decision, an affirmation of earlier decisions and the ban on Landis' participation in cycling for two years.

Floyd Landis was born on October 14, 1975, in Farmersville, Pennsylvania, to Paul and Arlene Landis. The Landis family was part of a devout Mennonite community in Lancaster County, in which many otherwise typical activities are often (but not always) forbidden, such as the wearing of "modern" clothes, using motorized transportation, and listening to radio and watching television. Floyd's own father was so concerned about his son's "frivolous" bicycle riding that he assigned the boy extra chores to keep him busy during the day. In response, Floyd changed his riding to the evening hours, often enjoying his hobby in the wee hours of the morning.

Nonetheless, Landis seemed to have been born for riding. At his first cycling competition, he reputedly showed up wearing "a garish jersey, a visored helmet, and a pair of brilliantly colored Argyle socks, pulled high," according to author Daniel Coyle in his book *Tour de Force*. When his opponents began making fun of him, he offered to buy dinner to anyone who could keep up with him in the race. No one did, and Landis won the race by more than 10 minutes.

In 1995, Landis moved to Southern California, expecting to find a more hospitable, year-around place to train and race. He soon developed a reputation for strength, endurance, and tenacity, finishing one race even after his tires had been completely worn away, riding only on the wheels' rims. Impressed by that type of reputation, seven-time Tour de France winner Lance Armstrong recruited Landis to ride with his team in 2002. Landis aided Armstrong in his 2002, 2003, and 2004 wins, and then went on to finish ninth himself in the 2005 race.

In May 2010, Landis finally admitted to the use of illegal steroids in the Tour de France, largely negating the long campaign he had fought to overturn his conviction for those actions. When his suspension expired on January 30, 2009, he returned to professional cycling again, with relatively modest success. He joined the OUCH Pro Cycling Team (now the UnitedHealthcare Pro Cycling Team) and finished 23rd in a field of 84 riders at his first competition, the Tour of California. He later moved to the Bahati Foundation Cycling Team which, over time and apparently partly because of its connection with

Landis, began to fall apart. His career came to an unfortunate conclusion when he entered the 2010 Cascade Cycling Classic as the sole representative of the Bahati team, failing to complete the event. In January 2011, he finally announced his retirement from the sport he loved so well. In an interview with *Cycling News*, he said, "I've spent five years trying to get back to a place that I can never really go back to, and it's causing more stress than is worth it. . . . I've been riding my bike a lot, trying to figure out life, which is the same reason I did it to start with, so I've come full circle."

Ernst Laqueur (1880–1947)

The 1930s were a decade of great progress in understanding the chemical structure and physiological activity of sex hormones. The first sex hormone ever discovered, estrone, was identified by German chemist Adolf Butenandt in 1929; Butenandt also isolated the first male sex hormone, androsterone, only two years later. These breakthroughs were of enormous significance because they provided researchers for the first time with a mechanism for understanding the process of sexualization in terms of concrete chemical compounds that could be studied, characterized, synthesized, and produced commercially.

This new information was of immense interest to a few large pharmaceutical companies, Organon, located in Oss, Netherlands; Ciba, headquartered in Basel, Switzerland; Schering, in Berlin, Germany; and Syntex, in Mexico. With the announcement of new discoveries about sex hormones, these companies began to pour financial and personnel resources into bringing hormone products to the commercial market. Among the most successful of the companies, in terms of research breakthroughs, was Organon. The company was founded in 1923 by Laqueur; Sall van Zwanenberg, owner of the Zwanenberg Slaughterhouse; and Dr. Jacques van Oss, a business consultant. Butenandt's research on sex hormones, as well as that of many other scientists, was supported by Organon. In perhaps its biggest commercial breakthrough, the company began producing its first product, insulin, in 1923. The discovery and synthesis of testosterone, the primary male sex hormone, were both the result of research by Organon-based researchers, primarily Karoly Gyula David, Elizabeth Dingemanse, Janos Freud, and Laqueur. In May 1935, this research team published a paper announcing the discovery and characterization of testosterone in a now classic paper, "On Crystalline Male Hormone from Testicles (Testosterone)."

Ernst Laqueur was born in Obernigk, near Breslau, Germany, on July 8, 1880, to Seigfried and Anna Levy Laqueur. He grew up in a prosperous Jewish family and attended school in Breslau. That region is now part of southwestern Poland. After high school, Laqueur attended both the University of Breslau and the University of Heidelberg, where he studied medicine. In 1905, he was awarded his medical degree by the former institution. In spite of his family history, Laqueur felt a greater affinity to his German nationality than to his religious affiliation and, in 1906, he, his wife, and their young daughter converted to the Evangelical religion. He is said to have taken this step to express his concern for a unified Germany in which religion would not be a decisive factor.

Between 1906 and 1910, Laqueur worked as an instructor and research assistant in physiology and pharmacology at the universities of Heidelberg, Königsberg, and Halle. In 1910, he was appointed professor of physiology at Halle, and two years later took a similar post at the University of Gröningen. When World War I broke out, Laqueur enlisted in the German army, where he served as a physician and instructor at the Army Gas School in Berlin. He also conducted research on gas warfare and treatment for gas poisoning at the Kaiser-Wilhelm Academy in Berling.

After the war, Laqueur was offered an appointment as professor of pharmacology and physiology at the Flemish- and German-sponsored University of Ghent, in Belgium. He never took that position, however, as he was almost simultaneously convicted of treason in absentia by the new Belgian government that took over the university after the way. In any case, Laqueur had become ill with typhoid and returned directly to Germany at the war's conclusion. He remained there until he accepted an appointment as an assistant to the highly regarded Dutch physician and medical researcher Isidore Snapper, in Amsterdam in 1919. Only a year later, he received his own appointment, as professor of pharmacology at the University of Amsterdam.

With the rise of National Socialism (Nazism) in Germany in the 1930s, Laqueur decided to give up his German citizenship and become a Dutch citizen. When the war first reached Holland in November 1940, he, along with all other Jewish professors, was removed from his office at the University of Amsterdam. The company he helped to found, Organon, was also sold to the German firm of Schering. Nonetheless, because he was originally a German citizen and he had served in the German army during World War I, he escaped many of the worst excesses experienced by other Jews in the Netherlands during the way. This "special treatment" resulted in some unpleasant feelings toward him after the war, and he never returned to full active participation in either the academic or the commercial world.

He did, however, continue to receive a number of honors and awards in recognition of his research accomplishments. In 1946, for example, he was invited to give the prestigious Harvey Lecture at the University of California at Los Angeles (UCLA). He followed this event with a tour of North and South America, during which he became quite ill and was hospitalized for an extended period in Argentina. He returned home to a continuing dispute with administrators at Organon, which was never resolved before he died while on vacation in Gletsch Furka, Switzerland, on August 19, 1947.

George J. Mitchell (1933–)

Mitchell was appointed in March 2006 by Major League Baseball commissioner Bud Selig to conduct an investigation of the use of illegal AAS by major league baseball players. The announcement followed closely upon the publication of a book, *Game of Shadows*, by *San Francisco Chronicle* reporters Mark Fainaru-Wada and Lance Williams. That book discussed in detail the distribution of illegal steroids by the San Francisco Bay area firm BALCO to a number of professional athletes, most prominently San Francisco Giants player Barry Bonds. The book was issued just prior to the season in which Bonds was expected to (and did) set a new major league baseball home run record for a single season.

George John Mitchell, Jr., was born in Waterville, Maine, on August 20, 1933, to George John Mitchell, Sr., a custodian at Colby College, and Mary Saad Mitchell, a textile worker. Mitchell helped put himself through secondary school by working as a janitor, like his father, before entering Bowdoin College, in Brunswick, Maine. He graduated with his bachelor's degree from Bowdoin in 1954 and enlisted in the U.S. Army, where he rose to the rank of first lieutenant. After leaving the army, he returned to Georgetown University, in Washington, D.C., from which he received his law degree in 1960. His first postgraduation job was with the U.S. Department of Justice, where he worked as a trial lawyer in the Antitrust Division. He left that position in 1962 to take a job as executive assistant to Sen. Edmund S. Muskie (D-Maine). He left that post in 1965 to take a job at the law firm of Jensen, Baird, Gardner and Henry, in Portland, Maine. He served with the firm for a dozen years, during which time he also remained active in politics. He ran for governor of the state in 1974, but lost the election to Republican James Longley. In 1977, President Jimmy Carter named Mitchell U.S. Attorney for the State of Maine.

In 1980, Mitchell's political career took a turn when he was appointed by Gov. Joseph Brennan to take the seat of former senator Edmund Muskie, who had been appointed Secretary of State by President Carter. He then won reelection to that seat in 1982, and again in 1988. During his last term in the Senate, he served as Majority Leader from 1989 to 1995. He left the

Senate at the end of his second term and declined a nomination by President Bill Clinton to a seat on the U.S. Supreme Court.

Mitchell's retirement did not, by any means, mean the end of his political career. In November 1995, President Clinton named Mitchell a special advisor on economic initiatives for Ireland. Mitchell produced a detailed report called for a number of steps that might lead to the end of the very long conflict between Great Britain and Ireland over the fate of Northern Island. Mitchell's work on the Irish problem eventually earned him a number of honors and awards, including the Presidential Medal of Freedom (the highest civilian honor that the U.S. Government can give); the Philadelphia Liberty Medal; the Truman Institute Peace Prize; and the United Nations (UNESCO) Peace Prize.

In 2000, President Clinton asked Mitchell to take on another international issue, the conflict between Israel and the Palestinian Authority. He served as chair of the Sharm el-Sheikh International Fact-Finding Committee, whose goal it was to develop a pathway for the peace process between the two entities. The process ultimately failed (as have all other peace efforts in the region), but Mitchell again won accolades from both sides for his efforts on behalf of the process.

Mitchell's work on behalf of Major League Baseball in 2006–2007 was conducted in spite of the decision by the Player's Union not to cooperate fully in his investigation. He is said to have interviewed only two players in person, although he and his staff eventually collected more than 115,000 pages of documents from more than 700 witnesses, including 60 former major league players. Key witnesses in the investigation were Kirk Radomski, a former Mets clubhouse attendant, and Brian McNamee, a former trainer for Roger Clemens, one of the finest pitchers in major league baseball history. As of 2012, repercussions of these investigations are continuing as Clemens appears before the U.S. House of Representatives on charges of lying to the U.S. Congress.

In 2009, Mitchell was called upon once more, this time by President Barack Obama, to serve as an intermediary in a contentious international issue, again the disagreements between Israel and the Palestinian Authority. Mitchell flew back and forth between Washington and the Middle East for two years attempting to make some progress between positions held by the two sides, again without success. In May 2011, he resigned that post and returned to private business.

In addition to his public service, Mitchell has continued to work in the private legal field. After leaving the Senate, he joined the Washington law firm of Verner, Liipfert, Bernhard, McPherson and Hand, where he was later chosen chairman. He has also been senior counsel at the law firm of Preti, Flaherty, Beliveau, Pachios, Orlick & Haley in Portland, and partner and chairman of the Global Board of DLA Piper, US LLP, a global law firm. Mitchell is the author of four books on his life experiences: *Men of Zeal: A Candid Inside Story of the Iran-Contra Hearings* (with William Cohen, 1988); *World on Fire: Saving an Endangered Earth* (1991); *Not For America Alone: The Triumph of Democracy and the Fall of Communism* (1997); and *Making Peace* (1999).

National Institute on Drug Abuse

6001 Executive Blvd., Room 5213
Bethesda, MD 20892-9561
Phone: (301) 443–1124; en español: (240) 221-4007
URL: http://www.drugabuse.gov/
E-mail: information@nida.nih.gov

The origins of the National Institute on Drug Abuse (NIDA) date to 1935 when the U.S. Public Health Service (USPHS) established a research facility on drug abuse in Lexington, Kentucky. In 1948, that facility was officially renamed the Addiction Research Center. Research on drug abuse was facilitated in the site of the original facility, called "Narco," which was adjacent to a prison that held drug offenders and was run cooperatively with the Federal Bureau of Prisons. The federal government's interest in drug abuse was expanded in 1971 when President Richard M. Nixon established the Special Action Office of Drug Abuse Prevention within the White Office. A year later, the Special Action Office initiated two programs, the Drug Abuse Warning Network (DAWN) and the National Household Survey on Drug Abuse (NHSDA), both of which continue today. DAWN is a public health surveillance system that monitors emergency department drug-related admissions. It is now a part of the Substance Abuse and Mental Health Services Administration (SAMHSA). NHSDA is now known as the National Survey on Drug Use and Health (NSDUH) and is also located in SAMHSA. Its function is to provide national and state-level data on the use of illegal drugs, tobacco, alcohol, and mental health to researchers and the general public.

The NIDA itself was created by the act of Congress in 1974 for the purpose of promoting research, treatment, prevention, training, services, and data collection on the nature and extent of drug abuse. In general, the activities of the NIDA can be classified into one of two major categories: the conduct and support of research on a variety of issues related to drug abuse and dissemination of this information both for the purposes of future research and to improve programs of prevention and treatment of drug abuse, as well as to inform decisions by state, local, and the federal government on drug abuse policies and practices. The agency's organizational charts reflect the way in which these activities are organized. Three of the main NIDA offices deal with extramural affairs (funding of outside research), science policy and communications, and management. The agency also consists of a number of divisions that deal with intramural research (research within the agency); basic neuroscience and behavioral research; clinical research and behavioral research; epidemiology, services, and prevention research; and pharmacotherapies and medical consequences of drug abuse. Special programs, working groups, consortia, and interest groups focus on more specific topics, such as HIV/AIDS;

childhood and adolescence issues; community epidemiology; women and sex/gender differences; nicotine and tobacco; neurosciences; and genetic issues.

The direction of NIDA activities over the period 2010–2015 has been laid out in the agency's *Strategic Plan*, published in September 2010. That report describes in detail the elements of the agency's four-pronged program over the coming five years: prevention, treatment, HIV/AIDS, and crosscutting priorities, activities that involve the interaction of drug abuse issues with other questions of international, national, and local concern. This publication is available online at http://www.drugabuse. gov/sites/default/files/stratplan.pdf.

The NIDA budget has remained relatively constant over the first decade of the 21st century. It rose slightly from 2011 ($1,048,776) to 2012 ($1,052,114) to 2013 ($1,054,001) with also a relatively constant number of full-time employee equivalents (386, 386, and 382, respectively). About 90 percent of that budget goes for extramural research ($902,696 in 2013), with the largest fraction of that designated for basic and clinical neuroscience and behavior research ($478,902).

As indicated above, dissemination of information is a major focus of the work carried out by the NIDA. Its publications include educational curricula, facts sheets, guidelines and manuals, journals, administrative and legal documents, posters, presentations, promotional materials, and reports. These publications can be reviewed on the agency's website at http://www.drugabuse. gov/publications by audience (students, teachers, parents, researchers, and health and medical professionals), by drug of abuse (e.g., alcohol, amphetamines, club drugs, LSD, marijuana, and steroids), by drug topic (such as addiction science, comorbidity, criminal justice, drugged driving, medical consequences, and relapse and recovery), by series (among which are Addiction Science and Clinical Practice, Brain Power, DrugFacts, Mind over Matter, and Research Reports), and by type.

The NIDA website also provides links to a number of resources for additional information about the subject of drug abuse and about the agency itself, including sections on NIDA in the News, NIDA Notes, meetings and events related to drug abuse topics, news releases, podcasts of NIDA-related programs, and electronic newsletters. The website is also available in a Spanish language edition.

Dick Pound (1942–)

Pound is described in his biography in the Canada's Sports Hall of Fame as the "ultimate champion" of the concept of purity in sport. For most of his adult life, Pound has campaigned to reduce or eliminate the influence of performance-enhancing substances and practices that supposedly provide an unfair advantage for their users over athletes who do not rely on such substances and practices. In 1999, he helped found the WADA, of which he became the organization's first president. He served in that post until 2007, when he chose not to run for an additional term at the agency.

Richard William Duncan Pound (almost universally known as "Dick Pound") was born in St. Catharines, Ontario, on March 22, 1942. He spent his childhood in a number of cities and towns ranging from Ocean Falls, British Columbia, to La Tuque and Trois-Rivieres, Quebec. After graduating from Mount Royal High School in Montréal, he matriculated at McGill University, where he went on to become a star in swimming. He set school records in every freestyle event and won three Canadian intercollegiate gold medals in each of his freshman, sophomore, and senior years. At one point in his career, he held every freestyle swimming record up to a distance of 220 m. He won the Canadian freestyle championship four times, in 1958, 1960, 1961, and 1962, and the Canadian butterfly championship in 1961. He swam on the Canadian team in the 1960 Olympic Games in Rome, where he finished sixth in the 100-m freestyle, and was fourth in the 4 × 400-m relay. In addition to his swimming accomplishments, Pound was also a first-class squash player, winning the Canadian intercollegiate championship twice. He was also a proficient golf and tennis player.

Pound received his bachelor of commerce and his bachelor of law degrees from McGill in 1962 and 1967, and his bachelor of arts degree from Sir George Williams University in 1963. He was licensed as a chartered accountant in 1964 and as a lawyer in 1968. Over the next decade, Pound worked as a chartered accountant and an attorney in Quebec and Ontario. He eventually reached the peak of both professions when he was named Queen's Counsel in 1991 and Fellow of the Order of Chartered Accountants, Quebec, in 2000. He currently works in the Tax Group of the law firm of Stikeman Elliott in Montréal, where his primary areas of practice are tax litigation and negotiations with tax authorities on behalf of clients, in addition to general tax advisory work and commercial arbitration. Pound has retained his association with McGill throughout his adult life, serving as lecturer and adjunct faculty member, governor, member of a number of administrative committees, and as chancellor of the university from 1999 to 2009.

For all of his accomplishments in the field of law, Pound is almost certainly best known for his role with the IOC and other amateur sports organizations. In 1978 he was elected a member of the IOC with special responsibility for negotiating sponsoring and television deals. He remained an active member of the committee for the next three decades, serving as chair of the Centennial Coin Programme, Centennial Working Group, Marketing Coordination Committee, and Olympic Games Study Commission, among other responsibilities. In all, he served a total of 18 years on the IOC, during 8 of which he was also vice-president of the organization.

In 1999, Pound was involved in the creation of the WADA, of which he was chosen the organization's first president. He held that post until his retirement in 2007, although he continues to serve on the organization's Foundation board. During his tenure, Pound became known for his very strong stands against the use of performance-enhancing substances and practices in sports, often making comments that were regarded as incendiary or provocative. One of his best-known ongoing feuds was with American cyclist Lance Armstrong, who objected to Pound's assertion in 2004 that "the public knows that the riders in the Tour de France and the others are doping." That feud reached new heights in 2005 when Armstrong apparently tested positive for erythropoietin and Pound demanded that his gold medal for the Tour de France that year be rescinded. Pound also had harsh comments about the use of performance-enhancing substances in other circumstances involving another cyclist, Floyd Landis, drug-using practices in the National Hockey League, the Austrian cross-country and Nordic ski teams, doping among professional golfers, and the growth of drug use in professional sports in general and American major league baseball in particular. In an interview for the WADA magazine *Play True*, Pound laid out his basic beliefs about the use of performance-enhancing substances in sports:

> Those who do not honour their promises, who cheat, undermine the entire ethical construct of sport. In many cases, it is also dangerous cheating. Either way, this cheating has no place in sport and must be confronted, not condoned or ignored.

Pound has received many awards and honors during his long career in the law and amateur sports. These include the Scarlet Key Honour Society and the Carswell Company Prize at McGill; 10 honorary doctorates from the United States Sports Academy, University of Windsor, University of Western Ontario, Laurentian University, Beijing Sports University, Lakehead University, Loughborough University, L'Université du Québec, Concordia University, and McGill; Officer of the Order of Canada; Officer of the National Order of Quebec; Gold and Silver Star of the Order of the Sacred Treasure, Government of Japan; and Laureus Spirit of Sport Award, WADA.

Leopold Ružička (1887–1976)

Ružička was a major participant in the attempt to identify the biochemical responsible for producing male secondary sexual characteristics in the 1930s. That research had a very long history, based on centuries-old knowledge that some substance, secreted by males in their urine, was responsible for the development of male sexual characteristics, such as body hair and a deep voice, as well as the ability to produce sperm. A number of breakthroughs in the late 19th and early 20th centuries culminated in the 1931 discovery by Adolf Butenandt of the hormone he called androsterone. Researchers knew, however, that an even more powerful substance responsible for male sexual characteristics remained undiscovered, and the race was on to find that substance. In the short period between May 27 and August 24, 1935, three separate groups of researchers reported the discovery and chemical structure of that substance, testosterone. One of those teams was led by Croatian biochemist Leopold Ružička, who later was awarded a share of the 1939 Nobel Prize in Chemistry (with Butenandt) for his research on polymethylenes and higher terpenes, chemical structures of which steroids are made.

Ružička was born Lavoslav Stjepan Ružička on September 13, 1887, in Vukovar, Hungary (then part of the Austro-Hungarian Empire, and now part of Croatia), to Stjepan Ružička, a cooper, and Ljubica Sever Ružička. After the death of his father in 1891, Ružička returned with his mother to her birthplace in Osijek, where he attended primary school and the classical gymnasium (high school). Although Ružička was not particularly interested in the science courses offered at Osijek, he took an interest in chemistry largely because he was intrigued by the nature of natural products, an interest that motivated most of his research throughout the rest of his life.

After graduation from Osijek, Ružička matriculated at the Technische Hochschule (technical high school) at Karlsruhe, where he took his first formal courses in chemistry. He proved to be well adapted to the subject and finished his courses in less than two years. His instructor at Karlsruhe was the famous German chemist Hermann Staudinger, who was only 26 at the time. Working together, Ružička and Staudinger essentially created the field of plant product chemistry, focusing their research at first on the structure and action of a group of compounds now known as pyrethrins, the major component of many insecticides. It was this line of research that led eventually to the primary focus of Ružička's research throughout his life. As part of that research, he and his colleagues submitted one of the classic papers in the history of steroid chemistry, "On the Artificial Preparation of the Testicular Hormone Testosterone (Androsten-3-one-17-ol)," to the journal *Helvetica Chimica Acta* on August 31, 1935.

In 1912, Staudinger was offered a position at the newly created Eidgenössische Technische Hochschule (Swiss Federal Institute of Technology, generally known simply as ETH), now one of the most prestigious scientific research institutes in the world. Ružička followed his mentor to ETH, where he took up a long-standing position in the field of organic chemistry. Some of his earliest works there were supported by the oldest perfume manufacturer in the world, Haarman & Reimer, of Holzminden, Germany. The firm obviously saw potential benefits in the line of research being pursued by Ružička at ETH, and this type of support was continued from other perfume and chemical firms throughout Ružička's career. Ružička left ETH in 1926 for a three-year stint at the University of Utrecht, in the Netherlands, after which he returned to Switzerland and ETH, where he spent the rest of his career. His decision to return to ETH was motivated both by the stronger chemical industry in Switzerland and by the offer of directorship of the institute. Ružička remained at ETH until his retirement in 1957.

In addition to his research, teaching, and administrative responsibilities, Ružička was especially interested in Dutch and Flemish art. His collection was at one time regarded as one of the finest collections of such works in the world. He is said to have remarked that his devotion to art actually reduced the amount of time and energy he was able to devote to chemical research. Ružička died in Mammern, Switzerland, on September 26, 1976.

During his lifetime, Ružička was awarded honorary doctorates from eight different institutions, four in science, two in medicine, one in natural science, and one in law. He also received seven prizes and medals and was elected to 24 honorary memberships in chemical, biochemical, and other scientific societies around the world. In 1957, the ETH established the Ružička Prize for outstanding work in the field of chemistry conducted by a young researcher.

Arnold Schwarzenegger (1947–)

Schwarzenegger is an Austrian-born former bodybuilder, actor, businessman, and 38th governor of the state of California. Before he became active in politics in the early part of the 20th century, he was probably best known at first for his bodybuilding accomplishments, having won the Mr. Olympia bodybuilding contest seven times, the first in 1967 when he was 20 years old. He was then acknowledged as having almost the perfect build for a bodybuilder, with a massive chest, arms, and legs. Even today, bodybuilding magazines and blogs point to Schwarzenegger as a sort of Mr. Perfect.

After retiring from bodybuilding competition, Schwarzenegger turned to movie making, and starred in a number of feature films that included *Hercules in New York* (under the name "Arnold Strong"); *Stay Hungry* (for which he won a Golden Globe in 1976); *Pumping Iron* (a bodybuilding film from 1977); *Conan the Barbarian* (1982) and *Conan the Destroyer* (1984); *The Terminator* (1984), *Terminator 2: Judgment Day* (1991), and *Terminator 3: Rise of the Machines* (2003); *Red Sonja* (1985); *Twins* (1988); *Total Recall* (1990); *Kindergarten Cop* (1990); *Junior* (1994); and *Eraser* (1996).

Beginning in the 1990s, Schwarzenegger was subjected to almost constant questioning about the possibility that he had used anabolic steroids to improve his muscle mass during his bodybuilding career. During his teenage years, it was very clear that he had developed from a well-built, but hardly extraordinary, young man into an adult with quite uncommon physical features. In response to such questioning, Schwarzenegger almost inevitably admitted to the use of anabolic steroids as something he had to do in order to compete. He points out that at the time he used steroids, it was not illegal to do so and virtually all bodybuilders took advantage of the contribution they made to improvement in body structure. He also notes that he used steroids only for short periods of time, usually in the build-up to a competition, and then ceased using them after the competition. (For Schwarzenegger's own words on this, see http://www.youtube.com/watch?v=ebRglq-CPsY.) In interviews on the topic, Schwarzenegger now makes it clear that he doesn't recommend the use of steroids among professional or amateur athletes. He insists, however, that athletes should continue to take advantage of any legal substances that will improve their own performances.

Arnold Alois Schwarzenegger was born in the village of Thal, Austria, on July 30, 1947, to Gustav Schwarzenegger, chief of police in Thal, and Aurelia Jadrny Schwarzenegger. He was an average student in primary and secondary school, with a special interest in soccer. He was introduced to weight training by his soccer coach and soon found that he preferred working out with barbells to kicking a soccer bell. His interest in bodybuilding was further encouraged by a number of films he saw that starred well-built male leads, such as Steve Reeves and Johnny Weissmuller. By the age of 14, he had decided to begin competing in bodybuilding competitions. He soon became absolutely committed to this pursuit, noting in later interviews that "[i]t would make me sick to miss a workout. . . . I knew I couldn't look at myself in the mirror the next morning if I didn't do it." As a result, he sometimes broke into the local gym where he worked out even when it was closed, just so as not to disrupt his schedule.

In 1965, Schwarzenegger joined the Austrian army, fulfilling the national requirement of one year of military service. Although his job is as a tank driver, he found enough time to continue his bodybuilding activities, winning the Junior Mister Europe title that year. A year later, after leaving the army, he added three more titles to his list: Mister Europe, Best Built Man in Europe, and International Powerlifting Championship. In 1967, he won the first of five Mr. Universe championships, which he later described as his "ticket to America." A year later, he finally realized a life-long dream of moving to the United States, where he made a meager living selling nutritional supplements and competing in bodybuilding contests. His hope of becoming a famous movie star was thwarted at first because of his thick accent. In fact, his voice had to be dubbed in after completion of the filming of his first movie, *Hercules in New York*, because he could not be understood in the original takes.

Schwarzenegger has been a lifelong Republican. He has said that he made that decision shortly after arriving in the United States, listening to a debate between presidential candidates Hubert Humphrey and Richard Nixon. He liked what Nixon had to say and said that if he (Nixon) was a Republican, then so was he (Schwarzenegger). Until after the turn of the century, however, Schwarzenegger's participation in political activities was quite limited. For example, he served on President George H. W. Bush's President's Council on Physical Fitness and Sports. He never, however, sought political office until 2003, when he announced that he was running for governor of California. That race was necessitated by a recall election against then-governor Gray Davis, who lost his seat in the election. Schwarzenegger was chosen to replace Davis, winning 48.58 percent of the vote compared to 31.47 percent for Democratic candidate Cruz Bustamante, and 13.41 percent for fellow Republican Tom McClintlock.

Schwarzenegger was reelected governor in 2006 with 55.9 percent of the vote, but declined to seek reelection in 2010. He announced instead that he was planning to return to his acting career, listing a number of scripts that he was then considering. That decision was put on hold in 2011 largely because of marital problems resulting from an affair that he had with the family housekeeper that had resulted in the birth of a child and divorce from his wife of 25 years, Maria. In 2012, he announced once more that he intended to begin acting again within a year.

The Taylor Hooton Foundation
P. O. Box 2104
Frisco, TX 75034-9998
Phone: (972) 403-7300
URL: http://taylorhooton.org/
E-mail: http://taylorhooton.org/contact-us/

The Taylor Hooton Foundation (THF) was founded in 2004 in honor of Taylor Hooton, who took his life on July 15, 2003, largely as the result of using anabolic steroids. The foundation is a 501(c)3 tax exempt organization that was created when Taylor's parents, relatives, and friends began to understand the profound effect that performance-enhancing drugs can have on the lives of individuals who use those substances. The foundation makes the point that such drugs are used not only by amateur and professional athletes but also by many men and women, boys and girls, who see the drugs as a way of improving their own self-image. For that reason, the foundation often refers to the drugs as appearance and performance enhancing drugs (APEDs). The foundation lists as its partners a number of sports organizations, including Major League Baseball, NFL, National Hockey League, National Baseball Hall of Fame, Minor League Baseball, National Athletic Trainers' Association, Canadian Football League, and New York Yankees baseball team.

THF lists six "core values" on its websites, including its commitment as a (1) family-based organization that (2) provides parents, coaches, and other adult influencers with knowledge and tools; and that honors (3) values, integrity, ethics (character), leadership, and respect; that help individuals (4) make the right choices with respect to healthy lifestyle; and that is, itself, (5) a good steward of funds; and that functions as (6) volunteer-oriented organization.

The THF website has three major components, one each designed for students, parents, and coaches. Each of these three segments of the foundation's program involves providing a detailed and accurate information on steroids, the risks posed by steroid use, the signs of steroid abuse, and nature and risks posed by dietary supplements, a glossary of terms, and an "expert's corner" through which one can obtain answers to specific questions. The foundation also promotes a concept of "Get Set" attitude toward avoiding steroid use, in which the term "set" stands for the three major components of a healthy lifestyle, healthy Sleep, healthy Eating, and healthy Training.

The Taylor Hooton Foundation is also very active in providing educational programs for students, adults, and coaches about AAS. For example, it offers two coaches courses 101 and 501 that deal, respectively, with an overview of topics related to the use of appearance and performance-enhancing drugs, and an advanced course on the same topic. On new online course called the Chalk Talk E-Learning Program goes even deeper into the topic of APEDs, including knowing the signs of steroid use and understanding methods for dealing with such problems in a sports and athletics setting.

The foundation also offers face-to-face multimedia instructional programs that have been presented thus far to more than 400,000 individuals in the United States, Canada, and Latin America. Audiences for such programs have included high schools, middle schools, colleges and universities, law enforcement personnel, parents groups, educators and coaches, and physicians and athletic trainers. These presentations may be accompanied by classroom presentations that are tied to the larger programs and provide for more intimate interaction between presenters and audience. The THF programs have been approved for continuing education credits for teachers, coaches, and counselors in Texas and Ohio and by the Texas Commission on Law Enforcement for law enforcement personnel.

Beginning in 2010, the foundation has given Taylor's Award to individuals who have made important contributions in educating students, parents, and coaches about the risks associated with AAS use. The first award in 2010 went to Major League Baseball commissioner Bud Selig, and in 2011, to University of Waterloo football coach Bob Copeland.

The Taylor Hooton Foundation also publishes a quarterly newsletter that carries additional information about its program and events. Subscribers can sign up for the newsletter on the foundation's website at http://taylorhooton.org/newsletter/.

United States Anti-Doping Agency
5555 Tech Center Dr., Suite 200
Colorado Springs, CO 80919-2372
Phone: (719) 785-2000
Toll free: (866) 601-2632
Fax: (719) 785-2001
Drug Reference Line: (800) 233-0393
URL: http://www.usantidoping.org/
E-mail: media@usada.org

Until the end of the 20th century, issues relating to the use of illegal substances among Olympic Games athletes from the United States were handled by the USOC itself, as one of its many responsibilities. During that time, a number of questions were raised both within the United States and in other parts of the world as to the effectiveness of the USOC in carrying out its drug testing program. As a result, on June 15, 1999, USOC president William J. Hybl appointed a Select Task Force on Drug Externalization, to determine if there was an alternative way of approaching drug abuse problems among U.S. athletes. That committee issued its report in December of the same year, recommending the creation of an entirely new agency, separate and distinct from the USOC, for the purpose of administering such a drug testing program. The United States Anti-Doping Agency (USADA) was established as a result of that recommendation. The USADA began operations on October 1, 2000. A year later, the U.S. Congress adopted legislation that officially recognized the USADA as "the official anti-doping agency for Olympic, Pan American and Paralympic sport in the United States" (now Public Law 107–67, section 644). The USADA is now the official antidoping agency for virtually all amateur athletics organizations in the United States, ranging from the American Archery Association, American Badminton Association, and American Canoe Association to the USA Swimming, USA Track & Field, and USA Wrestling.

The USADA's mission statement focuses on three primary objectives, the first of which is maintaining the integrity of athletics and sports by preventing and deterring the types of activities (such as illegal drug use) that violate the principles of true sports. A second and related objective is working to instill the principles of fair play among all athletes. Finally, the mission statement recognizes the rights of individual athletes to participate in fair competitions and, with success, to be "recognized as true heroes."

The focus of USADA's efforts largely mirrors those of the WADA, whose code of prohibited substances and methods of testing and test interpretation they follow closely. The USADA website provides detailed information about the way in which athletes are sampled for drug use, the types of tests conducted, the substances for which they are tested, the way in which test results are interpreted and announced, and the penalties issued in connection with the use of prohibited substances. The USADA also places special emphasis in drug testing on topics such as the therapeutic use of certain otherwise prohibited substances, the role of nutritional supplements in athletics and sport competitions, and the use of specialized energy drinks in sports and their possible connection with drug testing. An important additional activity of the USADA involves research on prohibited substances and drug testing programs. During the first decade of the 21st century, the agency budgeted an average of $2 million annually for research on these topics. It has also cooperated with professional sports agencies, such as Major League Baseball and the NFL, to promote additional research on prohibited substances and testing. In connection with these activities, the USADA annually sponsors the USADA Symposium on Anti-Doping Science, at which researchers present papers on their most recent studies on drug abuse in sports.

The USADA also conducts an active and extensive program of education about drug abuse in athletics and sports. That program includes print and electronic resources for athletes, parents, coaches, and others concerned about the use of illegal substances in sports. These materials include an Athlete Handbook, a comprehensive general resource on drugs and drug testing in athletics; the Athlete Pocket Guide, an abbreviate form of the Handbook; copies of the *USADA Protocol for Olympic and Paralympic Movement Testing, United States Olympic Committee Anti-Doping Policies, World Anti-Doping Agency (WADA) Code, USADA Whereabouts Policy*, and other WADA publications; *The Joy of Sports*, a general introduction to the subject of drugs and drug testing; *Journey–Struggling with Ethics in Sports*; the *USADA Outreach Education Brochure*; *What Sports Means in America*; and two educational curricula for 10–14- and 14–20-year-olds.

The USADA also provides extensive information to athletes themselves to educate them about the problems of illegal drug use and about drug testing. This outreach program includes information about forthcoming Olympic events, the WADA "Whereabouts" policy, exemptions for therapeutic uses of certain drugs, the Global Drugs Reference Online resource, retirement from sports, and athlete webinars. Some typical offerings in this category include webinars on athletes in the registered testing pool, athletes who are not in such a pool, the Florida

Road Cycling Association race series, and a program for masters track and field athletes. The USADA website also provides useful link to other organizations interested in the issue of drug abuse in athletics and sports, such as the Foundation for Global Sports Development, Steroid Analysis, the Taylor Hooton Foundation, Bike Pure, and P. E. Central.

World Anti-Doping Agency
Stock Exchange Tower
800 Place Victoria, Suite 1700
Montreal H4Z 1B7
Québec
Canada
Phone: +1 514 904 9232
Fax: +1 514 904 8650
URL: http://www.wada-ama.org/en/
E-mail: media@wada-ama.org

The World Anti-Doping Agency (WADA; in French: Agence mondiale antidopage) was established in 1999 in response to growing international concerns about the use of illegal substances by athletes participating in the Olympic Games. Evidence collected in preceding years had made it clear that drug use was out of control, not only in the Olympic Games, but also in a number of other amateur and professional sports. The event that precipitated the creation of the agency was a police raid conducted in 1998 by French police during the annual Tour de France cycling race in which very large quantities of illegal drugs were discovered among competitors and at competition sites. This event motivated the IOC to call a special conference in Lausanne, Switzerland, in February 1999 to discuss the problem of illegal substance abuse in sports. That conference eventually adopted a document establishing the WADA, to be funded by the IOC. The Declaration of Lausanne stated eight major objectives of the new agency, among them being "to promote and coordinate at international level the fight against doping in sport in all its forms including through in and out-of-competition"; "to reinforce at international level ethical principles for the practice of doping-free sport and to help protect the health of the athletes"; and "to promote and coordinate research in the fight against doping in sport." The document also called for the new agency to develop a list of substances prohibited for use in international athletic competitions, to create standards for drug testing, and to develop programs for drug education and treatment. The WADA was originally funded entirely by the IOC, although its funding now comes from both the IOC and a number of governmental agencies around the world.

The World Anti-Doping Program, developed and promulgated by the WADA, consists of three major elements: the World Anti-Doping Code; International Standards; and Model Rules, Guidelines, and Protocol. The World Anti-Doping Code was first adopted in 2004 prior to the opening of the 2004 Olympic Games in Athens. The code is a very long document that consists of sections dealing with a description of the actions that constitute a violation of the code; standards of proof for use of a illegal substance; a list of prohibited substances; methods of testing and analysis of samples; results management; rights to fair hearings and appeal processes; sanctions on individuals convicted of illegal substance use; rules of confidentiality; regulations for the doping of animals in sports competitions; programs for education and research; responsibilities of governmental and organizing agencies; and relevant definitions. Based on the first use of the code in the 2004 Games, the IOC authorized a review and revision of the code in 2007. Those revisions went into effect in 2009, and, as of late 2012, more than 600 governmental agencies had adopted the code for its own sports programs.

An essential key to the activities of WADA is the Prohibited List, a document that lists all substances that may not be used in athletic competition, along with certain prohibited methods, such as enhancement of oxygen transfer, gene doping, and various types of physical and chemical manipulation. Prohibited substances are subdivided into five major categories: anabolic agents; peptide hormones, growth factors and related substances; beta-2 agonists; hormone and metabolic modulators; and diuretics and other masking agents. The substances listed as prohibited are further subdivided into those that are prohibited during competitions and those that are prohibited both in an out of competition. The most recent edition of the Prohibited List is available online at http://www.wada-ama.org/Documents/World_Anti-Doping_Program/WADP-Prohibited-list/2012/WADA_Prohibited_List_2012_EN.pdf.

The WADA International Standards program consists of five documents to provide detailed information on topics described and discussed in the Anti-Doping Code: the prohibited list, methods of testing, testing laboratories, therapeutic use exemptions, and protection of privacy and personal information. The WADA Model Rules document translates general principles contained in the antidoping code and other documents into practical steps that national sport agencies can take to translate those principles into specific testing and interpretation activities. The WADA guidelines project consists of a number of specific documents dealing with topics such as blood sampling, alcohol testing, detection of doping with hGH, education program, laboratory testing results, and report and managing of specific testing results. The WADA protocol documents explain and clarify testing responsibilities among various antidoping organizations and agencies.

Antidoping testing is a complex and often controversial process that can have profound effects on international competitions. For example, the winners of two recent Tour de France competitions have been disqualified and stripped of their titles because of illegal substance use. In order to manage the testing process most efficiently, WADA has created a program known as the Anti-Doping Administration & Management System (ADAMS). ADAMS is an online program that permits all stakeholders in the testing process to keep track of every detail involved in the testing of athletes in a major competition (http://www.wada-ama.org/en/ADAMS/How-to-implement-ADAMS/).

In addition to its extensive online resources and references, WADA provides a host of other publications and materials, including a corporate press kit, doping control forms, an outreach model, global statistics, a digit library, and a list of participating federations and organizations. Among its print publications are an annual report, the "at-a-glance" series on specific doping issues, an athlete guide, a leaflet on the dangers of doping, the doping code, and *Play True* magazine, available in both print and electronic versions.

John Ziegler (ca. 1920–1983)

Ziegler was an American physician best known for introducing the use of anabolic steroids for performance enhancement to the United States in the 1950s. In 1954, he had traveled to Vienna as an advisor to the U.S. weightlifting team at the World Weightlifting Championships. The story is told that Ziegler shared drinks one evening with a member of the Russian team who asked him "What are you giving your boys," by way of inquiring about U.S. training practices. When Ziegler asked the same question of his Russian counterpart, he learned for the first time that those team members were receiving injections of testosterone. It was these injections that were responsible for the amazing increase in body mass and strength that Russian athletes were demonstrating at the time, not only at the weightlifting competition, but in other international events, such as the Olympic Games of 1956. Ziegler left Vienna convinced that he needed to try some comparable training regimen for members of the U.S. weightlifting community. He experimented by injecting himself, an American trainer named Bob Hoffman, and three team weight lifters with small amounts of testosterone. He was amazed at the success of the treatment in producing increased muscle mass and strength, but was troubled by the androgenic effects that were associated with the testosterone treatments. He made up his mind to search out or develop a new substance that had the muscle-building properties of testosterone, with the substance's undesirable side effects.

Ziegler's interest in anabolic steroids came about just as Ciba Pharmaceuticals was developing a drug along the lines of the product he was looking for. That drug, methandrostenolone (trade names: Averbol, Danabol, and Dianabol), was developed for the treatment of wasting in patients suffering from debilitating diseases and individuals suffering from severe burns. It proved to be hugely successful in helping such individuals regain body mass and strength. Ziegler immediately recognized the potential of the chemical for building body mass and strength in weight lifters and, perhaps, other athletes. He began to make the drug available to members of the weightlifting team and other athletes who asked for it. The problem was that the drug was so successful, that many of those to whom he gave it began using it in massive quantities, up to 10 times the amount he had recommended.

Over the years, Dianabol became increasingly popular as an anabolic steroid, and Ziegler became increasingly disillusioned about the misuse to which his clients made of the drug. By the beginning of the 1970s, he had essentially washed his hands of steroid use by athletics. In a 1972 interview with *Science* reporter Nicholas Wade, he said that he had "lost interest in fooling with IQ's of that caliber. Now it's [steroid use] about as widespread among these idiots as marijuana." In another interview for the *Journal of Sports History*, he added that "I wish to God now I'd never done it. I'd like to go back and take that whole chapter out of my life."

Birth data for John Bosley Ziegler are not generally available, and his birth information is given as sometime around 1920 somewhere in the Middle West. He entered the premedical program at Gettysburg College in 1938, graduating with his bachelor's degree four years later. Instead of immediately continuing his studies, he joined the U.S. Marine Corps and fought in the Pacific Zone for the rest of the war. During his time there, he suffered serious battle wounds that required extensive restorative surgeries when he returned home. After recovering from those surgeries, he enrolled at the University of Maryland Medical School, from which he earned his MD. He completed his residency and internship at Marine Corps hospitals in Norfolk, Virginia, and Mobile, Alabama, continuing with a two-year residency in neurology at the Tulane University School of Medicine. At the time, he had hoped to become a brain surgeon, but found that he did not have the manual skills for the specialty. Instead, he returned to Olney, Maryland, in 1954, where he opened a private practice specializing in the treatment of handicapped and severely injured patients and carrying out research at the nearby Ciba facility.

After he became disenchanted with his experience with anabolic steroids, Ziegler settled into the routine of general practice in Olney, where he remained until his death from heart failure in November 1983. Reminiscences of his life focus on his "restless, imaginative intellect" that prompted him to study everything from "nuclear medicine to hypnosis." As a way of pursuing this range of interests, he held a weekly salon at his home to which were invited an astonishing array of guests, ranging from "White House staffers to Marine generals and astrophysicists" (as mentioned by Shaun Assael in *Steroid Nation* [ESPN Books, 2007]). For many in the athletic and sports field, Ziegler will always be remembered as "Doctor Dianabol." To others who knew other sides of him, he will also be remembered as "Doc Ziegler," or, more simply, "Montana Jack" or "Tex," because of his tendency to dress up as a Westerner and his reputation as a "hell-raiser" around Olney.

This chapter provides some relevant data and documents dealing with the development of anabolic androgenic steroids (AAS), their use in medical and nonmedical settings, and regulations and court cases involving AAS. The Data section provides basic information on current and historical trends in AAS use and arrests in the United States and other parts of the world. The Documents section which follows is arranged in chronological order and includes excerpts from important committee and commission reports; from bills, acts, and laws; and from important legal cases.

Data

The World Anti-Doping Agency (WADA) annually collects data from all organizations that are members of the organization on the number of individuals for whom adverse drug testing were obtained and how many were found guilty of violating WADA drug regulations. Table 5.1 summarizes these data for 2010.

The U.S. Centers for Disease Control and Prevention conducts occasional surveys on a variety of risky behaviors in which American children and adolescents may become involved.

Without clear data on the levels of steroid abuse in youth sports, some activists think more states should follow the lead of New Jersey, which in 2007 became the first state to adopt a program of mandatory testing for high school athletes. (Dreamstime)

Table 5.1   2010 Anti-Doping Organization Activity Summary, as Reported by Code Signatory Anti-Doping Organizations

Anti-Doping Organization (International Federations)	Total Adverse Analytical Findings	Total Anti-Doping Rule Violations
International Federation American Football	0	0
Badminton World Federation	1	1
International Biathalon Federation	not provided	not provided
World Chess Federation	0	0
International Cricket Council	0	0
World Curling Federation	0	1
World Dancesport Federation	1	3
International Floorball Federation	3	3
International Go Association	0	0
International Golf Federation	1	0
Fédération Internationale de Gymnastique	2	5
International Handball Federation	0	0
International Hockey Federation	0	0
International Korfball Federation	0	0
International Luge Federation	0	0
Fédération Internationale de Natation	4	10
International Orienteering Federation	1	0
International Paralympic Committee	6	6
Federation of International Polo	0	0
International Powerboating Federation	0	0
International Powerlifting Federation	25	24
International Federation of Rowing Associations	0	0
International Rugby Board	9	5
International Sailing Federation (ISAF)	not provided	not provided
International Savate Federation	0	0
International Federation of Sport Climbing	0	0
World Squash Federation	0	0
International Table Tennis Federation	0	12
World Taekwondo Federation	0	0
World Taekwondo Federation	0	0
International Triathlon Union	23	2
Tug of War International Federation	0	1
World Underwater Federation	8	0
International Volleyball Federation	1	0
International Federation of Associated Wrestling Styles	15	12

Table 5.1 *(Continued)*

Anti-Doping Organization (National Anti-Doping Agencies)	Total Adverse Analytical Findings	Total Anti-Doping Rule Violations
Comité Olympique Algérien	1	0
Armenian National Anti-Doping Organization	0	0
Australian Sports Anti-Doping Authority	44	32
Nationale Anti-Doping Agentur Austria GmbH	17	27
National Anti-Doping Agency of Belarus	3	4
NADO Flanders	91	112
ONAD Communauté française de Belgique	50	25
Ministère de la Communauté germanophone de Belgique	0	0
Bermuda Sports Anti-Doping Authority	2	1
Bosnia and Herzegovina Anti-Doping Agency	0	0
Republic of Bulgaria Anti-Doping Centre	0	0
Canadian Centre for Ethics in Sport	30	26
Organisation Camerounaise de lutte contre le dopage dans le sport	0	0
Comision Nacional de Control de Dopaje Chile	2	2
China Anti-Doping Agency	43	35
Croatian Institute for Toxicology and Anti-Doping	8	9
Organo Nacional Antidopaje de la República de Cuba	1	1
Czech Anti-Doping Committee	18	20
Anti-Doping Denmark	19	19
Comité Olímpico Ecuatoriano	3	3
Egyptian Anti-Doping Organization	15	14
Estonian Anti-Doping Agency	4	3
Finnish Anti-Doping Agency	15	12
Agence française de lutte contre le dopage	217	238
Georgian Anti-Doping Agency	0	0
National Anti-Doping Agency of Germany	54	34
Hong Kong Anti-Doping Committee	6	7
Irish Sports Council	6	3
Italian Olympic Committee	55	119
Japan Anti-Doping Agency	6	5
Jordan Anti-Doping Organization	0	0
Korea Anti-Doping Agency	37	36
Kuwait Anti-Doping Committee	0	0
Agence Luxembourgeoise Antidopage	1	0
Anti-Doping Unit Ministry Youth and Sports—Mauritius	0	0
Nepal Olympic Committee	0	0
Anti-Doping Authority the Netherlands	83	23

(Continued)

Table 5.1 *(Continued)*

Anti-Doping Organization (National Anti-Doping Agencies)	Total Adverse Analytical Findings	Total Anti-Doping Rule Violations
Anti-Doping Norway	34	17
Anti-Doping Organization Pakistan	16	16
Autoridade Antidopagem de Portugal	53	59
Puerto Rico Anti-Doping Organization	1	1
Qatar Anti-Doping Commission	7	7
Romanian National Anti-Doping Agency	25	31
Russian Anti-Doping Agency	101	91
Saudi Arabian Anti-Doping Committee	14	2
Anti-Doping Agency of Serbia	17	18
Anti-Doping Singapore	0	0
Health and Doping Control and Supervision Committee	96	61
Swedish Sports Confederation	153	38
Anti-Doping Switzerland	not provided	11
Suriname Anti-Doping Autoriteit	0	0
Sports Authority of Thailand	29	27
Agence Nationale Antidopage Tunisie	6	10
UK Anti-Doping	21	24
US Anti-Doping Agency	56	23
Departamento Control Dopaje (Uruguay)	25	19
African RADO Zone IV	0	0

Anti-Doping Organization (Others)	Total Adverse Analytical Findings	Total Anti-Doping Rule Violations
SportAccord	2	not provided
Commonwealth Games Federation	11	6

*NOTE: The Adverse Analytical Findings (AAF) in this report are not to be confused with adjudicated or sanctioned Anti-Doping Rule Violations (ADRV). "Adverse Analytical Finding" is defined in the World Anti-Doping Code as "a report from a laboratory or other WADA-approved entity that, consistent with the International Standard for Laboratories and related Technical Documents, identifies in a Sample the presence of a Prohibited Substance or its Metabolites or Markers (including elevated quantities of endogenous substances) or evidence of the Use of a Prohibited Method." These figures may not be identical to Anti-Doping Rule Violations, as the figures given in this report may contain findings that underwent the Therapeutic Use Exemption (TUE) approval process. In addition, some Adverse Analytical Findings may correspond to multiple measurements performed on the same Athlete, such as in cases of longitudinal studies on testosterone, and some cases may be pending before the appropriate jurisdictions. Anti-Doping Rule Violations listed above may also include violations unrelated to AAFs (e.g., Refusals).

Source: World Anti-Doping Agency. 2010. *Anti-Doping Organization Activity Summary.* http://www.wada-ama.org/Documents/Resources/Statistics/ADO_Statistics/WADA_2010_ADO_Statistics_Report.pdf. Accessed on June 1, 2012.

The most recent such survey was published in 2010. Table 5.2 summarizes general characteristics of youth who used steroids illegally.

Table 5.3 provides data on steroid use by young adults by state and by certain localities.

Table 5.4 illustrates trends in the use of illegal steroids by high school-age boys and girls between 1993 and 2009.

Data on the use of anabolic steroids is readily available on an annual basis from the Monitoring the Future Study commissioned by the National Institute on Drug Abuse (NIDA). Similar data for adults are rare. One of the most complete such studies was conducted by the National Household Survey on Drug Abuse conducted also on a regular basis by the Substance Abuse and Mental Health Services

Table 5.2   Percentage of High School Students Who Took Steroids[1] by Sex, Race/Ethnicity, and Grade—United States, Youth Risk Behavior Survey, 2009

	Ever Took Steroids Without a Doctor's Prescription					
	Female		Male		Total	
Category	%	CI[2]	%	CI	%	CI
Race/Ethnicity						
White[3]	2.1	1.5–2.9	3.9	3.0–5.2	3.1	2.5–3.8
Black[3]	0.9	0.5–1.6	4.6	3.1–6.9	2.8	1.9–4.1
Hispanic	3.2	2.3–4.4	4.6	3.3–6.3	3.9	3.1–4.8
Grade						
9	2.3	1.7–3.0	4.0	2.9–5.3	3.2	2.7–3.8
10	2.3	1.6–3.2	4.3	3.1–5.8	3.4	2.7–4.2
11	2.5	1.7–3.6	4.4	3.3–5.7	3.4	2.8–4.2
12	1.6	0.9–2.7	4.6	3.3–6.3	3.1	2.3–4.1
Total	2.2	1.8–2.7	4.3	3.5–5.2	3.3	2.9–3.8

[1] Took steroid pills or shots without a doctor's prescription one or more times during their life.
[2] 95% confidence interval.
[3] Non-Hispanic

Source: Eaton, Danice K., et al. 2010. "Youth Risk Behavior Surveillance—United States, 2009." *MMWR.* 59(SS-5): whole, Table 48. (Injected drug data omitted.) Available online at http://www.cdc.gov/mmwr/pdf/ss/ss5905.pdf. Accessed on June 2, 2012.

Table 5.3   Percentage of High School Students Who Took Steroids[1] by Sex—Selected U.S. Sites, Youth Risk Behavior Survey, 2009

| | Ever Took Steroids Without a Doctor's Prescription | | | | | |
| | Female | | Male | | Total | |
Site	%	CI[2]	%	CI	%	CI
State surveys						
Alabama	3.3	1.9–5.8	7.5	5.3–10.7	5.6	3.9–8.1
Alaska	[3]		2.0	1.1–3.5	2.1	1.2–3.8
Arizona	3.4	2.2–5.4	4.5	3.0–6.6	4.2	3.2–5.5
Arkansas	3.5	2.1–5.8	9.3	6.4–13.3	6.4	4.6–8.9
Colorado	2.9	1.8–4.7	4.3	2.8–6.4	3.6	2.6–5.0
Connecticut	1.1	0.5–2.3	4.2	2.8–6.3	2.7	2.0–3.7
Delaware	2.3	1.6–3.4	4.6	3.2–6.4	3.7	2.9–4.7
Florida	2.3	1.8–2.8	5.4	4.6–6.5	3.9	3.4–4.5
Georgia	2.0	1.0–3.9	6.9	5.2–9.1	4.5	3.2–6.3
Hawaii	2.5	1.1–5.3	4.8	2.5–9.0	3.8	2.2–6.5
Idaho	2.4	1.6–3.8	3.2	2.1–4.9	2.9	2.0–4.1
Illinois	1.5	0.9–2.5	4.1	3.1–5.3	3.0	2.2–3.9
Indiana	3.0	1.7–5.2	3.5	2.2–5.4	3.2	2.4–4.4
Kansas	1.8	1.1–3.0	4.9	3.4–7.0	3.4	2.5–4.7
Kentucky	2.2	1.3–3.7	5.8	3.7–9.0	4.0	2.7–6.0
Louisiana	3.8	2.6–5.7	10.5	7.2–15.1	7.2	5.0–10.2
Maine	[3]		3.4	2.9–4.0	6.1	5.4–6.8
Maryland	1.9	1.2–3.2	5.2	3.9–6.9	3.9	3.2–4.7
Massachusetts	1.7	1.0–2.8	4.9	3.5–6.8	3.3	2.4–4.5
Michigan	2.0	1.2–3.4	5.7	4.5–7.2	4.1	3.4–4.9
Mississippi	2.9	2.0–4.3	3.7	2.4–5.6	3.3	2.5–4.5
Missouri	2.4	1.6–3.7	3.6	1.9–6.7	3.1	1.9–4.9
Montana	2.5	0.8–7.5	5.0	2.7–9.3	3.9	1.8–8.1
Nevada	3.1	2.1–4.5	4.3	2.9–6.4	3.7	2.8–4.9
New Hampshire	1.4	0.7–2.8	2.6	1.7–4.1	2.1	1.4–3.1
New Jersey	1.2	0.7–2.2	5.3	3.4–8.0	3.3	2.3–4.8
New Mexico	[3]		3.3	2.5–4.4	5.3	3.6–7.9
New York	[3]		2.4	1.5–3.8	5.0	3.5–7.0
North Carolina	2.3	1.4–3.8	5.3	3.6–7.6	3.8	2.7–5.4
North Dakota	[3]		1.6	0.7–3.5	2.7	1.3–5.4
Oklahoma	5.0	3.3–7.4	5.7	3.6–8.7	5.3	3.8–7.5
Pennsylvania	2.2	1.5–3.3	3.5	2.2–5.6	3.0	2.1–4.2
Rhode Island	1.7	1.0–2.9	3.4	2.2–5.4	2.6	2.0–3.4
South Carolina	2.1	0.9–4.7	4.4	2.7–7.0	3.4	2.2–5.1
South Dakota	1.0	0.4–2.3	3.0	2.1–4.4	2.1	1.4–3.0
Tennessee	2.4	1.5–3.7	4.4	3.2–6.0	3.4	2.6–4.4

Table 5.3   (Continued)

Site	Ever Took Steroids Without a Doctor's Prescription					
	Female		Male		Total	
	%	CI[2]	%	CI	%	CI
Texas	2.3	1.6–3.2	3.5	2.7–4.6	2.9	2.3–3.7
Utah	2.6	1.4–4.6	5.3	3.5–7.9	4.3	3.2–5.9
Vermont	1.1	0.9–1.4	2.9	2.4–3.5	2.2	1.8–2.5
West Virginia	4.1	2.4–7.0	7.4	5.7–9.5	6.0	4.8–7.6
Wisconsin	[3]		[3]		[3]	
Wyoming	3.9	3.0–5.2	6.6	5.4–8.1	5.3	4.5–6.3
Median	2.3		4.7		3.6	
Range		1.0–5.0		2.6–10.5		2.1–7.2
Local surveys						
Boston, MA	1.6	0.6–4.1	4.3	2.6–7.1	3.0	1.9–4.9
Broward County, FL	3.3	1.9–5.6	5.1	3.3–7.8	4.2	2.8–6.1
Charlotte-Mecklenburg, NC	1.2	0.7–2.3	3.4	2.1–5.4	2.3	1.6–3.5
Chicago, IL	1.9	0.7–4.8	6.8	3.7–12.1	5.0	3.1–8.0
Clark County, NV	2.9	1.8–4.7	4.5	2.6–7.6	3.7	2.5–5.4
Dallas, TX	2.3	1.2–4.5	4.0	2.5–6.5	3.2	2.1–4.8
Detroit, MI	3.9	2.5–5.9	7.5	5.2–10.7	5.8	4.0–8.2
Duval County, FL	3.7	2.5–5.2	10.2	7.8–13.2	7.3	5.8–9.3
Los Angeles, CA	2.7	1.5–4.8	4.1	2.1–7.8	3.5	2.3–5.2
Memphis, TN	2.0	1.1–3.9	3.3	2.0–5.3	2.6	1.8–3.8
Miami-Dade County, FL	2.0	1.2–3.4	5.5	4.0–7.5	3.8	2.9–5.0
New York City, NY	[3]					
Orange County, FL	3.3	2.1–5.3	2.9	1.8–4.8	3.1	2.2–4.4
Palm Beach County, FL	2.0	1.2–3.1	3.8	2.6–5.5	3.0	2.2–4.0
Philadelphia, PA	1.7	0.8–3.4	4.9	3.0–7.9	3.5	2.5–4.9
San Bernardino, CA	1.7	0.9–3.2	3.7	2.4–5.6	2.7	1.9–3.9
San Diego, CA	2.6	1.9–3.7	2.8	1.8–4.2	2.7	2.0–3.7
San Francisco, CA	2.4	1.4–4.0	3.4	2.5–4.8	3.2	2.4–4.2
Seattle, WA	2.7	1.9–4.0	4.0	2.7–5.9	3.8	2.9–5.1
Median	2.3		4.0		3.3	
Range		1.2–3.9		2.8–10.2		2.3–7.3

[1] Took steroid pills without a doctor's prescription one or more times during their life.
[2] 95% confidence interval.
[3] Not available.

Source: Eaton, Danice K., et al. 2010. "Youth Risk Behavior Surveillance—United States, 2009." MMWR. 59(SS-5): whole, Table 49. (Injected drug data omitted.) Available online at http://www.cdc.gov/mmwr/pdf/ss/ss5905.pdf. Accessed on June 2, 2012.

Table 5.4 Percentage of High School Students Who Used Selected Other Illicit Drugs by Sex, Race/Ethnicity, and Grade, Youth Risk Behavior Survey, 1991–2009

Drug Use Behavior and Year	Sex		Race/Ethnicity			Grade Level				All Groups
			Non-Hispanic							
	Male	Female	White	Black	Hispanic	9	10	11	12	
Lifetime Use of Illegal Steroids										
1993	3.1	1.2	1.9	2.4	3.0	2.1	2.0	2.2	2.3	2.2
1995	4.9	2.4	3.8	1.6	4.7	4.1	3.6	3.9	2.9	3.7
1997	4.1	2.0	3/1	1/5	3.4	4.3	3.0	2.7	2.5	3.1
1999	5.2	2.2	4.1	2.2	4.1	4.7	3.6	3.0	3.3	3.7
2001	6.0	3.9	5.3	3.2	4.2	5.8	4.9	4.3	4.3	5.0
2003	6.8	5.3	6.2	3.6	7.2	7.1	6.1	5.6	4.9	6.1
2005	4.8	3.2	4.2	2.4	3.9	4.8	3.9	3.7	3.3	4.0
2007	5.1	2.7	4.1	2.2	4.6	4.8	3.7	3.1	3.8	3.9
2009	4.3	2.2	3.1	2.8	3.9	3.2	3.4	3.4	3.1	3.3

Source: National Drug Control Strategy: Data Supplement 2011. Washington, D.C.: Office of National Drug Control Policy. [n.d.], Table 13, page 33. http://www.whitehouse.gov/sites/default/files/ondcp/policy-and-research/2011_data_supplement.pdf. Accessed on June 2, 2012.

Administration (SAMHSA) in 1994. Table 5.5 shows the main findings of that study, which included responses from 4,372 individuals.

Table 5.5 Adult Use of Anabolic Steroids, 1994

Ever Used Anabolic Steroids

Yes: 20 (0.5%)   No: 4532 (99.5%)

Used 3 or more years ago: 12 (0.3%)

Used 1 or more years ago, but less than 3 years ago: 6 (0.1%)

Used 6 or more months ago, but less than 1 year ago: 2 (0.0%)

Number of times used by injection: 6 (0.1%)

Age of first use of anabolic steroids:

10: 1	11: 2	12: 1	13: 1	14: 1
15: 2	16: 1	17: 1	18: 1	19: 2
24: 1	25: 1	27: 1	32: 1	

Missing or bad data, refused, or other non-response: 4355

Age of first opportunity to try anabolic steroids:

9: 1	10: 2	11: 3	12: 4	13: 7
14: 12	15: 13	16: 23	17: 20	18: 11
19: 6	20: 8	21: 6	22: 2	23: 1
24: 2	25: 3	26: 2	27: 1	29: 3
30: 1	32: 1	36: 1		

Missing or bad data, refused, or other non-response: 4237

Perceived Risk of Using Anabolic Steroids

Great risk: 2658 (60.8%)

Moderate risk: 1165 (26.6%)

Slight risk: 365 (8.6%)

No risk: 116 (2.7%)

Don't know: 26 (0.6%)

Multiple answers: 2 (0.0%)

No response: 30 (0.7%)

Perceived Risk of *Regularly* Using Anabolic Steroids

Great risk: 3609 (82.5%)

Moderate risk: 519 (11.9%)

Slight risk: 96 (2.2%)

No risk: 88 (2.0%)

Don't know: 29 (0.7%)

Multiple answers: 1 (0.0%)

No response: 30 (0.7%)

Source: National Household Survey on Drug Abuse, 1994. Steroid Use. http://www.icpsr.umich.edu/icpsrweb/SAMHDA/ssvd/studies/06949/variables?q=steroids&dataset=Part+A&paging.startRow=1. Accessed on June 26, 2012.

Documents

Drug Misuse: Anabolic Steroids and Human Growth Hormone (1989)

In 1989, the General Accounting Office conducted a study, at the request of Senator Joseph Biden (D-DE) on the use of anabolic steroids by amateur and professional athletes in the United States. The GAO study reported not only on the statistics of AAS use but also on the health effects related to the use of such substances. The major statistical findings reported were as follows:

A national-based study found that 6.6 percent of male 12th graders use or have used anabolic steroids. According to the authors of the study, if this use rate is applied to the national population of males enrolled in secondary schools, it suggests that between 250,000 and 500,000 adolescents in the country use or have used these drugs. In four other studies, while not nationally representative, a similar or higher rate of anabolic steroid use among males was found, with study estimates ranging from 5 percent to 11.1 percent. In three of the four studies, anabolic steroid use was found to be much lower among females, ranging from 1 percent to 2.5 percent.

. . .

The most frequent reasons cited for using steroids were (1) to increase strength, size, and speed and (2) to improve athletic performance. In the Arkansas study, 64 percent of steroid users reported that they wanted to increase strength, 50 percent wanted to increase size, and 27 percent wanted to improve physical appearance. In the national study of 12th graders, the largest percentage of users (47 percent) reported that their main reason for using the drug was to improve athletic performance. Another 27 percent of users reported "appearance" as the main reason for using anabolic steroids.

. . .

We identified only five studies on the extent of steroid use among college students. Two studies on general drug use in a representative sample of the general student body from five universities were carried out over a 15-year period, 1970–84. The first study reported results for 1970 and 1973; the second, for 1970, 1976, 1980, and 1984. In the general student body of the five schools, data for 1970 and 1973 showed that 0 to 2 percent of students had ever used steroids. When data from this study were examined for athletes only, 15 percent of athletes reported using anabolic steroids in 1970. This rate increased to 20 percent for 1976, 1980, and 1984. In 1984, only 1 percent of nonathletes in the study reported steroid use.

The third and fourth studies examined steroid use by sport. In the third study, which was conducted in 1980 and focused on intercollegiate swimmers at six universities, 6 percent of male swimmers reported steroid use. No female swimmers reported use. In the fourth study, involving 2,048 intercollegiate athletes conducted in the fall of 1984 at 11 universities, the national prevalence rate was found to be 4 percent for steroid use in athletes for eight different sports. The highest rate of use was found among male football players (9 percent), followed by male basketball, track, and tennis athletes (each 4 percent); 1 percent of female swimmers reported steroid use.

The fifth study, published in 1988, provided information on 1,010 male students at three universities. Results from this study also support a higher rate of steroid use among athletes than among nonathletes. Of varsity athletes at two of the three schools in the study, 17 percent reported steroid use. This rate is significantly higher than the 2 percent of all males who reported using steroids in the total survey sample of the three schools.

Source: United States General Accounting Office. August 1989. *Drug Misuse: Anabolic Steroids and Human Growth Hormone.* Washington, D.C.: United States General Accounting Office.

Anabolic Steroid Control Act of 1990

In 1990, the U.S. Congress passed and President George H. W. Bush signed a law adding anabolic steroids to the Controlled Substances Act. The main features of the act are as follows:
   Section 1 provides a short title for the act.

Sec. 2. Anabolic Steroid Penalties

(a) COACHES AND OTHERS PERSUADING OR INDUCING USE-Section 404 of the Controlled Substances Act (21 U.S.C. 844) is amended by inserting after subsection (a) the following:

'(b)(1) Whoever, being a physical trainer or adviser to an individual, endeavors to persuade or induce that individual to possess or use anabolic steroids in violation of subsection (a), shall be fined under title 18, United States Code, or imprisoned not more than 2 years, or both. If such individual has not attained the age of 18 years, the maximum imprisonment shall be 5 years.

'(2) As used in this subsection, the term 'physical trainer or adviser' means any professional or amateur coach, manager, trainer, instructor, or other such person, who provides any athletic or physical instruction, training, advice, assistance, or other such service to any person'.

(b) ADDITION OF ANABOLIC STEROIDS TO SCHEDULE III-Schedule III of section 202(c) of the Controlled Substances Act (21 U.S.C. 812(c)) is amended by adding at the end the following:

'(e) Anabolic steroids'.

(c) DEFINITION OF ANABOLIC STEROID-Section 102 of the Controlled Substances Act (21 U.S.C. 802) is amended by adding at the end the following:

'(41) The term 'anabolic steroid' means any drug or hormonal substance that promotes muscle growth in a manner pharmacologically similar to testosterone, and includes—

The act then names 23 specific chemicals and their derivatives to be considered as "anabolic steroids" under this act.

Sec. 3. Penalty for Distribution of Human Growth Hormone

Subsection (e) of section 303 of the Federal Food, Drug, and Cosmetic Act (21 U.S.C. 333) is amended—

(1) by striking 'anabolic steroid' each place it appears and inserting 'human growth hormone'; and

(2) by adding at the end the following:

'(3) As used in this subsection, the term 'human growth hormone' means somatrem, somatropin, or an analogue of either of them'.

Source: H.R.4658—Anabolic Steroids Control Act of 1990. The Library of Congress. Thomas. http://thomas.loc.gov/cgi-bin/query/z?c101:H.R.4658. Accessed on May 20, 2012.

H.R.3866—Anabolic Steroid Control Act of 2004

In 2004, the U.S. Congress passed and President George W. Bush signed a modification of the 1990 anabolic steroid legislation mentioned above. The primary change included in this legislation was the addition of more than 40 anabolic steroid chemicals to the list original from the original legislation. The law also had a few other minor sections, as indicated here.

Section 1 provides a short title for the act.

Sec. 2. Increased Penalties for Anabolic Steroid Offenses Near Sports Facilities

(a) IN GENERAL-Part D of the Controlled Substances Act is amended by adding at the end the following:

Anabolic Steroid Offenses Near Sports Facilities

'SEC. 424. (a) Whoever violates section 401(a)(1) or section 416 by manufacturing, distributing, or possessing with intent to distribute, an anabolic steroid near or at a sports facility is subject to twice the maximum term of imprisonment, maximum fine, and maximum term of supervised release otherwise provided by section 401 for that offense.

The term 'sports facility' is then defined.

Section 3 then directs the United States Sentencing Commission to consider appropriate sentences for individuals convicted of violating the provisions of this law.

Section 4 lists the new steroids to be included under Schedule III of the Controlled Substances Act.

Sec. 5. Reporting Requirement

Not later than 2 years after the date of the enactment of this Act, the Secretary of Health and Human Services, in consultation with the Attorney General, shall prepare and submit a report to the Judiciary Committee of the House and Senate, and to the Committee on Energy and Commerce of the House, evaluating the health risks associated with dietary supplements not scheduled under the amendments made by this Act which contain substances similar to those added to the list of controlled substances under those amendments. The report shall include recommendations on whether such substances should be regulated as anabolic steroids.

> **Source:** H.R.3866—Anabolic Steroid Control Act of 2004. U.S. Library of Congress. Thomas. http://thomas.loc.gov/ cgi-bin/query/D?c108:4:./temp/˜c108dl2hKY::. Accessed on May 20, 2012.

Anabolic Steroids Are Easily Purchased Without a Prescription and Present Significant Challenges to Law Enforcement Officials (2005)

In 2005, Representatives Henry Waxman (D-CA) and Tom Davis (R-VA) asked the U.S. Government Accountability Office (GAO) to collect information as to whether illegal anabolic steroids could be purchased in the United States, to identify the common sources of these drugs, and to discover the primary challenges posed in investigating, prosecuting, and deterring individuals involved in the

*illegal anabolic steroid business. The following are the primary find-
ings of GAO's research:*

Summary

Our investigators easily obtained anabolic steroids without a
prescription through the Internet. After conducting Internet
searches, they found hundreds of Web sites offering anabolic steroids commonly used by athletes and bodybuilders for sale. The
investigators then used an e-mail account in a fictitious name to
place 22 orders. From these orders, we received 10 shipments of
anabolic steroids; all were shipped from foreign countries. We
also received 4 shipments from within the United States but the
substances they contained, though marketed as anabolic steroids
or other "muscle building" products, were not anabolic steroids
according to the FDA. We are referring the evidence concerning
our purchases to DEA and to FDA for appropriate action.

The officials we spoke with told us that most anabolic steroids sold illegally in the United States come from abroad, and
that the Internet is the most widely used means of buying and
selling anabolic steroids illegally. They also reported that, because of the foreign origin of the steroids and the widespread
use of the Internet in steroid trafficking, extensive time and
resources are usually required to investigate and prosecute steroid cases. Further, the sheer volume of all types of imports
from abroad presents significant challenges in efforts to prevent
anabolic steroids from illegally entering the United States. Additionally, some officials noted the relatively low sentences that
result from application of the federal sentencing guidelines to
persons convicted of illegal steroid trafficking.

*[The GAO report then provided details about the ease with which
illegal anabolic steroids can be purchased in the United Sates, some
of which are reprinted here:]*

The 10 orders of anabolic steroids we received were obtained through Web sites that openly and boldly offer anabolic steroids for sale. Some of the Web sites offer a variety

of pharmaceutical drugs, while others sell anabolic steroids exclusively. They typically offer "private and confidential" sales of "discretely shipped" anabolic steroids that will "shape your body the way . . . you want it to look."

. . .

There is a readily available supply of steroids worldwide because, in most countries, anabolic steroids can be sold legally without a prescription. Thus, many foreign distributors do not violate the laws of their own country when they sell these substances to people in the United States. As a result, U.S. law enforcement agencies have difficulty in obtaining assistance from their foreign counterparts in investigations of such distributors.

Law enforcement officials also identified smuggling of anabolic steroids across international borders into the United States as an important part of the illegal distribution network and described how smugglers typically operate.

. . .

. . . the Internet is a primary vehicle for buying and selling anabolic steroids illegally. Internet Web sites, usually foreign based, advertise steroids for sale. Customers access these sites, inquire about purchases, and place orders. Sellers typically require advance payment through Western Union, PayPal, money orders, or credit cards. After receiving payment, sellers ship the steroids through international mail or an express carrier. . . .

The Internet also provides an easy means for sellers to market to young people. Moreover, according to some of the law enforcement officials we spoke to, sales of steroids and other synthetic drugs are used by some sellers as a "gateway" to sales of narcotics, such as cocaine. Typically, in such cases, the seller uses an initial series of steroid or designer drug transactions to gauge whether the buyer is a legitimate customer and is not an undercover law enforcement investigator. After the seller has gained assurances that the customer is legitimate through the initial steroid sales, narcotics are offered for sale.

To prosecute illegal steroid dealers, law enforcement officials must identify them and gather evidence of their trafficking activity. However, anabolic steroid dealers can capitalize on the anonymity afforded by the Internet to thwart efforts to identify them.

. . .

Law enforcement officials told us that although extensive time and resources are required to locate, charge, and convict criminal anabolic steroid dealers, the penalties under the Federal Sentencing Guidelines faced by persons convicted of such offenses do not reflect the seriousness of their crimes or provide adequate deterrence. Drug quantity is a principal factor in determining offense level and sentence for drug offenses under the sentencing guidelines . . . an offender responsible for selling 40,000 pills of a Schedule III substance other than an anabolic steroid, such as ketamine, would face a sentence of 33 to 41 months under the drug quantity rules of the sentencing guidelines. On the other hand, an offender convicted of selling 40,000 pills of an anabolic steroid would face a sentence of 0 to 6 months under those rules.

Source: United States Government Accountability Office. "GAO-06-243R Anabolic Steroids." http://www.gao.gov/new.items/d06243r.pdf. Accessed on June 3, 2012.

Clean Sports Act of 2005

For almost two decades, the U.S. Congress has been concerned about the use of anabolic and androgenic steroids by professional athletes. Individually and collectively, members of Congress have prodded professional baseball, football, basketball, and hockey leagues to "get their act together" and develop effective antidoping policies. When these entities have been slow to do so, Congress has threatened federal action against the leagues to enforce stronger drug testing policies. One such effort was the Clean Sports Act of 2005, sponsored by Senators John McCain and Ted Stevens in the Senate and Congressmen Tom Davis and Henry Waxman in the House. The following is Senator McCain's description of the act (which was introduced into the Congress, but was never passed).

The purpose of this bill is to protect the integrity of professional sports and, more importantly, the health and safety of our Nation's youth, who, for better or for worse, see professional athletes as role models. The legislation would achieve that goal by establishing minimum standards for the testing of steroids and other performance-enhancing substances by major professional sports leagues. By adhering to—and hopefully exceeding—these minimum standards, the Nation's major professional sports leagues would send a strong signal to the public that performance-enhancing drugs have no legitimate role in American sports.

This bill would prohibit our country's major professional sports leagues—the National Football League, Major League Baseball, the National Basketball Association, and the National Hockey League—from operating if they do not meet the minimum testing requirements set forth therein. Those standards would be comprised of five key components: the independence of the entity or entities that perform the leagues' drug tests; testing for a comprehensive list of doping substances and methods; a strong system of unannounced testing; significant penalties that discourage the use of performance-enhancing drugs; and a fair and effective adjudication process for athletes accused of doping. These elements are crucial components of any credible performance-enhancing drug testing policy.

More specifically, the bill would require all major professional sports leagues to have an independent third party administer their performance-enhancing drug tests. The legislation would further require that samples provided by athletes be tested by laboratories approved by the United States Anti-Doping Agency—USADA—and for substances banned by USADA. In addition, the bill would require not fewer than three unannounced tests during a league's season of play, and at least two unannounced tests during the off season. Under this legislation, if a player were to test positive for a banned performance-enhancing substance, that player would be suspended for 2 years for the first violation and banned for life for a second violation. Finally, if any player were to test positive, the professional sports league would be obligated to ensure that the player would have substantial due process rights including the opportunity for a hearing and right to counsel.

McCain explains some details as to how federal policy would be carried out.

The need for reforming the drug testing policies of professional sports is clear. However, I introduce this legislation reluctantly. Over a year ago, I stated publicly that the failure of professional sports—and in particular Major League Baseball—to commit to addressing the issue of doping straight on and immediately would motivate Congress to search for legislative remedies. Despite my clear warning and the significant attention that Congress has given to this stain on professional sports, baseball, and other professional leagues have refused to do the right thing.

. . .

I remain hopeful that professional sports will reform their drug testing policies on their own—a modest proposal in the eyes of reasonable people. However, the introduction of this bill demonstrates the continued seriousness with which Congress views this issue. It should be seen as a renewed incentive for the leagues to clean up their sports on their own without Government interference.

Source: *Congressional Record–Senate.* May 24, 2005, S5852. http://www.gpo.gov/fdsys/pkg/CREC-2005-05-24/pdf/ CREC-2005-05-24-pt1-PgS5852.pdf. Accessed on May 20, 2012.

———

Mitchell Report (2007)

On March 30, 2006, Major League Baseball commissioner Bud Selig, concerned about the growing evidence of illegal substance abuse in major league baseball, asked former Senator George J. Mitchell to head an investigation of drug abuse in professional baseball. Mitchell offered his report to Commissioner Selig on December 13, 2007. He later summarized the result of his research and his recommendations at a meeting of the U.S. House of Representatives Committee on Energy and Commerce on February 27, 2008. Some important features of Mitchell's testimony are reprinted here.

During the period discussed in my report, the use of steroids in Major League Baseball was widespread, in violation of federal law and baseball policy. Club officials routinely discussed the possibility of substance use when evaluating players. The response by baseball was slow to develop and was initially ineffective. The Players Association had for many years opposed a mandatory random drug testing program, but they agreed to the adoption of such a program in 2002, after which the response gained momentum.

. . .

Everyone involved in baseball over the past two decades—Commissioners, club officials, the Players Association, and players—shares to some extent in the responsibility for the steroids era. There was a collective failure to recognize the problem as it emerged and to deal with it early on. As a result, an environment developed in which illegal use became widespread.

. . .

The adoption of the recommendations set forth in my report will be a first step . . . and I will now summarize them.

. . .

First, there must be an enhanced capacity to conduct investigations based on non-testing evidence. Some illegal substances are difficult or virtually impossible to detect.

. . .

The Commissioner has accepted my recommendation to create a Department of Investigations, led by a senior executive, to respond promptly and aggressively to allegations of the illegal use or possession of performance enhancing substances. To do its job effectively, this department must establish credibility and cooperate closely with law enforcement agencies. I recommended that the Commissioner strengthen pre-existing efforts to keep illegal substances out of major league clubhouses by logging and tracking packages shipped to players at major league ballparks, conducting background checks and random drug tests on clubhouse employees, and adopting policies to ensure that allegations of a player's possession or use of performance enhancing substances are reported promptly to the Department of Investigations.

. . .

Second, improved educational programs about the dangers of substance use are critical to any effort to deter use. Over the last several years, the Commissioner's Office and the Players Association have made an increased effort to provide players and club personnel with educational materials on performance enhancing substances. Several suggestions for improvement in this effort are set forth in my report.

Third, although it is clear that even the best drug testing program is, by itself, not sufficient, drug testing remains an important element of a comprehensive approach to combat illegal use. The current program was agreed to in 2006 and will remain in effect until 2011. Any changes to the program therefore must be negotiated and agreed to by the clubs and the Players Association. In my report, I set forth the principles that presently characterize a state-of-the-art drug testing program, and I urged the clubs and the Players Association to incorporate them into baseball's program when they next deal with this issue.

Source: *Drugs in Sports: Compromising the Health of Athletes and Undermining the Integrity of Competition.* Hearing Before the Subcommittee on Commerce, Trade, and Consumer Protection of the Committee on Energy and Commerce. House of Representatives. One Hundred Tenth Congress, Second Session, February 27, 2008. Available online at http://www.gpo.gov/fdsys/pkg/CHRG-110hhrg49522/pdf/CHRG-110hhrg49522.pdf.

Effectiveness of Federal Anabolic Steroid Prevention Programs (2007)

In 2007, Representatives Henry Waxman (D-CA) and Tom Davis (R-VA) asked the U.S. General Accountability Office (GAO) to conduct a study to determine the effectiveness of federal programs designed to reduce illegal steroid use by young American adults. The GAO provided a report on their study in October 2007, focusing primarily on two federally funded programs, Athletes Training and Learning to Avoid Steroids (ATLAS) and Athletes Targeting Healthy Exercise & Nutrition Alternatives (ATHENA). Following are the general conclusions GAO drew about these programs.

[The GAO first attempted to identify factors that might be associated with illegal steroid use. It concluded that:]

Almost half of the studies we reviewed identified certain risk factors and behaviors linked to the abuse of anabolic steroids among teenagers. . . . Several studies found that the use of alcohol and other drugs—such as tobacco, marijuana, and cocaine—is associated with the abuse of anabolic steroids among teenagers, including teenage athletes and non-athletes. . . . Several studies we reviewed found no difference between athletes and non-athletes in their abuse of anabolic steroids. . . . A few studies we reviewed found a positive correlation between anabolic steroid abuse and risky sexual behaviors such as early initiation of sexual activity and an increased number of sexual partners. Some studies found that aggressive behaviors such as fighting were related to anabolic steroid abuse by both males and females. . . .

[Overall, the researchers concluded that:]

the cause-and-effect relationships between anabolic steroid abuse and other risky behaviors, such as violence, have not been determined.

[Researchers then investigated the success of federally funded programs to reduce steroid abuse:]

According to experts, available research does not establish the extent to which the ATLAS and ATHENA programs are effective over time in preventing anabolic steroid abuse among teenage athletes. Experts acknowledge that both programs appear promising in their ability to prevent the abuse of anabolic steroids among teenage athletes immediately following participants' completion of the programs. Assessment of the effectiveness of the ATLAS program 1 year later, however, found that the lower incidence of anabolic steroid use was not sustained, although participants continued to report reduced intentions to use anabolic steroids. The long-term effectiveness of the ATHENA program has not been reported.

[The GAO report concluded with a brief summary of information about long-term health effects of steroid use on adolescents:]

According to experts, there are several gaps in research on the health effects of teenage abuse of anabolic steroids. Experts report that while there is some research that has examined the health effects of anabolic steroid abuse among adults—for example, the harmful effects on the cardiovascular, hormonal, and immune systems—there is a lack of research on these effects among teenagers. There is also a lack of research on the long-term health effects of initiating anabolic steroid abuse during the teenage years. Some health effects of steroid abuse among adults, such as adverse effects on the hormonal system, have been shown to be reversible when the adults have stopped abusing anabolic steroids. Experts point out, however, that it is not known whether this reversibility holds true for teenagers as well. While some experts suggest that anabolic steroid abuse may do more lasting harm to teenagers, due to the complex physical changes unique to adolescence, according to other experts there is no conclusive evidence of potentially permanent health effects. Experts also report that the extent of the psychological effects of anabolic steroid abuse and, in particular, of withdrawal from steroid abuse, is unclear due to limited research.

Source: *Anabolic Steroid Abuse: Federal Efforts to Prevent and Reduce Anabolic Steroid Abuse among Teenagers.* Washington, D.C.: United States Government Accountability Office, October 2007. Available online at http://www.gao.gov/new. items/d0815.pdf. Accessed on June 2, 2012.

United States of America v. Marion Jones (2007)

In October 2006, Olympic gold and bronze medal winner Marion Jones pleaded guilty to lying about the use of steroids in preparation for athletic competitions. In preparation for her sentencing for this crime, prosecutors submitted a memorandum reviewing the primary elements of the case and their recommendation for her sentencing. The main points of that memorandum are as follows. (The judge accepted these recommendations in announcing Jones' sentence.)

[Prosecutors reviewed Jones' statements in two trials, one before the U.S. District Court for Northern California and the other before the U.S. District Court for southern New York. In each instance, they reviewed the facts presented at the trials and then drew the following conclusions:]

[Northern California case:]

The defendant's use of performance-enhancing drugs encompassed numerous drugs (THG, EPO, Human Growth Hormone) and delivery systems (sublingual drops, subcutaneous injections) over a substantial course of time. Her use of these substances was goal-oriented, that is, it was designed to further her athletic accomplishments and financial career. Her false statements to the IRS-CI agent were focused, hoping not only to deflect the attention of the investigation away from herself, but also to secure the gains achieved by her use of the performance-enhancing substances in the first place. The false statements to the IRS-CI agent were the culmination of a long series of public denials by the defendant, often accompanied by baseless attacks on those accusing her, regarding her use of these substances.

The context of the defendant's use of performance-enhancing substances, as detailed in the documents seized from BALCO, shows a concentrated, organized, long-term effort to use these substances for her personal gain, a scenario wholly inconsistent with anything other than her denials being calculated lies to agents who were investigating that same conduct.

[Southern New York case:]

Jones was very nearly a witness for the Government in the criminal trial before your Honor. It is difficult to articulate how catastrophic would have been her perjurious testimony had the Government not fortuitously learned, at the eleventh hour, of the falsity of her statements. The defendant's false statements derailed the Government's investigative efforts and were highly material to its criminal investigation.

[The government then set forth its recommendations for sentencing:]

For the reasons set forth above, the Court should impose a sentence within sentencing range of 0 to 6 months' imprisonment stipulated to by the parties.

Source: United States District Court, Southern District of New York. *United States of America v. Marion Jones.* "Government's Sentencing Memorandum." http://assets.espn. go.com/media/pdf/071221/jonessentencingmemo.pdf. Accessed on June 3, 2012.

Mandatory Steroid Testing for High School Students in New Jersey (2007)

Some individuals concerned about the dangers posed by steroid abuse among young people have argued for mandatory testing of all high school athletes. In 2007, New Jersey became the first state to adopt such a program. Since that time, only two other states have adopted similar laws, Illinois and Texas. All three states have experiences some common problems with their programs, perhaps the most important being cost. New Jersey, for example, spent $400,000 in the first four years of testing and found only one student who tested positive. Still, concerns about steroid abuse among high school athletes is such that the campaign for mandatory testing continues in a number of states. The New Jersey law reads as follows (extraneous citations are omitted).

18A:40A-22 Findings, declarations relative to substance abuse testing policies in public school districts.

1. The Legislature finds and declares that there are many school districts within the State with a growing problem of drug abuse among their students. The Legislature further finds that federal and State courts have held that it may be appropriate for school districts to combat this problem through the random drug testing of students participating in extracurricular activities, including interscholastic athletics, and students who possess school parking permits. The Legislature also finds that a random drug testing program may have a positive effect on attaining the important objectives of deterring drug use and providing a means for the early detection of students with drug problems so that counseling and rehabilitative treatment may be offered.

    18A:40A-23 Adoption of policy for random testing of certain students.

2. A board of education may adopt a policy, pursuant to rules and regulations adopted by the State Board of Education in consultation with the Department of Human Services, which

are consistent with the New Jersey Constitution and the federal Constitution, for the random testing of the district's students in grades 9-12 who participate in extracurricular activities, including interscholastic athletics, or who possess school parking permits, for the use of controlled dangerous substances as defined in N.J.S.2C:35-2 and anabolic steroids. The testing shall be conducted by the school physician, school nurse or a physician, laboratory or health care facility designated by the board of education and the cost shall be paid by the board. Any disciplinary action taken against a student who tests positive for drug use or who refuses to consent to testing shall be limited to the student's suspension from or prohibition against participation in extracurricular activities, or revocation of the student's parking permits.

18A: 40A-24 Public hearing prior to adoption of drug testing policy.

3. Each board of education shall hold a public hearing prior to the adoption of its drug testing policy. The policy shall be in written form and shall be distributed to students and their parents or guardians at the beginning of each school year. The policy shall include, but need not be limited to, the following:

   a. notice that the consent of the student and his parent or guardian for random student drug testing is required for the student to participate in extracurricular activities and to possess a school parking permit;
   b. the procedures for collecting and testing specimens;
   c. the manner in which students shall be randomly selected for drug testing;
   d. the procedures for a student or his parent or guardian to challenge a positive test result;
   e. the standards for ensuring the confidentiality of test results;
   f. the specific disciplinary action to be imposed upon a student who tests positive for drug use or refuses to consent to testing;

    g.   the guidelines for the referral of a student who tests positive for drug use to drug counseling or rehabilitative treatment; and

    h.   the scope of authorized disclosure of test results

Source: New Jersey State Statutes. Title 18A: Education. http://lis.njleg.state.nj.us/cgi-bin/om_isapi.dll?clientID=46259956&Depth=4&TD=WRAP&advquery=18A%2040A-22&headingswithhits=on&infobase=statutes.nfo&rank=&record={83BE}&softpage=Document42&wordsaroundhits=2&x=35&y=17&zz=. Accessed on June 28, 2012.

Anabolic Steroid Ban on Horse Racing in Kentucky (2008)

The discussion on the use of anabolic steroids as performance-enhancing substances in athletics has focused on humans in this book. The fact is that anabolic steroids have also been used on other animals involved in sports competitions, such as greyhounds and thoroughbred horses, quarter horses, and other breeds of horses. To a perhaps surprising degree, the use of anabolic steroids and other performance-enhancing drugs has largely been ignored in nonhuman competitors. In 2008, the Kentucky Horse Racing Commission changed that situation for at least one state by adopting new bans on the use of anabolic steroids in horses that are raced in the state. A description of the new regulations was included in the commission's 2008–2009 biennial report, as summarized here.

On Aug. 25, 2008, the KHRC approved the EDRC's [Equine Drug Research Council] recommendations to ban anabolic steroids for Thoroughbred and Standardbred racing and requested that Governor Beshear adopt the changes in state law through an emergency regulation.

Under the amendment to the drug regulation, anabolic steroids cannot be administered to a horse that is in competition. In addition, the presence of any naturally occurring anabolic steroid in a racehorse that is above natural levels will constitute a violation of the drug rule. The rule set forth naturally occurring physiological levels for boldenone, nandrolone, and testosterone which can be given for therapeutic reasons, but only under certain conditions.

The proposed regulation stated that a horse would be ineligible to race in Kentucky until at least 60 days after administration of a therapeutic anabolic steroid.

In addition, the EDRC recommended strengthening the penalties for detection of anabolic steroids and the KHRC acted on the recommendation by placing all anabolic steroids in the Class B Category when assessing penalties. A violation involving a Class B medication may carry a penalty of up to 60 days suspension. Under the previous drug rule, those steroids were treated as Class C medications, carrying a penalty of up to 10 days suspension.

The KHRC also approved the following EDRC recommendations relating to anabolic steroids to:

- Establish a 90-day grace period which started Sept. 5, 2008 in conjunction with Gov. Beshear signing the anabolic steroid ban into law, noting the KHRC would begin sending notices of positives to trainers and owners after the first 30 days of the grace period.

- Provide the capability for persons who claim a horse to be able to request that the horse be tested for anabolic steroids at the time the claim form is filed with the racetrack. The claimant will bear the cost of the test, but if the test results are positive, the claimant may void the claim.

- Provide the capability for trainers who ship horses to Kentucky shortly before the race to either follow the reporting requirements set forth in the regulation, certify that the horse has not received anabolic steroids in the last 60 days, or if the trainer cannot certify that the horse has not had anabolic steroids because they recently took the horse under their care, then the trainer must acknowledge and accept responsibility if a positive test result is returned for anabolic steroids.

Source: Kentucky Horse Racing Commission. *2008/2009 Biennial Report.* Lexington, KY: Kentucky Horse Racing Commission. Available online at http://www.khrc.ky.gov/reports/Biennial%20Report%202008-2009.pdf. Accessed on June 26, 2012.

———

UCI v. Alberto Contador Velasco & RFEC and WADA v. Alberto Contador Velasco & RFEC (2012)

Alberto Contador is a Spanish professional cyclist, widely regarded as one of the most skilled cyclists of his era. He is only one of five riders to have won all three major cycling competitions, the Tour de France, Giro d'Italia, and Vuelta a España. After his 2010 Tour de France win, he tested positive for the banned anabolic steroid clenbuterol. Contador disputed that finding, claiming that the positive tests for both his A and B samples was a consequence of having eaten contaminated steak. The alternative theory proposed by regulators was that Contador had consumed a nutritional supplement which contained clenbuterol as a contaminant. The World Anti-Doping Agency specifically warns athletes against taking nutritional supplements whose composition they do not positively know. After a 17-month period of legal wrangling, the Court of Arbitration for Sport in Lausanne, Switzerland, finally ruled that the original tests were accurate, that Contador had ingested a prohibited substance (clenbuterol) in a nutritional supplement, and that he was stripped of his 2010 victory and banned from professional cycling for a period of two years. The essence of the court's decision was as follows:

Findings of the Panel

[The Panel first considers whether the nutritional supplement theory is possible, and concludes that it is. It then moves on to the question of:]

(7) Is the Meat Contamination Theory More Likely to Have Occurred Than the Supplement Theory?

485. As has been shown above, the Panel has to assess the likelihood of different scenarios that—when looked at individually—are all somewhat remote for different reasons.

486. However, since it is uncontested that the Athlete did test positive for clenbuterol, and having in mind that both the meat contamination theory and the blood transfusion theory are equally unlikely, the Panel is called upon to determine whether it considers it more likely, in light of the evidence adduced, that the clenbuterol entered the Athlete's system through ingesting a contaminated food supplement. Furthermore, for the reasons already indicated, if the Panel is unable to assess which of the possible alternatives of ingestion is more likely, the Athlete will bear the burden of proof according to the applicable rules.

487. Considering that the Athlete took supplements in considerable amounts, that it is incontestable that supplements may be contaminated, that athletes have frequently tested positive in the past because of contaminated food supplements, that in the past an athlete has also tested positive for a food supplement contaminated with clenbuterol, and that the

Panel considers it very unlikely that the piece of meat ingested by him was contaminated with clenbuterol, it finds that, in light of all the evidence on record, the Athlete's positive test for clenbuterol is more likely to have been caused by the ingestion of a contaminated food supplement than by a blood transfusion or the ingestion of contaminated meat. This does not mean that the Panel is convinced beyond reasonable doubt that this scenario of ingestion of a contaminated food supplement actually happened. This is not required by the UCI ADR or by the WADC, which refer the Panel only to the balance of probabilities as the applicable standard of the burden of proof. In weighing the evidence on the balance of probabilities and coming to a decision on such basis, the Panel has to take into consideration and weigh all of the evidence admitted on record, irrespective of which party advanced which scenario(s) and what party adduced which parts of the evidence.

488. That said, the Panel finds it important to clarify that, by considering and weighing the evidence in the foregoing manner and deciding on such basis, the Panel in no manner shifted the burden of proof away from the Athlete as explained above (see supra §§ 243–265). The burden of proof only allocates the risk if a fact or a scenario can not be established on a balance of probabilities. However, this is not the case here.

489. Consequently, the Athlete is found to have committed an anti-doping violation as defined by Article 21 UCI ADR, and it remains to be examined what the applicable sanction is.

XII. The Sanctions

490. It is undisputed that it is the first time the Athlete is found guilty of an anti-doping rule violation.

491. As already mentioned, Article 293 UCI ADR reads as follows:

> *The period of* Ineligibility *imposed for a first anti-doping rule violation under article 21.1 (Presence of a* Prohibited Substance *or its* Metabolites *or* Markers*), article 21.2 (Use or* Attempted Use *of a Prohibited Substance or* Prohibited Method*) or article 21.6 (Possession of a* Prohibited Substance *or Prohibited Method) shall be 2 (two) years'* Ineligibility *unless the conditions for eliminating or reducing the period of* Ineligibility *as provided in articles 295 to 304 or the conditions for increasing the period of Ineligibility as provided in article 305 are met.* [typography as in original]

492. Pursuant to this provision, the period of ineligibility shall be two years. Accordingly, there is no discretion for the hearing body to reduce the period of ineligibility due to reasons of proportionality.

493. As none of the conditions for eliminating or reducing the period of ineligibility as provided in Articles 295 to

304 UCI ADR are applicable–in particular because the exact contaminated supplement is unknown and the circumstances surrounding its ingestion are equally unknown–the period of ineligibility shall be two years.

Source: "Arbitral Award Delivered by Court of Arbitration for Sport." http://www.tas-cas.org/d2wfiles/document/5648/5048/0/Award20FINAL202012.02.10.pdf. Accessed on June 26, 2012.

6 Resources

The use of performance-enhancing drugs such as steroids has been the subject of a great many books, reports, and print and online articles. Space does not permit a complete or exhaustive listing of those resources. The items presented here do, however, provide a general overview of the types of materials available on the subject. The resources are listed in four general categories: books, periodicals, reports, and Internet resources. Because some items are available in more than one format, they may be listed here in differing, but comparable, categories. The acronym "AAS" stands for *anabolic-androgenic steroid abuse*.

Books

Assael, Shaun. 2007. *Steroid Nation: Juiced Home Run Totals, Anti-aging Miracles, and a Hercules in Every High School: The Secret History of America's True Drug Addiction*. New York: ESPN Books.

> In a well-written narrative style, the author reviews the origins and development of steroid abuse problems in the nation's major professional sports, as well as in a range of amateur venues.

Marion Jones sprints a preliminary heat of the women's 100-meter dash during the U.S. Outdoor Track and Field Championships in Indianapolis, Indiana, on June 23, 2006. The former Olympic track champion's 2010 book *On the Right Track* chronicled the doping that helped her win—and lose—Olympic medals and serve prison time. (Matthew Stockman/Getty Images)

Bahrke, Michael S., and Charles Yesalis, eds. 2002. *Performance-enhancing Substances in Sport and Exercise.* Champaign, IL: Human Kinetics.

> The 29 chapters in this anthology deal with topics such as the history of doping in sports, anabolic and androgenic steroids, the physiological effects of AAS, blood doping, amphetamines, ephedrine as an ergogenic aid, drug testing in sports and athletics, and designer and future performance-enhancing drugs.

Beamish, Rob. 2011. *Steroids: A New Look at Performance-enhancing Drugs.* Santa Barbara, CA: Praeger.

> The author reviews the history of the use of anabolic steroids in sports and athletics and discussed the current status of that issue.

Bjornlund, Lydia D. 2011. *How Dangerous Are Performance-enhancing Drugs?* San Diego, CA: ReferencePoint Press.

> A review of the drug abuse problem in athletics and sports designed for young adult readers.

Burns, Christopher N., ed. 2006. *Doping in Sports.* New York: Nova Science Publishers.

> This short book reviews current laws, regulations, and policies dealing with the use of performance-enhancing substances in sports, with a separate chapter on the drug ephedra.

Buti, Antonio, and Saul Fridman. 2001. *Drugs, Sport and the Law.* Mudgeeraba, QLD: Scribblers.

> Legal issues have become a significantly more important part of both amateur and professional sports in the past few decades. The authors consider the agencies that have developed to impose and test for violations of doping policies and practice, examine carefully the traditional reasons provided for having such policies and practices, and review some of the legal challenges that have and will be raised against drug testing programs.

Clark, Dan. 2011. *Gladiator: A True Story of 'Roids, Rage, and Redemption.* New York: Scribner.

> The author, commonly known as Nitro on the American Gladiators television program, tells of his experiences with the use of AAS.

Cohen, Robert W. 2009. *Baseball's Hall of Fame: Or Hall of Shame?* Las Vegas: Cardoza Publishers.

> One part of this book focuses on biographical sketches of some of the greatest baseball players of all times. A second part of the book then discusses the use of illegal substances by some of those individuals and asks how that practice affected their level of playing accomplishments.

Conte, Victor, and Nathan Jendrick. 2008. *Balco: The Straight Dope on Steroids, Barry Bonds, Marion Jones, & What We Can Do to Save Sports.* New York: Skyhorse.

> The authors review the recent cases involving the use of steroids by Barry Bonds, Marion Jones, and other elite athletes and suggest some steps that must be taken to reduce or eliminate the use of AAS by professional athletes.

Dennis, Mike, and Jonathan Grix. 2012. *Sport under Communism: Behind the East German "Miracle."* New York: Palgrave Macmillan.

> The authors analyze the reasons that sports teams and individuals from East Germany were among the most successful in the world over a three-decade period at the end of the 20th century.

Fainaru-Wada, Mark, and Lance Williams. 2006. *Game of Shadows: Barry Bonds, BALCO, and the Steroids Scandal That Rocked Professional Sports.* New York: Gotham Books.

> The authors tell the story of the use by Bonds of illegal performance-enhancing drugs supplied to him by agents of the Bay Area Laboratory Cooperative (BALCO) company.

Fourcroy, Jean L., ed. 2009. *Pharmacology, Doping and Sports: A Scientific Guide for Athletes, Coaches, Physicians, Scientists and Administrators*. London; New York: Routledge.

> The essays in this book all deal with technical aspects of the testing for illegal substances, the procedures used by athletes to avoid being detected in their use of illegal drugs, and related issues.

Ghigo, Ezio, Fabio Lanfranco, and Christian J. Strasburger, eds. 2011. *Hormone Use and Abuse by Athletes*. New York: Springer Science+Business Media.

> This book deals with all types of hormonal substances used by amateur and professional athletes, but contains a number of important chapters focusing on anabolic androgenic steroids (AAS).

Gold, Mark S. 2007. *Performance-enhancing Medications and Drugs of Abuse*. Binghamton, NY: Haworth Medical Press.

> This book is a reprint of volume 25, number 1 of the journal *Journal of Addictive Diseases*, which includes chapters on performance-enhancing drugs in general, nicotine, anabolic steroids, and related substances.

Goldberg, Ray. 2012. *Taking Sides. Clashing Views in Drugs and Society*, 10th ed. New York: McGraw-Hill.

> The author reviews all sides of the debate over the use of performance-enhancing drugs in sports in a "debate-style format." His goal is to "stimulate student interest and develop critical thinking skills."

Grace, Fergal, and Julien Baker, eds. 2012. *Perspectives on Anabolic Androgenic Steroids (AAS) and Doping in Sport and Health*. Hauppauge, NY: Nova Science Publishers.

> This book provides essays on the use of AAS in sports and athletics from the standpoint of sports medicine research, medical practice, behavioral science, molecular physiology, sociology, and the ethics of sports doping.

Haggard, Jesse. 2008. *Demystifying Steroids.* Bloomington, IN: AuthorHouse.

The author points out that steroids have a host of important legitimate uses in medicine, including treatment of cancer, multiple sclerosis, and HIV infection. He suggests that the bad reputation that steroids have as a result of their misuse in sports is unearned and harmful to their many beneficial applications.

Hamidi, Mehrdad, Mohammad-Ali Shahbazi, and Hajar Ashrafi. 2012. *Drug Abuse in Sport: Doping.* New York: Nova Science Publishers.

The authors provide an excellent review of the history of efforts by sportsmen and -women to enhance their performances with drugs and other substances. They also review the current status of the use of illegal substances in amateur and professional athletics.

Healey, Justin. 2008. *Performance Enhancing Drugs.* Thirroul, NSW: The Spinney Press.

This book provides a broad, general introduction to the subject of steroid abuse with a review of the history of steroid use in amateur and professional athletics, some effects of steroid use, and laws and regulations designed to deal with the problem.

Hunt, Thomas M. 2011. *Drug Games: The International Olympic Committee and the Politics of Doping, 1960/2008.* Austin: University of Texas Press.

The author reviews the history of illegal drug use by participants in the Olympic Games dating from at least 1960. He discusses the issues involved in getting sports organizations to recognize the extent of the problem and the responses developed to athletic drug abuse.

Jendrick, Nathan. 2006. *Dunks, Doubles, Doping: How Steroids Are Killing American Athletics.* Guilford, CT: Lyons Press.

The author argues that the use of AAS is causing far more damage to the health of athletes that almost anyone is willing to recognize today and that by the end of the century, illegal drug use will be seen as one of the nation's worst medical problems.

Jones, Marion. 2010. *On the Right Track: From Olympic Downfall to Finding Forgiveness and the Strength to Overcome and Succeed.* New York: Howard Books.

Track star Marion Jones discusses her own history with drug abuse and explains how that experience changed her life.

Kiesbye, Stefan. 2007. *Steroids.* Detroit: Greenhaven Press.

This book is part of Greenhaven's Contemporary Issues series for young adults, in which important social issues are described and discussed from a variety of standpoints.

Lednicer, Daniel. 2011. *Steroid Chemistry at a Glance.* Hoboken, NJ: Wiley.

This chemistry text provides a complete introductory to the chemistry of steroidal compounds. It is of interest and value to anyone with an advanced degree in chemistry.

Lenehan, Pat. 2003. *Anabolic Steroids and Other Performance-enhancing Drugs.* London; New York: Taylor & Francis.

This excellent introduction to the topic of performance-enhancing drugs contains chapters on the history of performance-enhancing drugs in general, and steroids in particular, along with a detailed review of their current medical and performance-enhancing uses. An important section discusses in detail some of the medical and biological effects produced on the human body by steroids and related drugs.

Llewellyn, William. 2011. *Anabolics*, 10th ed. Jupiter, FL: Molecular Nutrition.

One of the best-known, most widely used, and highly respected reference books in the field of anabolic steroids, this manual provides extensive introductory information about anabolic steroids and related substances, including their chemical structure and function and physiological actions and side effects. The major part of the book is devoted to a thorough review of nearly 200 anabolic substances.

Llewellyn, William, and Ronny Tober. 2010. *Underground Anabolics*. Jupiter, FL: Body of Science.

The author reviews the history of AAS use in sports and athletics and provides intriguing details as to how the underground business of supplying steroids works in today's world.

Locks, Adam, and Niall Richardson, eds. 2012. *Critical Readings in Bodybuilding*. New York: Routledge.

See especially Chapter 3, "Accounting for Illicit Steroid Use: Bodybuilders' Justifications." AAS are mentioned and discussed elsewhere in the book also.

Master, Roy. 2010. *Higher, Richer, Sleazier: How Drugs and Money Are Changing Sport Forever*. Crows Nest, NSW: Allen & Unwin.

Former coach and now sports journalist Roy Masters laments the downfall of Australian sports from the days when it was dominated by idealistic amateurs to the present time when money and drugs are driving forces behind athletics.

McNamee, Mike, and Verner Møller, eds. 2011. *Doping and Anti-doping Policy in Sport: Ethical, Legal and Social Perspectives*. Abingdon, UK; New York: Routledge.

The papers in this volume were presented at the third annual conference of the Network of Humanistic Doping Research, held at Aarhus University in August 2009. They cover topics such as the burden of proof in endogenous substance cases, some implications of imperfect testing procedures, privacy rights and doping procedures, the ethics of testing citizens in recreational gyms, and steroid issues in the court of public opinion.

McVeigh, R., ed. 2013. *Anabolic Steroids and Other Performance and Image-enhancing Drugs*. New York: Wiley-Blackwell.

This collection of essays covers topics such as a historical perspective, a global review of use prevalence, profiles of individuals who use such drugs, how performance-enhancing drugs work, health effects of performance-enhancing drugs, and some country-by-country case studies.

Millar, David. 2011. *Racing Through the Dark: The Rise and Fall of David Millar*. London: Orion Books.

The author describes his life as a promising young cycling prospect who falls prey to the all-consuming culture of drug use in the profession, eventually leading to his arrest for the use of illegal substances.

Mitchell, George J. 2007. *Report to the Commissioner of Baseball of an Independent Investigation into the Illegal Use of Steroids and Other Performance-enhancing Substances by Players in Major League Baseball*. [New York]: Office of the Commissioner of Baseball.

This now out-of-print book provides all the details of the Mitchell investigation of the use of illegal drugs by major league baseball players, along with his conclusions and recommendations for dealing with this problem.

Møller, Verner, M.J. McNamee, and Paul Dimeo, eds. 2009. *Elite Sport, Doping, and Public Health*. Odense: University Press of Southern Denmark.

The papers in this anthology review the growth of illegal substance abuse in professional (elite) sports over the past few decades, with a consideration of the ways in which that growth has expanded to include a much larger portion of the general population.

Nieschlag, Eberhard, Hermann M. Behre, and Susan Nieschlag, eds. 2012. *Testosterone: Action, Deficiency, Substitution*, 4th ed. Cambridge, UK; New York: Cambridge University Press.

>   This standard text provides detailed information on all aspects of testosterone, from its chemical structure and synthesis to its biological effects and side effects.

Piehl, Norah. 2010. *Performance-enhancing Drugs*. Farmington Hills, MI: Greenhaven Press/Gale Cengage Learning.

>   The 11 essays in this book are intended to provide an introduction to the issue of performance-enhancing drugs to young adults.

Radomski, Kirk. 2009. *Bases Loaded: The Inside Story of the Steroid Era in Baseball by the Central Figure in the Mitchell Report*. New York: Hudson Street Press.

>   The author was formerly an employee of the New York Mets baseball team who supplied players with illegal performance-enhancing substances. He was later a major participant in the review of major league baseball drug use conducted by George Mitchell.

Roach, Randy. 2011. *Muscle, Smoke & Mirrors*. Volume II. Bloomington, IN: AuthorHouse.

>   This book is the second volume in a long and detailed history of the sport of bodybuilding, with strong emphasis on the role that the use of illegal drugs has had in changing the direction and very nature of the sport.

Roberts, Paul K., ed. 2010. *Steroid Use and Abuse*. New York: Nova Biomedical Books.

>   The papers in this anthology provide an overview of the chemical and physiological properties of AAS, as well as a discussion of their licit and illicit uses.

Rogers, Peter D., and Brian H. Hardin, eds. 2007. *Performance Enhancing Drugs*. Philadelphia; London: Saunders.

This book is a reprint of the volume 54, number 4 issue of *Pediatric Clinics of North America*. It includes articles on the specialized problems of performance-enhancing drugs among children and adolescents.

Rosen, Daniel M. 2008. *Dope: A History of Performance Enhancement in Sports from the Nineteenth Century to Today*. Westport, CT: Praeger.

This book's seven chapters are divided into the time periods from 1860 to 1959, 1960 to 1969, 1970 to 1979, 1980 to 1989, 1990 to 1999, and 2000 to the present, with an outlook for the future.

Thieme, Detlef, and Peter Hemmersbach, eds. 2010. *Doping in Sports*. Heidelberg; New York: Springer.

This book is part of Springer's Experimental Pharmacology series dealing with the technical aspects of most major performance-enhancing drugs, including all of the important AAS.

Thorne, Gerard. 2009. *Anabolic Primer: Ergogenic Enhancement for the Hardcore Bodybuilder*. Mississauga, ON: Robert Kennedy.

The author points out that developing one's natural assets in the field of bodybuilding has certain inherent limitations, and when those limitations are reached, it is necessary to turn to anabolic steroids to further increase one's strength. He reviews the possibilities available to bodybuilders.

Tilin, Andrew. 2011. *The Doper Next Door: My Strange and Scandalous Year on Performance-enhancing Drugs*. Berkeley: Counterpoint.

The author provides the story of his own experimentation with performance-enhancing drugs over a single year.

Tod, David, and David Lavallee, eds. 2012. *The Psychology of Strength and Conditioning*. London; New York: Routledge.

See especially Chapter 9 on "The Misuse of Anabolic-androgenic Steroids" for a discussion of this issue.

Waddington, Ivan, and Andy Smith. 2009. *An Introduction to Drugs in Sport: Addicted to Winning?* Abingdon; New York: Routledge.

The authors review the complex relationships between drug use and amateur and professional sports, with special attention to topics such as sports law, policy, and administration; case studies in football and cycling; the role of sports federations, such as the World Anti-Doping Association; and the relevance of the profession of sports medicine.

Willey, Warren. 2007. *Better Than Steroids!* Victoria, BC: Trafford Publishing.

The author provides a good review of the effect of steroids on the human body, but then goes on to outline a training program that he says will provide even better and safer results for the bodybuilder or other person interested in improving one's strength, endurance, speed, and other physical qualities.

Articles

Acevedo, P., et al. 2011. "A Ten-year Assessment of Anabolic Steroid Misuse among Competitive Athletes in Puerto Rico." *The West Indian Medical Journal.* 60(5): 531–535.

This article is of particular interest, partly because it is one of the few studies of steroid abuse in the Caribbean, but also because it was conducted over such a long period of time.

Amos, Anne, and Saul Fridman. 2009. "Drugs in Sport: The Legal Issues." *Sport in Society: Cultures, Commerce, Media, Politics.* 12(3): 356–374.

The authors point out that drug testing has now become an integral part of most sports competition, but that some fundamental legal questions remain to be answered about the basis and interpretation of such tests.

Bahrke, Michael S., Charles E. Yesalis, and James E. Wright, III. 1990. "Psychological and Behavioural Effects of Endogenous Testosterone Levels and Anabolic-Androgenic Steroids Among Males." *Sports Medicine*. 10(5): 303–337.

In a review of more than 50 years of studies on the physical effects of AAS, the authors conclude that the relationship between testosterone levels and aggressive behavior is inconsistent in humans (although not in experimental animals) and depends on a number of factors that include the length of time drugs are taken and the type of testosterone derivative used.

Basaria, Shehzad, Justin T. Wahlstrom, and Adrian S. Dobs. 2001. "Anabolic-androgenic Steroid Therapy in the Treatment of Chronic Diseases." *The Journal of Clinical Endocrinology & Metabolism*. 86(11): 5108–5117.

This article reviews the evidence for the use of AAS in the treatment of chronic diseases, especially the problems of palliative care and weight loss. They note potential serious side effects associated with the use of AAS in such settings, but conclude that AAS use is still desirable in many such instances.

Beaver, Kevin M., et al. 2008. "Anabolic-androgenic Steroid Use and Involvement in Violent Behavior in a Nationally Representative Sample of Young Adult Males in the United States." *American Journal of Public Health*. 98(12): 2185–2187.

In a sample of 6,823 adolescents, violent behavior was statistically more common among AAS users than among a control population that did not use the drugs.

Bhasin, Shalender, et al. 2006. "Drug Insight: Testosterone and Selective Androgen Receptor Modulators as Anabolic Therapies for Chronic Illness and Aging." *Nature Clinical Practice Endocrinology & Metabolism*. 2(3): 146–159.

The authors point out that there is unequivocal experimental and clinical evidence that testosterone and other AAS increase muscle mass and strength and, therefore, have a host of potential medical benefits in a variety of chronic disorders. They go on to say that experiments on these substances have been hampered by concerns about the long-term effects of AAS on the human body.

Black, Terry. 1996. "Does the Ban on Drugs in Sport Improve Societal Welfare?" *International Review for the Sociology of Sport.* 31(4): 367–381.

The author points out that bans on the use of drugs in sports are usually based on arguments that such bans make competitions more equitable and that they protect the health of athletes. He presents reasons for believing that neither of these assumptions is true and that drug bans may actually make contests less equitable and increase the health risk of athletes.

Brown, G. A., M. Vukovich, and D. S. King. 2006. "Testosterone Prohormone Supplements." *Medicine and Science in Sports and Exercise.* 38(8): 1451–1461.

A number of suppliers have marketed prohormones as sources of testosterone in the body that can be used in place of traditional AAS. These researchers report that such prohormones are not effective in producing the results claimed by advertisers.

Brown-Séquard, Dr. 1889. "Note on the Effects Produced on Man by Subcutaneous Injections of a Liquid Obtained from the Testicles of Animals." *The Lancet.* 2(3438): 105–107. Available online at http://www.thelancet.com/journals/lancet/article/PIIS0140-6736(00)64118-1/fulltext (subscription required).

This article is the original report by Brown-Séquard of self-injection of the fluid taken from animal testicles and its effects on the author.

Calfee, Ryan, and Paul Fadale. "Popular Ergogenic Drugs and Supplements in Young Athletes." *Pediatrics.* 117(3): e577–e589.

> In this review article, the authors summarize current knowledge about the AAS substances currently used by young athletes, known physical and psychological effects, risks posed by the drugs, and legal status of the drugs.

Clark, Ann S., and Leslie P. Henderson. 2003. "Behavioral and Physiological Responses to Anabolic-androgenic Steroids." *Neuroscience and Biobehavioral Reviews.* 27(5): 413–436.

> The authors describe a series of experiments in which laboratory animals have been provided with supraphysiological doses of AAS to determine the effect on a variety of behaviors, including aggression, anxiety, reward behavior, sexual behavior, and locomotion.

Clement, Christen L., et al. 2012. "Nonprescription Steroids on the Internet." *Substance Use & Misuse.* 47(3): 329–341.

> In a study of popular websites between March 2006 and June 2006, the authors found that prescription AAS were readily available without prescription on most websites, with only about 5 percent of such websites providing accurate information about health risks associated with the use of these substances.

Cohen, Jason, et al. 2007. "A League of Their Own: Demographics, Motivations and Patterns of Use of 1,955 Male Adult Non-medical Anabolic Steroid Users in the United States." *Journal of the International Society of Sports Nutrition.* 4(12). Available online at http://www.jissn.com/content/4/1/12.

> The authors report on a study in which users of AAS recruited from Internet sites that sell the drugs report on their own history of AAS use. They find that most individuals did not begin using AAS during adolescence, nor is their use particularly associated with athletics, but is motivated by desires to improve one's body in order to improve one's self-image.

Devine, John William. 2011. "Doping Is a Threat to Sporting Excellence." *British Journal of Sports Medicine.* 45(8): 637–639.

The author writes in response to an article by Savulescu, Foddy, and Clayton (see 273) supporting the use of AAS in athletics. He says that the use of AAS should be disapproved both because of deleterious health effects on users, as well as the threat they pose to "displaying the relevant types of sporting excellence."

Dotson, Jennifer L., and Robert T. Brown. 2007. "The History of the Development of Anabolic-androgenic Steroids." *Pediatric Clinics of North America.* 54(4): 761–769.

The authors trace the long history of the discovery of anabolic steroids and their use by humans for a variety of purposes, including their most recent use by athletes for the purposes of performance enhancement.

Fitch, Kenneth D. 2008. "Androgenic-anabolic Steroids and the Olympic Games." *Asian Journal of Andrology.* 10(3): 384–390.

The author reviews the history of the use of AAS in Olympic Games going back to the 1960s. He then notes how developments in the field of drug design are likely to create new problems of detection of such drugs in future Olympic Games.

Franke, Werner W., and Brigitte Berendonk. 1997. "Hormonal Doping and Androgenization of Athletes: A Secret Program of the German Democratic Republic Government." *Clinical Chemistry.* 43(7): 1262–1279.

Doctoral theses, government documents, grant reports, scientific papers, and other classified documents collected after the collapse of the East German government in 1990 describe a secret program to use AAS in the nation's Olympic and other international sports programs.

Freeman, Erica R., David A. Bloom, and Edward J. McGuire. 2001. "A Brief History of Testosterone." *The Journal of Urology.* 165(2): 371–373.

The authors review and discuss a few of the most important events in the history of steroids, dating to John Hunter's earliest experiments in the late 18th century.

Harmer, P. A. 2010. "Anabolic-androgenic Steroid Use among Young Male and Female Athletes: Is the Game to Blame?" *British Journal of Sports Medicine.* 44(12): 26–31.

The author reviews studies of the use of AAS by young British athletes and finds that sports programs and desires to improve one's athletic performance are not the primary driving force behind steroid use by those included in the studies.

Hartgens, Fred, and Harm Kuipers. 2004. "Effects of Androgenic-anabolic Steroids in Athletes." *Sports Medicine.* 34(8): 513–554.

This paper is of special interest because it challenges some accepted notions about the effects of using AAS by athletes, largely because insufficient scientific data is available (or was available at the time of this study) to draw strong conclusions. In particular, they point out that the levels of steroids used by athletes in real life are probably significantly greater than those used in controlled studies of the substances.

Hoberman, John M., and Charles E. Yesalis. 1995. "The History of Synthetic Testosterone." *Scientific American.* 272(2): 76–81.

The authors trace the history of the development of synthetic testosterone products from the work of Brown-Séquard in the 1880s to the mid-1990s, with a discussion of the use of these compounds in medical science as well as by professional and amateur athletes.

Hoffman, Jay R., and Nicholas A. Ratamess. 2006. "Medical Issues Associated with Anabolic Steroid Use: Are They Exaggerated?" *Journal of Sports Science and Medicine.* 5(2): 182–193.

Hoffman, Jay R., et al. 2009. "Position Stand on Androgen and Human Growth Hormone Use." *Journal of Strength and Conditioning Research.* 23(suppl 5): S1–S59.

> This extensively documented paper outlines the official position on the use of human growth hormone and anabolic steroids in strength conditioning, sports, and other athletic activities of the National Strength and Conditioning Association.

Ip, Eric J., et al. 2011. "The Anabolic 500 Survey: Characteristics of Male Users Versus Nonusers of Anabolic-androgenic Steroids for Strength Training." *Pharmacotherapy.* 31(8): 757–766.

> The authors studied 506 self-identified AAS users recruited through online sources to determine the correlation of steroid abuse with other psychiatric disorders. They found that steroid users ranked significantly higher on all measures used, including anxiety disorder, recent cocaine use, substance dependence disorder, and sexual abuse.

Irving, Lori M., et al. 2002. "Steroid Use among Adolescents: Findings from Project EAT." *Journal of Adolescent Health.* 30(4): 243–252.

> The authors report on a study of 4,746 middle and high school students in St.Paul/Minneapolis public schools and find that 5.4 percent of male students and 2.9 percent of female students report having used AAS. Factors associated with AAS use include poor self-esteem, depression, and poor information about health issues.

Kanayama, Gen, et al. 2006. "Body Image and Attitudes Toward Male Roles in Anabolic-androgenic Steroid Users." *American Journal of Psychiatry.* 163(4): 697–703.

> In a study of 89 weight lifters, 48 of whom used AAS and 41 of whom did not, investigators found major differences

in muscular dysmorphia (discomfort with one's own body image) and adoption of male role model characteristics. Those men who used AAS for the longest period of time tended to show the greatest difference from short-term and nonusers of the drugs.

Kanayama, Gen, James I. Hudson, and Harrison G. Pope, Jr. 2008. "Long-term Psychiatric and Medical Consequences of Anabolic-androgenic Steroid Abuse: A Looming Public Health Concern?" *Drug and Alcohol Dependence.* 98(1–2): 1–12.

The authors point out that individuals who started using AAS in the 1980s are now reaching middle age, and researchers are beginning to ask what long-term effects AAS use may start to show up. They indicate that the limited evidence so far suggests increased risk for cardiac problems, little risk for prostate cancer, and increased risk for a variety of psychiatric disorders such as mood disorders and progression to other forms of substance abuse.

Kicman, A. T. 2008. "Pharmacology of Anabolic Steroids." *British Journal of Pharmacology.* 154(3): 502–521.

The author provides a good review of the chemical and biological function of anabolic steroids and suggests that it is easy to overestimate their harmful effects. What is more important, he says, is to remind athletes who use AAS that they are not invulnerable to their harmful effects.

Kochakian, Charles D. 1990. "History of Anabolic-androgenic Steroids." *NIDA Research Monographs.* 102: 29–59.

This monograph provides a detailed and exhaustive history of the discovery of testosterone and related anabolic steroids, along with a discussion of their use for the rejuvenation and revitalization of males in a variety of therapies.

Kuhn, Cynthia M. 2002. "Anabolic Steroids." *Recent Progress in Hormone Research.* 57: 411–434.

The author takes note of the disparity between scientists' conviction that the use of AAS has no significant effect on the growth of muscle tissue and the equally avid belief of athletes that the opposite is quite true, and that AAS significantly improve muscle mass and strength. She argues that the difference between these two views lies in the difference in dose used in scientific experiments and in the everyday use of AAS by athletes.

Lardon, Michael T. 2008. "Performance-enhancing Drugs: Where Should the Line Be Drawn and by Whom?" *Psychiatry (Edgmont)*. 5(7): 58–61.

The author raises some questions as to how the question stated in the article title can be answered, stressing, for example, the recognition of the point at which restorative function of drugs ends and performance enhancement begins.

Leme de Souza, Guilherme, and Jorge Hallak. 2011. "Anabolic Steroids and Male Infertility: A Comprehensive Review." *BJU International*. 108(11): 1860–1865.

The authors provide what they describe as an "absolutely unique" and complete review of everything that is currently known about the effect of anabolic steroids on the male reproductive system.

Lippi, G., M. Franchini, and G. Banfi. 2011. "Biochemistry and Physiology of Anabolic Androgenic Steroids Doping." *Mini Reviews in Medicinal Chemistry*. 11(5): 362–373.

The authors provide a technical review of the biochemistry and physiology of anabolic-androgenic steroids in the human body.

McCabe, Sean Esteban, et al., 2007. "Trends in Non-medical Use of Anabolic Steroids by U.S. College Students: Results from Four National Surveys." *Drug and Alcohol Dependence*. 90(2–3): 243–251.

The authors used four national surveys to determine trends in AAS use in 1993, 1997, 1999, and 2001. They found that lifetime prevalence for drug use was less than one percent throughout the period of the survey and that prevalence data did not change to any great extent during that time. They found that AAS was correlated primarily with participation in collegiate athletics and alcohol use disorder, as defined by the *Diagnostic and Statistical Manual, IV* of the American Psychiatric Association.

Pagonis, Thomas A., et al. 2006. "Psychiatric Side Effects Induced by Supraphysiological Doses of Combinations of Anabolic Steroids Correlate to the Severity of Abuse." *European Psychiatry*. 21(8): 551–562.

In a study of 320 bodybuilders and amateur and recreational athletes, researchers found that individuals who used AAS were significantly more likely to develop a range of psychological disorders and that the severity of the disorders correlated with the amount of AAS used.

Parkinson, Andrew B., and Nick A. Evans. 2006. "Anabolic Androgenic Steroids: A Survey of 500 Users." *Medicine and Science in Sports and Exercise*. 38(4): 644–651.

Noting that information about the nonmedical, self-administered use of AAS is "sparse and poorly documented," the authors conducted a survey of 500 self-identified AAS users. They found a number of interesting points, including the fact that more than three quarters of respondents were "noncompetitive bodybuilders and nonathletes." A significant number used a larger dose of AAS than had previously been recorded, and more than 10 percent used hazardous and/or unsafe drug injection practices.

Pope, Harrison G., et al. 2004. "Anabolic Steroid Users' Attitudes Towards Physicians." *Addiction*. 99(9): 1189–1194.

Among 80 weightlifters included in this survey, more than half had never revealed their use of AAS to their physicians. Although they tended to trust their physicians' general knowledge of medical information, they trusted other sources (friends, fellow lifters, their drug suppliers) more than they did their physicians about AAS information.

Savulescu, J., B. Foddy, and M. Clayton. 2003. "Why We Should Allow Performance Enhancing Drugs in Sport." *British Journal of Sports Medicine.* 38(6): 666–670.

The authors provide historical context to argue that "Performance enhancement is not against the spirit of sport; it is the spirit of sport." (Also see Devine, above.)

Schroeder, E. Todd, et al. 2005. "Six-week Improvements in Muscle Mass and Strength During Androgen Therapy in Older Men." *The Journals of Gerontology, Series A.* 60(12): 1586–1592.

The authors report on a study of 32 men between the ages of 66 and 78 who were given intensive AAS treatment for six weeks. The treatment improved their muscle mass and strength, although it had no effect on their leg muscle power or walking speed.

Schultheiss, Dirk, John Denil, and Udo Jonas. 1997. "Rejuvenation in the Early 20th Century." *Andrologia.* 29(6): 351–355.

The authors discuss scientific research designed to improve the functioning of human organs by the transplantation of tissue from lower animals, especially with the goal of improving male sexual functioning by transplanting testicular tissue from guinea pigs, rats, monkeys, and other animals.

Schwarzenbach, Heidi. 2011. "Impact of Physical Activity and Doping on Epigenetic Gene Regulation." *Drug Testing and Analysis.* 3(10): 682–687.

The author points out that AAS have biochemical and physiological effects on the human body that go well beyond those normally described in the literature, one of which involves changes in certain genetic expressions controlling the development of muscle tissue, the release of neurotransmitters, and the function of certain growth factors.

Setchell, Brian P. 1990. "The Testis and Tissue Transplantation: Historical Aspects." *Journal of Reproductive Immunology.* 18(1): 1–8.

The author provides a detailed review of the early history of transplantation experiments designed to test the effects of male hormones on physiological and behavioral characteristics.

Shah, J. 2002. "Erectile Dysfunction Through the Ages." *BJU International.* 90(4): 433–441.

This article is of interest because it reviews some of the ways in which people, stretching back over millennia, have used concoctions made from male sexual parts to increase virility and achieve other masculine characteristics.

Sjöqvist, Folke, Mats Garle, and Anders Rane. 2008. "Use of Doping Agents, Particularly Anabolic Steroids, in Sports and Society." *The Lancet.* 371(9627): 1872–1882.

The authors review research on the use of AAS by athletes and point out that the problem of illegal AAS use has now spread more widely to the general society. They review some of the most common psychiatric side effects associated with AAS use, especially violent behavior.

Talih, Farid, Omar Fattal, and Donald Malone, Jr. 2007. "Anabolic Steroid Abuse: Psychiatric and Physical Costs." *Cleveland Clinic Journal of Medicine.* 74(5): 341–344, 346, 349–352.

The authors call attention to a variety of psychiatric problems that may develop with extended AAS use and suggest that these problems can best be treated by withdrawal of the drugs, with the use of ancillary treatments in some cases.

Tattersall, R. B. 1994. "Charles-Edouard Brown-Séquard: Double-hyphenated Neurologist and Forgotten Father of Endocrinology." *Diabetic Medicine.* 11(8): 728–731.

> The author reviews the professional accomplishments of one of the early researchers in the field, suggesting that he is deserving of the title of "Father of Endocrinology." Only his late experiments on self-injection of testes-derived fluids that led to the cult of the Elixir of Life diminished his reputation and perhaps deprived him of full recognition of his accomplishments.

Thiblin, Ingemar, and Anna Petersson. 2004. "Pharmacoepidemiology of Anabolic Androgenic Steroids: A Review." *Fundamental & Clinical Pharmacology.* 19(1): 27–44.

> The authors attempt to draw some conclusions about the nature of AAS users and the effects of the drugs on those users from a review of previous research. Their study illustrates the numerous methodological problems that make it difficult to state firm generalizations that can be drawn from these studies.

Reports

Adolescent Steroid Use. [Washington, DC]: Department of Health and Human Services. Office of Inspector General, February 1991. Available online at http://oig.hhs.gov/oei/reports/oei-06-90-01080.pdf.

> This report is largely of historical interest, but it does present a comprehensive and complete overview of the status of adolescent steroid use at one point in American history.

Mitchell, George J. *Report to the Commissioner of Baseball of an Independent Investigation into the Illegal Use of Steroids and Other Performance Enhancing Substances by Players in Major League Baseball.* December 13, 2007.

This report was produced by former Senator George J. Mitchell at the request of Major League Baseball (MLB) commissioner Bud Selig in March 2006. The report reviews the evidence Mitchell collected in hundreds of interviews with players and other stakeholders, along with a number of recommendations for changes in MLB drug testing policies.

State of New Jersey. Office of the Attorney General. July 7, 2011. *Report of the Attorney General's Steroids Study Group*. Available online at http://dspace.njstatelib.org/xmlui/bitstream/handle/10929/16699/p7662011.pdf?sequence=1. Accessed on May 21, 2012.

This report was issued after a study conducted on the illegal use of anabolic steroids by a number of members of the New Jersey state law enforcement departments, a study initiated by a series of reports in the *Newark Star-Ledger* newspaper.

Steroids Working Group. United States Sentencing Commission. [n.p.] March 2006. *2006 Steroids Report*.

This report was mandated by the Anabolic Steroid Control Act of 2004, in which Congress directed the U.S. Sentencing Commission to review existing sentencing guidelines for steroid abuse and to consider changes in those guidelines to reflect the current status of steroid use in the United States. The report concluded that the status of AAS use in the United States in 2004 was essentially the same as it had been in the Commission's earlier review in 1990.

Internet

"9151: Medical and Illicit Use of Anabolic Steroids." http://www.netce.com/coursecontent.php?courseid=684. Accessed on June 11, 2012.

This website provides course materials for the topic named in its title. The course is part of the online educational program of Continuing Medical Education (CME), whose purpose is to provide course material on a wide variety of topics of interest and value to healthcare professionals.

"About the Drug: What Are Performance Enhancers?" *Duke Pharmacology.* 150. http://www.rise.duke.edu/phr150/ Performance/about.html. Accessed on May 24, 2012.

This website provides valuable basic information about performance-enhancing drugs, a service of the Duke University Medical Center Raising Interest in Science Education (RISE) project.

"Adolescent Steroid Abuse." http://www.cwru.edu/med/ epidbio/mphp439/Steroids.htm?nw_view=1361059836&.. Accessed on February 16, 2013.

This website focuses on topics of special interest about steroid abuse for teenagers. In addition to a good general introduction, it has a number of appendices dealing with definitions of steroids, steroid research, consequences of steroid abuse, steroid addiction, and steroid programs.

"Anabolic Steroid Abuse—Topic Overview." WebMD. http:// men.webmd.com/tc/anabolic-steroid-abuse-topic-overview. Accessed on May 21, 2012.

WebMD is one of the major health and medical-oriented websites with complete and reliable information on a wide variety of topics, including anabolic steroids.

"Anabolic Steroids." MedlinePlus. http://www.nlm.nih.gov/ medlineplus/anabolicsteroids.html. Accessed on May 22, 2012.

This page is part of the highly respected website, Medline Plus, which provides information on the topic in addition to related issues, journal articles, directories, organizations, and other websites.

"Anabolic Steroids." NIDA for Teens. http://teens.drugabuse.gov/facts/facts_ster1.php. Accessed on May 22, 2012.

>This website provides a general introduction to the problem of steroid abuse for teenagers by the National Institute of Drug Abuse.

"Anabolic Steroids Information." *Anabolic Bible*. http://www.anabolic-bible.org/ShowPage.aspx?callpage=Introduction. Accessed on May 23, 2012.

>This website calls itself the "ultimate resource for information on anabolic steroids." It contains sections on the effects of anabolic steroids, the history of anabolic steroids and their use for medical and nonmedical purposes, the chemistry and pharmacology of steroids, and side effects of AAS use.

"Anabolic Steroids: News for the Treatment Field." Substance Abuse and Mental Health Services Administration. http://kap.samhsa.gov/products/manuals/advisory/pdfs/anabolicsteriods.pdf. Accessed on May 22, 2012.

>This website is an electronic version of the SAMHSA "Substance Abuse Treatment Advisory" series, providing general information on the topic of steroid abuse, as well as some useful references and additional resources.

"Anabolic Steroids and Sports: Winning at Any Cost." New York State Department of Health. http://www.health.ny.gov/publications/1210/. Accessed on June 3, 2012.

>This publication of the New York State Department of Health presents a general introduction to the nature of anabolic steroids, their use in athletic competition, and their potential effects on users.

"Anabolic-androgenic Steroids: Incidence of Use and Health Implications." *President's Council on Physical Fitness and Sports Research Digest*. Series 5, No. 5, March 2005. Available online at http://connection.ebscohost.com/c/articles/19611571/anabolic-androgenic-steroids-incidence-use-health-implications. Accessed on May 24, 2012.

This bulletin provides a broad, general overview of the nature of AAS, how they are used and misused, and their prevalence in the U.S. population as of 2005.

Antonovich, Michael. "The FIM's Assault on Performance Enhancing Drugs." http://motocross.transworld.net/ 1000124312/features/the-fims-assault-on-performance-enhancing-drugs/. Accessed on May 24, 2012.

The author describes efforts by the FIM (Fédération Internationale de Motocyclisme), ruling organization for motocross sports, to introduce drug testing into a sport that had previously not been overly concerned about the potential problems of AAS abuse.

"Articles." e-steroid.com. http://www.e-steroid.com/steroid-articles/. Accessed on May 22, 2012.

Although primarily a website for the sale of steroids, this resource has an excellent collection of articles on a variety of AAS-related topics, such as the current U.S. Congress investigation of former major league baseball pitcher Roger Clemens and stories of recent athletes who have failed drug tests.

"Articles." Steroidology.com. http://www.steroidology.com/category/articles/. Accessed on May 23, 2012.

Another website designed primarily to sell steroids, this page also has a number of interesting articles on the history of AAS, the effects of AAS on sports, post-cycle therapy, the side effects of steroids, and steroid testing.

Balko, Radley. January 23, 2008. "Should We Allow Performance Enhancing Drugs in Sports?" *Reason* magazine. http://reason.com/archives/2008/01/23/should-we-allow-performance-en/singlepage. Accessed on May 24, 2012.

This web page contains the text of a presentation made by Balko, senior editor of *Reason* magazine in 2008, in which he claims that the debate over AAS is really about "paternalism and control" of sports agencies over the individuals who play for them.

"DrugFacts: Steroids (Anabolic-androgenic)." National Institute of Drug Abuse. http://www.drugabuse.gov/publications/drugfacts/steroids-anabolic-androgenic. Accessed on May 22, 2012.

This NIDA fact sheet provides basic information on the nature of AAS, their health effects, and methods for withdrawal from their use.

"The Elixir of Life." HubPages. http://leahlefler.hubpages.com/hub/The-Elixir-of-Life-A-Brief-History-of-Testosterone. Accessed on May 19, 2012.

The author provides a brief history of the use of testosterone for health-enhancing experiences, beginning with the discoveries of Charles-Édouard Brown-Séquard and their spread across Europe and into the United States.

Fahey, Thomas D. "Anabolic-androgenic Steroids: Mechanism of Action and Effects on Performance." *Encyclopedia of Sports Medicine and Science.* http://www.sportsci.org/encyc/anabster/anabster.html. Accessed on May 23, 2012.

This article is a reprint from the 1998 edition of the *Encyclopedia of Sports Medicine and Science*, with a detailed general overview of the mechanisms and effects of AAS.

Frounfelter, Gregory G., and Greg E. Bradley Popovich. "Ethical Considerations Regarding Anabolic-Androgenic Steroid Use." http://faculty.css.edu/tboone2/asep/EthicalConsiderations.html. Accessed on May 24, 2012.

The authors briefly review the chemistry and physiology of AAS use, but focus on moral issues related to such use, with special attention to the role of medical care providers.

Haskew, Mike. "Seeking Peak Performance." *Health Scope Magazine.* http://www.healthscopemag.com/HS2.11/08_Supplements.pdf. Accessed on May 24, 2012.

This article provides an introduction and review of AAS for amateur and professional athletes, pointing out both the benefits and risks associated with such use.

"Health Effects of Steroids." fitnessmith. http://www.fitnessforworld.com/article/article3.htm. Accessed on May 24, 2012.

This article provides a review of the intentional and unintentional physical and psychological effects of using AAS.

Herper, Matthew. "The Case for Performance-enhancing Drugs in Sports." *Forbes.* http://www.forbes.com/sites/matthewherper/2011/05/20/the-case-for-performance-enhancing-drugs-in-sports/. Accessed on May 24, 2012.

The author explains why he favors the legalization of performance-enhancing drugs in athletics.

"History of the Development of Anabolic Androgenic Steroids." *Muscular Development.* http://www.musculardevelopment.com/articles/chemical-enhancement/3706-history-of-the-development-of-anabolic-androgenic-steroids.html. Accessed on May 18, 2012.

This website provides an excellent introductory overview of the history of the use of anabolic steroids for enhancement of masculine characteristics.

Horwitz, Steven. "Performance Enhancing Drugs." http://www.momsteam.com/team-of-experts/steven-horwitz-dc/performance-enhancing-drugs. Accessed on May 24, 2012.

This website contains three good articles on specific aspects of AAS, "Ten Signs of Steroid Abuse," "What Are Anabolic Steroids And How Do They Work?," and

"Anabolic Steroids: Your Child's Road to the Gold or to the Grave?"

Kaminstein, David S. "Steroid Drug Withdrawal." Medicine Net.com. http://www.medicinenet.com/steroid_withdrawal/article.htm. Accessed on May 22, 2012.

The author describes and discusses the physical and psychological symptoms associated with withdrawal from the use of steroid drugs.

Katz, Jeffrey. "Should We Accept Steroid Use in Sports?" npr. http://www.npr.org/2008/01/23/18299098/should-we-accept-steroid-use-in-sports. Accessed on February 16, 2013.

Six experts on the topic of steroid use in sports argue pros and cons (three on each side) about the morality and ethics of allowing athletes to use steroids.

Kishner, Stephen. "Anabolic Steroid Use and Abuse." Medscape Reference. http://emedicine.medscape.com/article/128655-overview. Accessed on May 22, 2012.

This highly respected Internet resource provides useful and technical information on the chemistry, physiology, and pharmacology of AAS, with extended discussion of topics such as the biopharmacology of testosterone, testosterone esters and derivatives, adverse effects, clinical uses, and AAS abuse.

Lamb, David R. "The Consequences of Anabolic Steroid Abuse." *Performance Playbook.* http://www.fhsaa.org/sites/default/files/orig_uploads/health/pdf/gatorade_steroidabuse.pdf. Accessed on May 22, 2012.

This one-page fact sheet lists a number of medical effects that may result from the continued use of AAS.

Lee, Yu-Hsuan. "Performance Enhancing Drugs: History, Medical Effects & Policy." http://leda.law.harvard.edu/leda/data/780/LeeY06.pdf. Accessed on June 1, 2012.

This excellent paper, written by a Harvard undergraduate, reviews many of the most important elements in the interaction among sports and athletics, the medical effects of AAS use, and the development and implementation of policy dealing with drug use in sports.

"Liver Damage and Increased Heart Attack Risk Caused by Anabolic Steroid Use." Medical News Today. http://www.medical-newstoday.com/releases/38069.php. Accessed on May 23, 2012.

This article summarizes a report on the use of AAS with patients suffering from wasting as a result of HIV infection. The steroids did provide the expected increase in body mass and strength, but had the side effect of increasing the risk of liver and coronary damage, a result that should be of concern to non-AIDS patients, such as those who use AAS for weight lifting and bodybuilding purposes.

"Notable Players Linked to PEDs." ESPN.com. http://sports.espn.go.com/mlb/news/story?id=4366683. Accessed on May 24, 2012.

This website lists a number of professional athletes who have been implicated in or admitted to the use of performance-enhancing drugs.

Ormsbee, Michael, and Matt Vukovich. "Performance Enhancing Drugs." IDEA Health and Fitness. http://www.ideafit.com/fitness-library/performance-enhancing-drugs. Accessed on May 24, 2012.

The authors suggest that the use of AAS in the United States has become essentially a fait accompli, and that athletes now need to become aware of the health effects that may be associated with AAS use.

Perez, A.J. "Cops' Use of Illegal Steroids a 'Big Problem'." AolNews.http://www.aolnews.com/2010/12/26/illegal-steroid-use-among-police-officers-a-big-problem/. Accessed on May 22, 2012.

> This report points out that individuals in law enforcement appear to be involved in the illegal use of AAS at a higher rate than the general population. The writer describes specific problems in Trenton, New Jersey; South Bend, Indiana; and Orlando, Florida, in which steroids were involved in inappropriate police actions.

"Performance Enhancing Drugs." Mayo Clinic. http://www.mayoclinic.com/health/performance-enhancing-drugs/HQ01105. Accessed on May 24, 2012.

> The Mayo Clinic staff provides an introduction to AAS, with a detailed description of some of the most important drugs along with warnings about their use.

"Play Healthy." http://playhealthy.drugfree.org/default.aspx. Accessed on May 24, 2012.

> This website is maintained by MLB to provide youngsters with information about drug abuse, with special guidance for coaches, parents, and others concerned about the use of AAS in athletics.

"Position Statement on Anabolic Steroids." National Federation of State High School Associations Sports Medicine Advisory Committee. http://www.nfhs.org/content.aspx?id=3357. Accessed on May 24, 2012.

> The position statement puts forward the views of the National Federation of State High School Associations (NFHS) about AAS use, indicating that the organization is "strongly" opposed to such use among high school athletes.

Presto, Greg. "11 Questions about Performance-enhancing Drugs." Men's Health. http://www.menshealth.com/health/performance-enhancing-drugs?fullpage=true. Accessed on May 24, 2012.

The author raises some practical questions associated with the use of AAS by athletes and ordinary individuals, such as when steroid use jumped from bodybuilding to mainstream sports, is there a connection between steroid use and hand–eye coordination, and what are the risks associated with human growth hormone?

Quinn, Elizabeth. "Steroids—Anabolic—Androgenic Steroids in Sports." About.com. http://sportsmedicine.about.com/od/performanceenhancingdrugs/a/AnabolicSteroid.htm. Accessed on May 23, 2012.

This article presents a good, general introduction to the topic of AAS and their use and misuse by athletes and in competitive sports, with a number of useful links to other related pages.

"Research Reports: Anabolic Steroid Abuse." National Institute on Drug Abuse. http://www.drugabuse.gov/publications/research-reports/anabolic-steroid-abuse. Accessed on May 21, 2012.

This August 2006 publication covers topics such as the meaning of anabolic steroids and related compounds, the prevalence of steroid use in the United States, health effects of steroid use, treatments available for steroid abuse, and additional sources of information on the subject.

"Should the Use of Performance-enhancing Drugs in Sports Be Legalized?" Debates: Health. http://debates.juggle.com/should-the-use-of-performance-enhancing-drugs-in-sports-be-legalized. Accessed on May 24, 2012.

This online debate site allows individuals to present their own views on this topic. In this case, 21 writers oppose legalization, while 4 write in favor of legalization.

"Sports and Drugs." ProCon.org. http://sportsanddrugs.procon.org/. Accessed on May 24, 2012.

This superb website offers an extended pros and cons discussion on the use of AAS in sports with a number of distinct pages on various aspects of the issue. An excellent source of the debate over the topic along with a good source of information about the topic.

"Steroid Abuse." http://www.steroid-abuse.org/about-us.htm. Accessed on May 21, 2012.

This website is sponsored by an unidentified group of researchers, medical doctors, and steroid drug users who wish to provide information about the problems associated with steroid abuse to the general public. Topics included on the website include side effects, alternatives to steroid use, prevalence, special effects on women, body image, and psychological and emotional effects.

"Steroid Abuse in Today's Society." Office of Diversion Control. U.S. Department of Justice. http://www.deadiversion. usdoj.gov/pubs/brochures/steroids/professionals/index.html. Accessed on May 21, 2012.

This website is the online electronic version of the Office of Diversion Control's (ODC) popular publication on steroid abuse, including a discussion of the nature of anabolic steroids, reasons for their misuse, sources of anabolic steroids, physical and psychological effects, and laws and penalties for steroid abuse.

"Steroid Abuse Help." http://www.steroidabusehelp.com/. Accessed on May 22, 2012.

This website provides information on the illegal use of AAS and provides links to current articles on the subject. Its main purpose, however, is to provide help for individuals with a steroid abuse problem by providing a toll-free help line and other resources.

"The Steroid Book." http://www.directionsact.com/pdf/drug_ news/The_Steriod_Book.pdf. Accessed on May 24, 2012.

This unattributed book lists no author and no publisher, but it contains a great deal of valuable information about the nature and use of AAS. The introduction of the book says that it is intended for "people working in needle and syringe programs." The book also contains some useful references and a helpful glossary.

"Steroid Law.com." http://www.steroidlaw.com. Accessed on February 16, 2013.

This website is maintained by Rick Collins, who calls himself "the nation's leading legal expert on anabolic steroids and muscle building supplements." It provides a vast amount of information on legal issues relating to the use of AAS.

"Steroids." herbs2000.com. http://www.herbs2000.com/medica/4_steroids.htm. Accessed on May 19, 2012.

Available on a number of websites, this essay describes in detail the history of steroids and their use for anabolic and androgenic purposes.

"Steroids (Anabolic)." National Institute of Drug Abuse. http://www.drugabuse.gov/drugs-abuse/steroids-anabolic. Accessed on May 21, 2012.

This NIDA website provides general information on anabolic steroids, including recent news and articles, resources, and links to other sources on the topic.

Stöppler, Melissa Conrad. "Steroid Abuse." MedicineNet.com.

The author provides a general introduction to the problem of steroid abuse, with special emphasis on intended and unintended consequences of the drug's use.

Svare, Bruce B. "What We Can Do to Prevent Steroid Abuse." National PTA. http://www.pta.org/2085.htm. Accessed on May 22, 2012.

This article from the 2008 National PTA magazine outlines some steps that parents and schools can take to reduce steroid use among adolescents.

Szalavitz, Maia. "Performance-enhancing Drugs O.K. in School, but Not in Sports, Students Say." Time. http://healthland.time.com/2012/05/09/performance-enhancing-drugs-o-k-in-school-but-not-in-sports-students-say/. Accessed on May 24, 2012.

This article reviews a recent research report in which college students say that it is permissible for students to use performance-enhancing drugs in the classroom (e.g., to get better scores on tests), but not in competitive athletics.

"Testosterone, Epitestosterone and the Doping Tests." Cycling News. http://autobus.cyclingnews.com/news.php?id=features/2006/testosterone_testing. Accessed on June 3, 2012.

This article explains how the ratio between two hormones, testosterone and epitestosterone, is used in standard anti-doping tests.

Weaver, Jean. "Steroid Addiction a Risk for Young Athletes." msnbc.com. http://www.msnbc.msn.com/id/7348758/ns/health-mental_health/t/steroid-addiction-risk-young-athletes/. Accessed on May 22, 2012.

This online MSNBC.com article reviews current concerns about the misuse of AAS, particularly among adolescents who may use the drugs to improve their body image.

Wedro, Benjamin. "Anabolic Steroid Abuse." MedicineNet.com. http://www.medicinenet.com/anabolic_steroid_abuse/article.htm. Accessed on May 21, 2012.

This technical website provides basic information on definitions of steroids and other AAS, reasons for using steroids, physical and psychological effects of using steroids, and treatment and prevention of steroid abuse.

"The World Anti-Doping Code. The 2008 Prohibited List. International Standard." http://www.wada-ama.org/rtecontent/document/2008_List_En.pdf. Accessed on May 20, 2012.
This website provides the official list of prohibited substances, as determined by the World Anti-Doping Agency, as of 2008.

The discovery and general use of steroids dates only to the late 19th century. Yet, the roots of the steroid abuse story go back much farther in history. This chapter lists some of the most important events that have occurred throughout that history.

At least 6000 BCE   Humans learn of the demasculinizing effects of castration by trial and error, a bit of agricultural knowledge that survives for millennia without any theoretical basis.

776 BCE   Date of the first Olympic Games in Greece. Competitors at the games are thought to have ingested the testicles of male animals to gain strength, speed, and endurance to aid them in their participation in the games.

1760s+   Scottish physician John Hunter studies the effects of transplanting testicular tissue from male chickens to female chickens and to demasculinized males (capons). He discovers that both females and capons develop male characteristics, such as growing a comb and displaying crowing behavior.

1840s   German physiologist Arnold Berthold conducts a series of experiments in which he found that castrated roosters had combs and wattles reduced in size, reduced aggressive behavior toward other males, and reduced interest in hens. His

Ben Johnson claims victory over Carl Lewis and Linford Christie in the 100-meter final at the 1988 Olympics in Seoul. Johnson was later disqualified when a drug test revealed traces of anabolic steroids. (AP/ Wide World Photos)

experiments were among the first studies on endocrine-determined behavior in animals.

1889   At the age of 72, Mauritian-born physiologist Charles-Édouard Brown-Séquard reports having injected himself with fluid taken from the testes of dogs and guinea pigs, after which he experiences a significant renewal of physical strength and mental abilities.

1896   Austrian physiologists Oskar Zoth and Fritz Pregl publish a paper describing their experiments in injecting themselves with testicular extracts from animals. They suggest the possibilities that such procedures may be effective in increasing the skills needed by athletes in a variety of sports.

1902   English physiologists William Bayliss and Ernest Starling discover the action of the first hormone, secretin. The name hormone, meaning "I arouse to activity," is suggested to Starling by a colleague, William B. Hardy.

1918   Austrian physiologist Eugen Steinach performs the first "Steinach operation," a type of vasectomy which he believed would restore a man's sexual prowess and overall good health. The Steinach operation soon becomes widely popular throughout the Western world as a method of "rejuvenation" for men.

1920s–1930s   Russian-born French surgeon Serge Abrahamovitch Voronoff attempts to improve male sexual function by grafting tissue from monkey testicles into human male testicles. The procedure is very popular for a while, but soon falls into disuse and notoriety.

1928   The International Association of Athletics Federations adopts the world's first sports association drug policy, one that was virtually impossible to enforce because methods for testing for most drugs were not yet available.

1929   German chemist Adolf Butenandt isolates the first sex hormone, estrone, obtained from the urine of pregnant women. Two years later he isolates the first male sex hormone, which he names *androsterone* (*andro*: "male," *ster*: "sterol," *one*: ketone family).

1930s Swiss physician Paul Niehans develops the theory of cellular therapy, in which the healthy cells of an animal organ are transplanted into the unhealthy organ of a human to improve the functioning of the latter. Niehans specialized in such procedures to improve the sexual functioning of older men.

1934 Croatian biochemist Leopold Ružička synthesizes androsterone, an accomplishment that contributed to his receipt of a share of the 1939 Nobel Prize in Chemistry.

1935 Researchers at the Dutch pharmaceutical firm of Organon, led by Ernst Laqueur, announce the discovery of a crystalline substance with a physiological effect more pronounced than that of androsterone, which they call testosterone.

1935 Only a few months after the Organon discovery, research teams led by Butenandt and Ružička announce in two separate articles the first synthesis of testosterone from cholesterol. The development makes possible, at least in principle, the production of testosterone on a commercial scale.

1935 American medical researcher Charles D. Kochakian discovers that androsterone has anabolic as well as androgenic effects, establishing for the first time the possibility of using the substance for muscle- and tissue-building purposes.

1937 Clinical tests on the use of testosterone for the treatment of hypogonadism begin. At the same time, interest in the use of testosterone to improve masculine characteristics is already underway, often in a less rigorous and controlled manner.

1939 The Nobel Prize in Chemistry is divided equally between Adolf Friedrich Johann Butenandt "for his work on sex hormones" and Leopold Ružička "for his work on polymethylenes and higher terpenes" (compounds of which steroids and related compounds are produced).

Early 1940s Anecdotal evidence suggests that the physiological effects of testosterone injections were tested by German researchers on prisoners of war, members of the military, and on Adolf Hitler himself. One purpose of the experiments was to increase aggressiveness in German troops.

1941   An 18-year-old trotting horse by the name of Holloway with a rapidly diminishing skill at racing is treated with testosterone injections. Over the following few months, he shows marked improvement in his racing skills and, at the age of 19, sets a new record for the one-mile distance of 2 minutes 10 seconds. Holloway is, thus, the first "athlete" for whom positive "doping" in a competitive event has been confirmed.

1945   American writer Paul de Kruif publishes *The Male Hormone*, a book in which the anabolic and androgenic effects of testosterone products are described. The book is probably the first widespread introduction to the topic for the general public worldwide.

Late 1940s   Testosterone injections are used for therapeutic purposes in undernourished survivors of German concentration camps at the conclusion of World War II.

Early 1950s   Sports teams in the Soviet Union and other Soviet bloc nations begin the use of anabolic androgenic steroids (AAS) in training programs for many of their national athletic teams.

1954   The first results of the Soviet training programs with AAS use appear in the 1954 Olympic Games when Russian weight lifters sweep most medal awards in their divisions.

1954   U.S. Olympic trainer John Ziegler learns of the Soviet of AAS use in training programs and obtains samples of drugs used by the Soviets from their makers, Ciba Pharmaceuticals.

1958   The U.S. Food and Drug Administration approves the use of a version of the AAS used by Soviet trainers that contains fewer androgenic effects and greater anabolic effects. Approval is granted for use with the elderly and burn victims, but it rapidly becomes popular among bodybuilders, weight lifters, and other athletes for off-label purposes. Produced by

Ciba Pharmaceuticals, the drug is called Dianabol (chemically, methandrostenolone).

1966   The Fédération Internationale de Football Association (Federation of International Football Associations, or FIFA) and Union Cycliste Internationale (International Cycling Association) both adopt drug testing policies.

1967   In response to concerns about the increasing use of drugs in athletic competitions, the International Olympic Committee (IOC) establishes the Medical Commission to study the problem of doping, develop methods for testing for the use of illegal substances, and to develop alternative methods of helping athletes.

1968   The IOC conducts the first tests for illegal substances at the summer and winter games in Mexico City and Grenoble, France, respectively. AAS drugs are not included because adequate tests for them are not yet available. There is one positive test in the summer games and none in the winter games.

1974   The German Democratic Republic ("East Germany") adopts official policies requiring the use of AAS in training programs for the nation's athletes.

1975   The IOC aids AAS to their list of banned drugs.

1976   The Olympic Games at Montréal are the first such competitions to include testing for AAS. At the Games, East German women win 11 of 13 individual gold medals, adding to the suspicion that they have been taking steroids in preparation for the contests.

1981   Steroid "guru" Daniel Duchaine issues *The Original Underground Steroid Handbook for Men and Women*, describing the use of AAS for bodybuilding, weight lifting, and other activities, as well as a list of substances to be used for that purpose. He issued an expanded and updated version in 1988.

1983   Officials at the Pan American Games in Caracas implement unannounced drug testing. At least two dozen athletes from the United States and other nations withdraw from the games before they begin. In addition, 23 medals are withdrawn after their winners test positive for prohibited drugs. Among those who lose their medals is weight lifter Jeff Michels, who is stripped of three gold medals.

1984   Former musician Victor Conte and colleagues found the Bay Area Laboratory Cooperative, better known as BALCO. Originally formed as a blood and urine analysis facility, the company is reputed to have become involved in supplying illegal supplements to a number of famous athletes, including Barry Bonds, Jason Giambi, Marion Jones, and Bill Romanowski.

1986   The National Collegiate Athletic Association (NCAA) adopts a drug testing policy for all sports under its control. The policy includes anabolic steroids.

1987   The National Football League (NFL) begins testing players for AAS, the earliest such policy in American professional sports leagues.

1988   U.S. sprinter Ben Johnson is stripped of his world record gold-medal-winning victory in the Olympics 100-meter (m) dash after testing positive for the AAS Stanozol.

1988   The U.S. Congress passes and President Ronald Reagan signs the Anti-Drug Abuse Act of 1988, which bans the sale of AAS for other than medical purposes. It also provides penalties for the sale of AAS within 100 feet of schools.

1988   The National Association for Stock Car Auto Racing (NASCAR) announces a drug testing policy based on "reasonable suspicion" that a drug is being used.

1990   The World Health Organization (WHO) reports on a large, multicenter research study that confirms that some AAS are effective as a male contraceptive.

1990   The U.S. Congress adopts the Anabolic Steroid Control Act of 1990, which places anabolic steroids under Schedule III of the Controlled Substances Act.

1991   Major League Baseball (MLB) Commissioner Fay Vincent issues a seven-page memorandum banning the use of certain illegal substances in the league. The substances for which athletes will be tested are amphetamines, cocaine, marijuana, opiates, and phenylcyclidine (PCP). AAS are not yet included in the list.

1991   Winfried Leopold, chief swimming coach of the East German Olympic swimming team, admits that the use of AAS has been an integral part of the nation's training program for more than two decades.

1992   Former professional football player Lyle Alzado dies of a rare form of brain cancer. He blamed his medical condition on AAS that he had been using for more than 20 years. (No medical evidence is currently available for a connection between the two.)

1997   MLB Commissioner Bud Selig issues a memorandum banning drug use that is almost identical with the one issued by Fay Vincent six years earlier. Again, AAS are not included in the list of banned drugs.

1998   St. Louis Cardinals player Mark McGwire establishes a new MLB record by hitting 70 home runs. He acknowledges that he has been using a steroid precursor chemical for some time. AAS are still not illegal in MLB.

1999   The World Conference on Doping in Sports is held in Lausanne, Switzerland. It adopts the Lausanne Declaration on Doping in Sport, which announces the forthcoming formation of an international antidoping agency (now called the World Anti-Doping Agency [WADA]).

1999   The National Basketball Association (NBA) modifies its drug policy, first announced in 1983, to include anabolic androgenic steroids.

1999   The U.S. Major League Soccer organization announces a ban on the use of AAS.

2000 Upon recommendation of the United States Olympic Committee Select Task Force on Externalization, the U.S. Anti-Doping Agency is created to "uphold the Olympic ideal of fair play, and to represent the interests of Olympic, Pan American Games, and Paralympic athletes."

Early 2000s American chemist Patrick Arnold invents the first two synthetic AAS not listed on antidoping schedules, norbolethone and tetrahydrogestrinone (also known as THG or "The Clear").

2001 MLB institutes its first random AAS drug testing policy at the Minor League level. At this point, no Major League player may be tested for AAS.

2002 As part of its collective bargaining agreement, and at the insistence of the U.S. Senate, MLB institutes a random experimental testing program for AAS at the Major League level. No penalty may be assessed for anyone who tests positive for AAS drugs.

2003 MLB institutes a mandatory random drug testing program for AAS for all major and minor league players.

2003 The WADA announced a new World Anti-Doping Code that lists substances banned in international competitions, provisions for testing for such substances, and related antidoping issues. The code is first put into use at the 2004 Olympic Games in Athens.

2004 The U.S. Congress passes the Anabolic Steroid Control Act of 2004, which updates and revises the earlier 1990 law placing steroids under Schedule III of the Controlled Substances Act. The act lists 59 specific substances to be listed under the schedule.

2005 MLB adopts a schedule of penalties for players who test positive for drugs, beginning with a 10-day suspension without pay for the first positive test, 30-day suspension for the second positive test, 60-day suspension for the third positive test, and a one-year suspension for the fourth positive test.

2005   MLB player Jose Canseco releases a new book, *Juiced: Wild Times, Rampant 'Roids, Smash Hits & How Baseball Got Big*, describing his own experiences with AAS and claiming that 85 percent of all MLB players regularly use AAS drugs.

2006   The National Hockey League institutes a drug testing program, although it announces that it believes it has "no drug problem."

2006   MLB appoints former U.S. Senator George Mitchell to head a committee studying the use of anabolic steroids in MLB.

2007   American cyclist Floyd Landis is stripped of his 2006 Tour de France championship for testing positive for elevated testosterone levels.

2007   The NFL expands and tightens its drug policy by adding certain substances to its prohibited list and expanding the number of players to be tested annually.

2007   The IOC strips runner Marion Jones of three gold medals and two bronze medals won in the 2000 Olympics because of her use of AAS.

2007   A federal grand jury in San Francisco indicts San Francisco Giant baseball player Barry Bonds for lying about the use of steroids.

2008   Runner Marion Jones is sentenced to six months in prison for her use of illegal AAS. (See **2007**.)

2008   Former MLB pitcher Roger Clemens and his trainer Brian McNamee testify before the U.S. House of Representatives Committee on Oversight and Government Reform that Clemens never used anabolic steroids.

2008   The State of Kentucky bans the use of AAS in horse racing in the state.

2009   The Belgium Nationals Bodybuilding Championships are canceled when all 20 competitors flee the site of competition when antidoping officials show up unannounced to do surprise steroid testing.

2010   Mark McGwire (**1998**) and Floyd Landis (**2007**) both admit that they used illegal AAS throughout their professional sports careers.

2010   A federal grand jury in Washington, D.C. indicts Roger Clemens (**2008**) for lying to a Congressional committee about his use of illegal steroids during his career in MLB.

2011   A jury finds Barry Bonds (**2007**) guilty of obstruction of justice, but reaches no decision on three more serious counts against the former MLB player.

2012   The Court of Arbitration for Sport strips Spanish cyclist Alberto Contador of his 2010 Tour de France championship for testing positive for anabolic steroids.

2012   MLB pitcher Roger Clemens (**2008**; **2010**) is found innocent of all charges of using illegal drugs during his career.

2012   American cyclist Lance Armstrong is stripped of seven Tour de France titles for failing to pass drug tests conducted following those races. He had earlier been banned from Olympic sports for life by the United States Anti-Doping Agency.

2013   Armstrong publicly admits on television that he has not been truthful about his use of illegal substances in his Tour de France races.

Discussions of steroids may involve terminology that is unfamiliar to the average person. In some cases, the terms used are scientific, technical, or medical expressions, used most commonly by professionals in the field. In other cases, the terms may be part of the so-called street slang that users themselves employ in talking about the drugs they use, the paraphernalia associated with drugs, or the experiences associated with steroid use. This chapter lists and defines a few of the terms needed to understand explanations provided in this book.

AAS A common acronym standing for "anabolic androgenic steroids."

addiction A chronic condition in which a person's body has developed a dependence on some exogenous chemical, generally accompanied by physical changes in the brain.

anabolic Having reference to a substance that builds new tissue.

anabolism The metabolic process by which simple compounds, such as sugars and amino acids, are combined in the

A muscular man strikes a pose at a gym in November 2009. Long associated with professional bodybuilders, the use of anabolic steroids to "burn fat," create lean muscle, and improve overall appearance has become a widespread phenomenon in evidence at local gyms and amateur bodybuilding competitions nationwide. (R. Gino Santa Maria/Dreamstime) body to produce more complex compounds, such as carbohydrates and proteins.

analog Chemical, a compound that is structurally similar to some other compound. Testosterone analogs have chemical structures similar to those of testosterone itself.

androgenic Having reference to a substance that produces typical male secondary sexual characteristics.

androstenedione A naturally occurring hormone from which testosterone is formed in the body.

aromatization A chemical process by which excess testosterone in the body is converted into the female hormone estrogen.

atrophy The process by which the mass and strength of body tissue decreases, often as the result of lack of use or because of the use of an exogenous chemical.

basement drug A counterfeit drug.

blending The process of combining the use of steroids with the use of other drugs.

catabolism The metabolic process by which complex compounds in the body, such as carbohydrates and proteins, are broken down into simpler organic compounds, such as sugars and amino acids.

chemical analog *See* **analog**.

cycling The schedule on which an individual uses steroids.

cycloalkane An organic (carbon-containing) compound consisting of only carbon and hydrogen atoms joined to each other in a six-carbon ring.

designer drug/steroid A synthetic compound that is created in the laboratory to have physiological effects similar to those of some natural or other synthetic compound.

diuretic Any substance that increases the output of urine from the body.

doping The process of using an illegal substance, such as steroids, in an athletic competition.

drug test A chemical analysis of some bodily fluid, usually blood or urine, to detect the presence of certain specified chemicals, such as illegal drugs.

endogenous Created within the body.

epitestosterone An isomer (structurally similar form) of testosterone produced naturally in the body, but with different physiological effects from testosterone.

ergogenic Performance enhancing.

exogenous Created outside of the body.

gonane A grouping of four cycloalkane rings joined to each other forming the core of a steroid molecule.

gynecomastia A process in which males develop unusually large mammary glands, resulting in the development of atypically large breasts.

hormone A chemical substance (protein) produced in one part of the body that travels to another part of the body and produced a physiological effect at that site.

hypertrophy The increase in the size or bulk of an organ or tissue.

lean mass The mass of muscle in the body.

libido Sex drive.

macrocycle The elements that make up a year-long training program, usually including preparation, competition, and transition phases.

megadosing The process of ingesting very large quantities of a substance, such as a steroid, often far beyond that considered safe by the medical profession.

microcycle The elements that make up a brief period in a training cycle, usually one week.

off-label use Any use of a prescription pharmaceutical for which it was not originally and specifically approved.

organotherapy Strictly, the treatment of a disease with extracts from the organs (usually the glands) of an animal. Also, the consumption of animal organs by athletes in an attempt to gain physical traits associated with those organs (such as the consumption of testicles to increase masculine traits of strength and endurance).

periodization The process of arranging a training schedule into discrete segments so as to achieve some maximum effect. *Also see* **macrocycle, microcycle**.

plateau A condition in which the continued use of AAS no longer has an increased effect on a person's body.

plyometrics A type of athletic training designed to improve one's ability to move rapidly and powerfully.

prohormone A chemical substance that is a precursor to a hormone produced in the body, but that has little or no hormonal effects in and of itself.

pyramiding The process by which the number of drugs taken or the quantity of one drug, or both, is gradually increased to some maximum point, followed by a gradual tapering off.

'roid rage An uncontrollable and often unpredictable outburst of anger, frustration, combativeness, or other negative emotion brought about by the use of steroids.

shotgunning The practice of taking steroid drugs according to some irregular schedule.

stacking The process in which a person uses two or more AAS in combination with each other.

steroid An organic (carbon-containing) compound consisting of a core of four cycloalkane rings joined to each other. In popular parlance, the term often refers to the specific category of anabolic steroids.

supraphysiological Having to do with quantities of a substance greater than is normally found in the body.

tapering The process of slowly reducing the amount of drugs taken over some given period of time.

T/E drug test A common drug test used with athletes that measures the ratio of testosterone to epitestosterone in the body.

testosterone A hormone secreted primarily by the testes, responsible for the development of male sex organs and secondary sexual characteristics, such as deepening of the body, body hair, and increase in body and muscle mass.

virilization The process in which a female begins to develop male sexual characteristics, often the result of using anabolic androgenic steroids.

withdrawal symptoms The appearance of unusual or abnormal physical and/or psychological characteristics as the result of discontinuing the use of some chemical substance.

About the Author

David E. Newton holds an associate's degree in science from Grand Rapids (Michigan) Junior College, a BA in chemistry (with high distinction) and an MA in education from the University of Michigan, and an EdD in science education from Harvard University. He is the author of more than 400 textbooks, encyclopedias, resource books, research manuals, laboratory manuals, trade books, and other educational materials. He taught mathematics, chemistry, and physical science in Grand Rapids, Michigan, for 13 years; was professor of chemistry and physics at Salem State College in Massachusetts for 15 years; and was adjunct professor in the College of Professional Studies at the University of San Francisco for 10 years. Previous books for ABC-CLIO include *Global Warming* (1993), *Gay and Lesbian Rights—A Resource Handbook* (1994, 2009), *The Ozone Dilemma* (1995), *Violence and the Mass Media* (1996), *Environmental Justice* (1996, 2009), *Encyclopedia of Cryptology* (1997), *Social Issues in Science and Technology: An Encyclopedia* (1999), *DNA Technology* (2009), and *Sexual Health* (2010). Other recent books include *Physics: Oryx Frontiers of Science Series* (2000), *Sick!* (4 volumes; 2000), *Science, Technology, and Society: The Impact of Science in the 19th Century* (2 volumes; 2001), *Encyclopedia of Fire* (2002), *Molecular Nanotechnology: Oryx Frontiers of Science Series* (2002), *Encyclopedia of Water* (2003), *Encyclopedia of Air* (2004), *The New Chemistry* (6 volumes; 2007), *Nuclear Power* (2005), *Stem Cell Research* (2006), *Latinos in the Sciences, Math, and Professions* (2007), and *DNA*

Evidence and Forensic Science (2008). He has also been an updating and consulting editor on a number of books and reference works, including *Chemical Compounds* (2005), *Chemical Elements* (2006), *Encyclopedia of Endangered Species* (2006), *World of Mathematics* (2006), *World of Chemistry* (2006), *World of Health* (2006), *UXL Encyclopedia of Science* (2007), *Alternative Medicine* (2008), *Grzimek's Animal Life Encyclopedia* (2009), *Community Health* (2009), and *Genetic Medicine* (2009).